D1766161

DATE DUE FOR RETURN

NEW ACCESSION
CANCELLED

2 6 MAY 1993

3 0 MAY 2000

CONSTRUCTING BROTHERHOOD

CONSTRUCTING BROTHERHOOD

✳

CLASS, GENDER, AND FRATERNALISM

✳

MARY ANN CLAWSON

PRINCETON UNIVERSITY PRESS

PRINCETON, NEW JERSEY

QMW LIBRARY
(MILE END)

Copyright © 1989 by Princeton University Press
Published by Princeton University Press, 41 William Street,
Princeton, New Jersey 08540
In the United Kingdom: Princeton University Press,
Guildford, Surrey

All Rights Reserved

Library of Congress Cataloging-in-Publication Data
Clawson, Mary Ann, 1947–
Constructing brotherhood : class, gender, and fraternalism /
Mary Ann Clawson.
p. cm.
Includes index.
ISBN 0–691–09447–0
1. Men—United States—Societies and clubs—History—
19th century. 2. Freemasonry—United States—
History—19th century. 3. Friendly societies—United States—
History—19th century. 4. Artisans—United States—
Societies, etc.—History. 5. Men—Europe—Societies
and clubs—History. 6. Freemasonry—Europe—History.
7. Friendly societies—Europe—History. 8. Artisans—Europe—
Societies, etc.—History. I. Title.
HS2275.C53 1989
366'.088041—dc19   88–38418

This book has been composed in Linotron Monticello

Clothbound editions of Princeton University Press books
are printed on acid-free paper, and binding materials are
chosen for strength and durability
Paperbacks, although satisfactory for personal
collections, are not usually suitable for
library rebinding

Printed in the United States of America by
Princeton University Press,
Princeton, New Jersey

CONTENTS

ACKNOWLEDGMENTS

THE intellectual and emotional debts incurred in the writing of this book are enormous and go back much farther than the project itself. Its spirit and approach are very much the product of intellectual influences encountered before I began graduate school. At Carlton College, Carl Weiner taught me to do social history and to love it, and Kim Rodner helped me to understand the need for more explicit theoretical articulation of sociological and historical problems. Both these processes were continued when I met and studied with George Rawick.

The Sociology Department of the State University of New York at Stony Brook provided a supportive atmosphere for my development as a graduate student. During my years there, Stony Brook faculty often worried that the program provided insufficient guidance and structure to its students. I believe, on the contrary, that this laissez-faire atmosphere, along with the resources offered by faculty, should be recognized for its role in enabling the development of so many fine sociologists. I am grateful to my dissertation committee, Michael Schwartz, Charles Perrow, Terry Rosenberg, and Robert Marcus for supporting my right to work on a topic of my own choosing no matter how foolish it seemed to them. A special thanks to Michael Schwartz, who manages at one and the same time to be an inspiring model and a wonderful friend.

Three people appeared at crucial moments to get me to the other side of this project. Margaret Cerullo's early and infectious enthusiasm for my work, rendered believable by the fact that she hardly knew me at the time, provided powerful encouragement at a moment when I could have drifted. She also led me to Julia Demin, whose insight and intelli-

ACKNOWLEDGMENTS

gence both freed and anchored me. Finally, Charles Lemert,
whose advice, support, and commitment enabled me to survive in academia.

In addition, I want to thank the following friends and col-
leagues for help and support of many different kinds over
the years: Laura Anker, Leonore Davidoff, Alex and Wanda
Dupuy, Martha Ecker, Sue Fisher, Naomi Gerstel, Steve
Hart, Linda Kopf, Bob O'Gorman, Gail Radford, Ron
Schatz, Frank Sirianni, Mary Sirianni, and Robert Zuss-
man.

Funding from the American Association of University
Women and the American Council of Learned Societies, as
well as a sabbatical from Wesleyan University provided me
with the blocks of time I needed. Irene Spinnler, Pat Arnold, and Nora Moulter have made the Wesleyan Sociology
Department office a cheerful and comfortable place as well
as a source of logistical support. I especially want to thank
the readers for Princeton University Press, whose excellent
comments made this a much better book, and Gail Ullman,
my editor, for her intelligence, patience, and good advice.

Portions of Chapter One are adapted from an earlier article, "Early Modern Fraternalism and the Patriarchal Family," *Feminist Studies*, 6:2 (Summer, 1980). Chapter Three
includes material from "Fraternal Orders and Class Formation in the Nineteenth Century United States," *Comparative
Studies in Society and History*, 27:4 (October, 1985), and a
version of Chapter Six appeared as "Nineteenth-Century
Women's Auxiliaries and Fraternal Orders" in *Signs*, 12:1
(Autumn, 1986). I thank these journals for their permission
to use this material.

Laura Clawson's life has been contemporaneous with the
life of this project, and she had to put up with the highs and
lows it engendered long before she could understand them.
I'm grateful for her presence in my life, and especially for the
way she always encourages me to believe in myself. Dan
Clawson has given me detailed and insightful comments on

every draft of every chapter, helped me with typing and word processing, and kept the house running. I want to thank him for cheering me up, saving me from countless disasters, large and small, and for being my best friend always.

CONSTRUCTING BROTHERHOOD

INTRODUCTION

Fraternalism as a Social Form

In seventeenth-century France, journeymen began to form *compagnonnages*, or journeymen's associations. Through these organizations, they attempted to defend their collective interests against the masters and to provide food, lodging, and guidance for one another as they traveled the country searching for work. In the compagnonnage's elaborate initiation rite the young journeyman symbolically entered a new kin group by renouncing his name of origin and being "baptized" with a new name, known only to his fellow compagnons.

✳

Eighteenth-century British society saw the emergence of Freemasonry as an institutional force. Beginning in the seventeenth century, English and Scottish gentlemen had sought admission into the lodges of practicing stone masons, and from this peculiar practice grew the Masonic system, distinguished by its remarkable combination of social prestige and class diversity. At a time when differences of rank were almost universally accepted as basic to the social order, gentlemen and even nobles joined with merchants and craftsmen in a rite of leveling that ended in their symbolic *elevation* to the idealized status of Master Mason.

✳

In 1881, in Belleville, Illinois, union activist miners joined forces with a fiercely anti-union attorney and mine owner to establish the Garfield Lodge of the Knights of Pythias. The Pythians were a fraternal order, a kind of social organization that enjoyed an overwhelming popularity in this era; of fifty-five organizations and voluntary associations listed in the

3

Belleville City Directory of 1884, thirty-five were local branches of national fraternal organizations. During this same period, hundreds of thousands of American workers became members of the nation's largest labor organization, the Knights of Labor, while many thousands of farmers joined first the Grange (Patrons of Husbandry) then the Farmers' Alliance.

✳

By the end of the nineteenth century, fraternal agents were organizing lodges for a living, paid on commission, like traveling salesmen, to sell the product of lodge membership. In 1915 one such agent, William J. Simmons, came up with a particularly vivid theme for a new order: a recreation of the Ku Klux Klan as a membership organization. The fact that its founder's idea took on a political life of its own should not obscure its origins as one variation of a tried-and-true money-making scheme. In the 1920s, not long after the hapless Simmons had his inspiration, James J. Davis, Supreme Dictator of the Loyal Order of Moose, demonstrated the fraternal order's economic potential by selling his interest in the order for over half a million dollars.

WHAT unites these historically varied associations is the fact that all of them were organized fraternally, brought into being by ritual and based upon the social metaphor of brotherhood. From that seemingly uncomplicated observation derives the subject of this book: the significance of fraternalism, especially Masonic or quasi-Masonic fraternalism, as an unexamined theme in the social and cultural experience of Western Europe, Britain, and the United States. Two points are basic to my argument.

First, fraternalism is an identifiable social and cultural form. It may be defined in terms of four characteristics—a "corporate" idiom, ritual, proprietorship, and masculinity—that appear with remarkable consistency in the guilds, journeymen's societies, and confraternities of late medieval and early modern Europe, the Masonic lodges of eighteenth-

4

century Britain, and the trade unions and fraternal social organizations of nineteenth-century America.

Second, the persistent use of the fraternal form as a mode of organization has been an unrecognized social fact. To the great majority of historians who have even noticed it, the presence of fraternal association has been as uninteresting as it was insignificant. Indeed, the fraternal aspect of any given organization or movement, taken in isolation, can seem trivial, but when we consider the range of organizations that made use of fraternal identity, it is remarkable that it has gone unexplored for so long.

Over centuries of European and American history, fraternalism exerted a persistent appeal, forming the basis for guilds, workers' organizations, political societies, and social groups. For the most part, these organizations have been treated separately and without regard to their fraternal character—the guild as an economic institution, the confraternity in religious terms, the Knights of Labor as a union or political organization. In each case scholars have tended to strip away the epiphenomenal fraternal "trappings" so as to concentrate on the religious, economic, or political "core," which is then seen as the only meaningful part of the institution. This lack of awareness is most pronounced in the study of nineteenth-century American society, where a Masonic type of fraternalism served as the organizational model for trade unions, agricultural societies, nativist organizations, and political movements of every conceivable ideological stripe, as well as for literally hundreds of social organizations.

What is amazing is that even the best and most authoritative of recent historians of social movements have written the history of these organizations without attempting to address their fraternal character. In his book on the Farmers' Alliance, for example, Lawrence Goodwyn emphasizes the importance of a movement culture without considering the heritage of fraternalism as a component of that culture.[1]

---

[1] One indication of this is that the terms ritual, secrecy, brotherhood, lodge,

Leon Fink's study of the Knights of Labor acknowledges that the Knights were organized as a fraternal order, pointing to the linkages between membership in social orders like the Masons, Odd Fellows, and Pythians and participation in the Knights and their opponents. But Fink makes no attempt to *comprehend* the character of the fraternalism that was so much a part of the social and cultural environment of Gilded Age communities.[2]

Late-nineteenth-century American fraternal institutions, like their predecessors, articulated a vision of unity and brotherhood among men of disparate social statuses. But their ability to do this, given the social context in which they flourished, is both fascinating and problematic. The period from the mid-1870s to the 1890s was one of "prolonged,

---

or fraternal and its variants do not even appear in the index. Lawrence Goodwyn, *Democratic Promise: The Populist Movement in America* (New York: Oxford University Press, 1976).

[2] Leon Fink, *Workingmen's Democracy: The Knights of Labor and American Politics* (Urbana, Ill.: University of Illinois Press, 1983). Several scholars have made important contributions to a conceptualization of fraternalism, including Natalie Zemon Davis, John Gillis, William H. Sewell, Jr., Sean Wilentz, and especially E. J. Hobsbawm in his remarkable essay on secret societies and quasi-Masonic brotherhoods in *Primitive Rebels* (New York: W. W. Norton, 1965).

In addition, note the distinction between "fraternity" as a political ideal and "fraternalism" as an institutionalized and historically specific mode of association. Wilson Carey McWilliams's *The Idea of Fraternity in America* (Berkeley, Ca.: University of California Press, 1973) is the definitive treatment of the former. I share with McWilliams a common recognition that (a) the fraternal relation, grounded in the model of kinship, represents a form of masculine solidarity, and that (b) it contains and expresses hierarchical as well as egalitarian assumptions about human relations. But these insights are not as central to the development of McWilliams's argument as to mine.

McWilliams's goal is to trace the theme of fraternity in the history of American political discourse, and thus to consider whether it represents a desirable and feasible political ideal. My purposes are more delimited and historicized: to conceptualize fraternal*ism* as a form of association, depict its institutionalization in American culture through the medium of Freemasonry, and explore the social and cultural significance of Masonic fraternalism in the articulation of class and gender relations in the nineteenth-century United States.

intense, bitter, and spreading class conflict," a period in which, David Montgomery argues, the working class achieved a plane of "moral universality."[3] Yet it also witnessed the growth of fraternal orders as organizations that attracted a multiclass membership of massive and steadily increasing proportions. In 1900, for example, the two largest organizations, the Masons and Odd Fellows, had one million members each, and at least four others had over 500,000 members, drawn from a total adult male population of 21.9 million. At the most straightforward level, fraternal orders are important because of the large number of people who were members. In a more determinative sense, the fraternal order, like any other structure comprising a set of institutionalized relationships, represents a resource—of organization, of coordination and of the potential capacity to mobilize for desired ends.

Here the concept of resource is key—the idea, advanced by social movement theorists such as Charles Tilly, Anthony Oberschall, and Jo Freeman, that the types and levels of resources available to a constituency group are crucial in explaining its ability to mobilize. Similarity in people's life experiences or structural location is one necessary basis for a social movement, but cannot by itself explain either emergence or success. If a group lacks appropriate means and opportunities, it will be unable to engage in effective collective action no matter how compelling the grievances it experiences. Successful social movements typically draw upon a variety of resources, but of these, resource mobilization theorists identify the character and extent of pre-existing social networks as one of the key variables affecting the emergence of movements and shaping their actions.

At the most basic level, social networks allow for communication, a prerequisite for even the most "spontaneous" of activities. As Freeman has written, "Masses alone do not form movements, however discontented they may be . . . If

[3] David Montgomery, "Labor and the Republic in Industrial America: 1860–1920," *Le Mouvement Social*, no. 111 (April–June, 1980): p. 204.

INTRODUCTION

they are not linked in some manner . . . the protest does not become generalized but remains a local irritant or dissolves completely. If a movement is to spread rapidly, the communication network must already exist."[4] Communication, however, is but a first step. Movements operate at an advantage when they can make use of already existing structures of action instead of having to build from scratch. The trust and confidence developed through informal acquaintance can facilitate cooperative activity while the more formal structures of ongoing social institutions can provide the resources of leadership and expertise.

The associational life of a protest or interest group is thus crucial to its ability to mobilize. The civil rights movement, for example, was made possible by the social networks created by the black colleges and the black church, and thus already in place.[5] Similarly, feminist scholars identify same-sex association as a key variable affecting the relative position of men and women. Men typically have access to extensive social networks outside the family, which privilege them vis-à-vis their female relatives. The extent of women's networks varies, and with this women's autonomy and well-being; the societies that most closely approach sexual egalitarianism seem to be those in which women possess forms of organization outside the family and paralleling those of men.[6] Viewed from such a perspective, the significance of fraternalism becomes clearer.

But it is not enough to recognize that the fraternal order

---

[4] Jo Freeman, "Origins of Social Movements," in Jo Freeman, ed., *Social Movements of the Sixties and Seventies* (New York: Longman, 1983), p. 9.

[5] Ibid., pp. 10–13; Aldon D. Morris, in *The Origins of the Civil Rights Movement: Black Communities Organizing for Change* (New York: Free Press, 1984), extensively documents the role of the black church in the civil rights movement.

[6] Michelle Zimbalist Rosaldo, "Woman, Culture and Society: A Theoretical Overview," in Michelle Zimbalist Rosaldo and Louise Lamphere, eds., *Woman, Culture and Society* (Stanford, Ca.: Stanford University Press, 1974); Peggy Sanday, *Female Power and Male Dominance: On the Origins of Sexual Inequality* (Cambridge: Cambridge University Press, 1981).

8

is a resource, a potential contribution to a group's capacity to organize and mobilize itself. We must ask: who is mobilized? who is included, who is excluded, and on what basis do they understand themselves to be a group? Resource mobilization theory has tended to take as its object of study, and thus to assume, pre-existing collectivities with relatively fixed identities. It then asks: how will this group be mobilized? what are the institutional contingencies that make collective action more or less likely? under what circumstances will blacks organize to resist racism, workers form unions, women demand the vote? Such a perspective assumes that the identity and self-understanding of the group is given, preordained. It fails to examine "the constitution of the collectivity itself"; it fails to recognize that "the historical production of social categories" is in itself problematic and in need of analysis.[7]

The growing literature on class formation was the first to undertake such an analysis: first, through the development of a body of historical work that takes class formation as its implicit subject (beginning with E. P. Thompson's *The Making of the English Working Class*), and second, through more explicit attempts to theorize the bases of class formation. All these accounts emphasize that the emergence of class is a historically variable process as dependent for its emergence on the political economy, culture, and organizational structure of particular societies as it is on the abstract logic of the accumulation process. We may then ask, in a nonteleological fashion, how people responded to the transformations brought about by capitalist development. Under what circumstances does class emerge, in Ira Katznelson's words, "as a way of organizing, thinking about, and acting

---

[7] Craig Calhoun, *The Question of Class Struggle: Social Foundations of Popular Radicalism during the Industrial Revolution* (Chicago: University of Chicago Press, 1982), p. 144; Tim Carrigan, Bob Connell, and John Lee, "Toward a New Sociology of Masculinity," *Theory and Society* 14:5 (1985): p. 552.

on society"?[8] And, what was the relationship of class to alternative principles of collective identity and action such as race, ethnicity, and, particularly important to this work, gender?

Gender relations are equally the product of historical processes, comparable though not precisely parallel to those of class formation. On the one hand, it is undeniably the case that all societies structure and conceptualize social relations around gender, a fundamental principle of human organization. Thus there is no question whether gender will emerge as a social category. Nonetheless gender, like class, constitutes a system of institutionalized power relations, a terrain of struggle, and an interpretive framework for the construction of social life. In each aspect, it is historically variable, its character in any given society the product of complex interactions between and among men and women struggling to make use of the political, economic, and cultural resources available to them.[9]

In principle, class and gender exist as separate bases of oppression and thus as alternative points of personal and collective interest around which solidarity might be constructed. In practice the relationship is far more complex, as gender, class, and other modes of domination interact to create historically specific social and cultural systems. Identification based upon class, gender, race, and ethnicity may appear as a set of discrete alternatives; but more commonly, the density of historical experience intertwines them in intricate and consequential ways. It is this process that inter-

[8] Ira Katznelson, "Working-Class Formation: Constructing Cases and Comparisons," in Ira Katznelson and Aristide Zolberg, eds., *Working-Class Formation: 19th Century Patterns in Western Europe and the United States* (Princeton, N.J.: Princeton University Press, 1986), p. 3. In general, see this volume for a systematic and comparative attempt to conceptualize class formation.

[9] Judith M. Gerson and Kathy Peiss's "Boundaries, Negotiations, Consciousness: Reconceptualizing Gender Relations," *Social Problems* 32:4 (April, 1985), is an excellent statement of this perspective on gender. See also Carrigan et al., "Sociology of Masculinity."

ests me: I seek to understand both class and gender as socially constructed and contested identities that interact with one other. Fraternalism offers a privileged point of access into this issue because it allows us to ask, in historically specific terms, how the kinds of organizations that nineteenth-century American men belonged to affected class mobilization and gender identity.

First, fraternal orders were organizations, and thus social resources. The question then arises: to whom did the resource of fraternal organization belong and to what uses could it be put? That is, what social categories were being validated, and what denied? Because the fraternal order as an institution is so centrally "about" social bonding, the question of whom fraternal organizations include and whom they exclude, what groups they help to unite and what groups they help to isolate, becomes especially significant.

Typically, fraternal forms of association have reached across boundaries, tending to unite men from a relatively wide social, economic, or religious spectrum. At the same time, fraternalism bases itself on a principle of exclusion, from which it derives much of its power. This seeming contradiction highlights the fact that the fraternal order cannot be understood as simply a random assemblage of people. Rather, it was a cultural and associational form with an implicit content, a guiding logic. If the fraternal order was a potential resource for social action, it was by no means a neutral resource. All social action is symbolic and reflexive. But fraternalism, as an institution explicitly defined by ritual, especially demands to be analyzed as a historically-shaped symbolic form. Its significance resides not only in the social networks it created, reinforced, or displayed, but in the meanings it articulated, the cultural context it provided for social action.

Several principles orient my analysis of fraternalism as a cultural form. First, cultural constructs—products, events, texts—play a cognitive as well as an interpretive role. The cultural "organization of experience" is not just a retrospec-

11

INTRODUCTION

tive making sense of it, but is, in Robert Wuthnow's words, "constitutive of meaningful experience itself." "Reality" and consciousness are themselves socially created through "the selective organization of objects and events into patterns and through the location of objects and events in symbolic frames of reference."[10] That is, cultural constructs shape how we view the world and what we can know. Selectivity is central to this process; every culture is the product of "absence, omission, neglect, and suppression" as well as of "invention and inclusion."[11]

Second, cultural construction is both a consensual and a conflictual process. It rests upon the availability of shared forms of discourse and shared meaning systems, without which communication would be impossible. Still, that discourse, while shared, is not unitary but inflected with the differing perceptions and interests of its participants. Indeed, the power of a cultural product may depend precisely on its ability to engage people at different levels of meaning, to resolve symbolically the contradictory experiences of everyday life.

Third, because of its cognitive significance, culture is a resource and thus both an object and a terrain of struggle. Because the ability to define reality is a form of power, the struggle to define "reality" is a political one. Gramsci's concept of hegemonic structuring best captures both the structural limits and the play of oppositional forces that infuse cultural discourse. In Gramsci's account, the dominant class does structure consciousness, in the sense that it exercises a disproportionate influence over the definition of social reality. Yet, significantly, this "reality" is a contested one, constantly challenged by the experiences, needs, demands, and imputations of subordinate groups. Thus, cultural products, "in their multiplicitous and varied forms, are not only pat-

[10] Robert Wuthnow, *The Consciousness Reformation* (Berkeley, Ca.: University of California Press, 1976), p. 62.
[11] Susan G. Davis, *Parades and Power: Street Theatre in Nineteenth-Century Philadelphia* (Philadelphia: Temple University Press, 1986), p. 15.

12

terned by social forces—they . . . [are] part of the very building and challenging of social relations."[12]

Within such cultural processes, rituals have a special character. On the one hand, like other forms of communication, ritual is cognitive. Its selective focus "draws people's attention to certain forms of relationship and activity—and at the same time, therefore, deflects their attention from other forms, since every way of seeing is also a way of not seeing." It thus defines "as authoritative certain ways of seeing society."[13] But ritual is analogous to art; it must exert an aesthetic appeal if people are to be drawn to its repetitive reenactment. Like art, ritual can both express and generate sensibilities, styles of feelings, aesthetically satisfying interpretations of social experience. At the same time, ritual is a collective experience that creates social relationships as it creates meaning. The cognitive "truth" of ritual is thus confirmed for its members not simply by its seeming factuality or intellectual consistency, but by the aesthetic power of the images it offers and the character of the social relations that are created and cemented by the ritual experience.[14]

Fraternalism was one of the most widely available and persistently used forms of collective organization in European and American history from the Middle Ages onward. Any explanation of this must take into account its ritual character. Initiations and other ceremonies were dramatic enactments. Like the street parades that Susan Davis writes about, they were "dramas of social relations" in which "performers define who can be a social actor" and thus "what society was or might be."[15] In the case of Masonic fraternalism, I would argue, the image of one particular social actor, the artisan, dominated the reality-defining drama/discourse of fraternal ritual.

[12] Ibid., p. 5.
[13] Steven Lukes, "Political Ritual and Social Integration," *Sociology* 9:2 (May, 1975): p. 301.
[14] Calhoun, *Question of Class Struggle*, p. 16.
[15] Davis, *Parades and Power*, p. 6.

INTRODUCTION

THIS book argues that Masonic fraternalism exerted a special appeal to anyone seeking to establish or reaffirm a symbolic relationship to the figure of the producer-proprietor, especially as it was exemplified by the contradictory figure of the artisan. Masonic fraternalism has often been seen simply as a product of the Enlightenment, an expression of eighteenth- and nineteenth-century liberalism. But Masonry was not merely liberal, because it contained a critique of individualism and an antidote to it as well as an affirmation of it. This complexity derived from proprietorial, especially artisanal, culture, which, as recent historians have noted, stands in a singularly problematic relationship to an emergent capitalist order.

Masonic fraternalism valorized craft labor and material productivity. In traditional liberal fashion it justified social inequality by presenting it as a system open to talent, a ladder that anyone and everyone could ascend. But it simultaneously recognized the dislocations of capitalist development through its promise of mutual aid. It thus offered the vision of a society in which individual advancement and social solidarity were complementary rather than antagonistic—and attempted to create that society in miniature.

It is important to realize that in offering such a vision, Masonic fraternalism drew upon an additional resource, the fact that the identity of the artisan was a gendered identity of a historically specific type. The individualism that was one of its contradictory components was a characteristic that the natural rights philosophers accorded only to men; at the same time, fraternal mutuality was inspired by a vision of masculine camaraderie derived from the workshop and the tavern. In late nineteenth-century America this collective identity was subject to assault from two directions. Industrial development and the growing assertion of a feminine vision of social and affective life threatened to undermine major institutions of male solidarity, thus making fraternal institutions doubly attractive.

Originating in the corporate bodies of medieval and early

modern Europe, given a powerful and appealing reinterpretation via the Masonic movement, the fraternal order played an important role in organizing the social and cultural life of American communities in the nineteenth and early twentieth centuries. It was, then, important both for its role in creating and consolidating social ties and for its promotion of particular values, identities, and implicit models of society. This book will argue that through its construction of ties based upon images of masculinity and craftsmanship, the mixed-class, all-male American fraternal order worked to deny the significance of class difference and to offer gender and race as appropriate categories for the organization of collective identity. An understanding of American fraternalism's appeal and influence must be based upon (1) an analysis of its European antecedents and (2) the transformation of those earlier themes in the context of American culture and socioeconomic development.

The lodges of nineteenth- and twentieth-century America were the descendants of an earlier European fraternalism, examined in Chapter One. Guilds, journeymen's societies, religious confraternities, and village youth brotherhoods were all forms of fraternal association, making it one of the most widespread and culturally central modes of organization in late medieval and early modern Europe. In societies where kinship remained the primary basis of solidary relations, fraternal association was effective because it used quasi-kin relations to extend bonds of loyalty and obligation beyond the family, to incorporate people into kin networks, or to create new relations having something of the force of kinship.

Freemasonry was the particular vehicle by which fraternalism entered American society. Chapter Two looks at the Masonic reworking of earlier European fraternal institutions, while Chapter Four outlines the development of an American fraternalism heavily influenced by the Masonic model. Freemasonry involved the transformation of the traditional craft brotherhood into a social and convivial institution patronized by men drawn from an unusually wide spectrum of British society—from aristocrats and gentlemen to artisanal masters and even journeymen. The creation of Freemasonry expressed in a particularly vivid way the broader social importance of craft labor, which contributed not just to scientific advance but to commercial and manufactured wealth. By symbolically *becoming* masons, members of the British elite expressed their commitment to the emerging market economy and to the social value of craft labor and material productivity. They identified the craft worker as a heroic figure and valorized the artisanal culture from which he emerged even as they infused it with their own goals and values.

In Chapters Three, Four, and Five I develop an argument about the consistency of the relationship between fraternalism and artisanal identity. The two major forms of fraternalism in nineteenth-century America were workplace-based organizations—trade associations and fraternally organized unions and benefit societies—and a social fraternalism based upon Freemasonry. Although they followed separate paths of development, the continuing interplay between the two kinds of organizations reveals their essential kinship. Chapter Three examines the social composition of lodges while Chapter Four traces their history. Fraternal orders were indeed open-class organizations, but their membership was most heavily concentrated among two core groups: skilled workers and proprietors, that is, among the two groups for whom the identity of artisan remained crucial.

In Chapter Five I look at the connection between social fraternalism and its origins in the craft workshop. Outstanding recent work in both European and American social history reveals the central role of artisans in shaping early working-class experience. Economically pressured, their work reorganized and transformed, artisans nonetheless persisted in the sometimes contradictory values of self-improvement, mutuality, fellowship, and pride of craft, values that were fostered and sustained by the masculine culture of the workshop. The fraternal order abstracted those characteristics from their social foundations in the relations of the craft workshop and the community of artisanal workers and presented them as the basis for a larger social solidarity. As the kinds of workplace solidarity that had been available to masters and workers early in the nineteenth century became increasingly untenable, fraternalism, through its re-creation of an idealized artisanal world, could make a special and analogous appeal to the entrepreneurs and skilled workers who formed the largest segment of lodge membership.

If fraternalism was unusually congenial to American society in its approach to class relations, it stood at odds with the culture in another way. In its character as a masculine organization, it not only maintained sexual segregation, it also rejected many of the century's most deeply held convictions about gender, especially the belief in the spiritual role of women and men's dependence upon them. Chapter Six looks at fraternal attitudes toward womanhood, with their origins in an earlier Masonic era, then outlines the orders' attempts to deal with the feminine disapproval and resistance that their practices elicited.

Chapter Seven makes the argument that by the late nineteenth century fraternal orders could no longer be regarded as simple voluntary associations. Instead, they had become entrepreneurial organizations that operated so as to maximize membership growth and financial profit or stability. To this end, most orders employed agents who worked on commission to organize lodges much as a traveling salesman would sell any other product. In this case the chief product distinguishing one order from another was the ritual, a mini-drama that was acted out by the members of each local lodge. The orders altered and revised their rituals periodically in attempts to make them more appealing and thus to improve their competitive position. Through this process, fraternal orders acted as providers of something approaching mass media entertainment. In their creation and dissemination of ritual dramas, they were marketing a standardized entertainment product that was reproduced socially and organizationally rather than electronically, as radio, films, and records would be. Fraternal rhetoric continued to emphasize the relation of brotherhood, the ideal of a noncontractual mutuality, but fraternal sociability occurred within organizations that were increasingly centralized and entrepreneurial in character.

THIS book should be understood as a project of conceptualization, of advancing a formulation that is necessarily suggestive rather than definitive. I have chosen to focus on social fraternalism in the belief that the fraternal impetus would be most available to scrutiny in those organizations where it was the major raison d'être. My hope is that scholars looking at the whole range of fraternally inspired organizations will be motivated to incorporate and refine my formulation, to consider in greater depth how fraternalism's formal qualities interacted with variations in the identities of participants, social and historical context, and organizational goals and resources.

Reworked and transformed by each generation, fraternalism remained available as a cultural resource with a characteristic vocabulary, interactional style, and set of preoccupations. Fraternalism used ritual to create solidarity, to articulate group identity, and to address concerns about class, gender, and other kinds of social difference. As a result, it is a particularly appropriate vehicle for the study of class and gender relations, as well as a social form of intrinsic interest to sociologists and historians.

PART ONE

✳

EUROPEAN
DEFINITIONS

ONE

The Fraternal Model

NINETEENTH-CENTURY American fraternal orders made constant reference to the past, portraying themselves as the modern embodiments of age-old traditions. The re-creation of cultural traditions is a highly selective process, as much a work of invention as of preservation or replication. The lodges of nineteenth-century America were so remote, both temporally and organizationally, from the fraternalism of early modern Europe that any attempt to draw connections between the two warrants skepticism. Yet that is precisely what I intend to do. The connections that I draw are not causal, certainly not genealogical in the sense that nineteenth-century fraternalists meant when, for example, they traced the origins of Freemasonry back to the building of King Solomon's Temple. It is not necessary to draw precise organizational links in order to identify continuities of theme and style and to recognize that fraternalism, as a distinctive form of association, was a widely available resource for organizing and understanding the social world, a central part of the repertoire of popular action in Europe and America for some five hundred years.

The power of the fraternal form is most clearly visible in the popular culture of early modern Europe, where it pervaded almost all facets of daily life. In this chapter I use a synthetic overview of early modern fraternalism to accomplish two ends: first, to convey the appeal of fraternalism through an analysis of its many uses within a variety of social contexts, and second, to identify and explore the common features of fraternal association so as to construct an ideal-typical definition of fraternalism as a social form.

21

The key to understanding early modern fraternalism and the appeal of fraternalism more generally, lies in the recognition of kinship as a wide-reaching and socially-constructed mode of social organization. Only when we see the fundamental role played by familial relationships can we understand both the appeal and the utility of fraternal association as a means of extending the organizing power of kinship. And only then can we perceive that the assumptions about mutual obligation and masculine authority underlying the patriarchal family system of early modern Europe, structure the character of fraternalism as well.

The importance of kinship is most apparent in pre-state societies, where it is the central social relation that organizes "economic, political, and ceremonial, as well as sexual activity. One's duties, responsibilities, and privileges vis-à-vis others are defined in terms of mutual kinship or lack thereof. The exchange of goods and services, production and distribution, hostility and solidarity, ritual and ceremony, all take place within the organizational structure of kinship."[1] Friendship, mutuality, and the possibility of stable social relations are in this view nearly synonymous with kinship, a sentiment that was almost as frequently expressed in medieval Europe, where the common term for kinfolk was simply "friend," as it was in the pre-state societies described by anthropologists.[2]

[1] Gayle Rubin, "The Traffic in Women: Notes on the 'Political Economy' of Sex," in Rayna R. Reiter, ed., *Toward an Anthropology of Women* (New York and London: Monthly Review Press, 1975), pp. 169–70. See also Marshall D. Sahlins, *Tribesmen* (Englewood Cliffs, N.J.: Prentice-Hall, 1968), pp. 74–75.

[2] Marc Bloch, *Feudal Society*, trans. L. A. Manyon (Chicago: Phoenix Books, 1964), pp. 123–24. For additional discussions of the relationship between kinship and friendship, see John Bossy, "Blood and Baptism: Kinship, Community and Christianity in Western Europe From the Fourteenth to the Seventeenth Centuries," in Derek Baker, ed., *Sanctity and Secularity: The Church and the World* (New York: Harper and Row, 1973); and Lawrence Stone, "The Rise of the Nuclear Family in Early Modern England: The Patriarchal Stage," in Charles Rosenberg, ed., *The Family in History* (Philadelphia: University of Pennsylvania Press, 1975).

In early modern Europe, kinship occupied a less central place in social organization as the growth of state-organized societies involved a largely successful attempt to shape kin relations and transfer resources from kin to class-based control.[3] Nonetheless, the passage quoted above comes much closer to indicating the attitude to kinship, the attachment to its traditional forms, and the vigorous attempts to create new ones that endured among the common people of late medieval and early modern Europe, than do our necessarily attenuated modern conceptions of kin relations and their significance.

As the persistence of fraternalism and other fictive kin relations demonstrates, the attachment to kinship as a mode of organizing and understanding social relations was not easily relinquished. The efforts of the state and the church to shape kinship to their own ends were often resisted. Attachment to kinship was expressed in the early modern period in three ways. The first was through strong involvement in large kin groups, which persisted in many rural areas until well into the sixteenth and seventeenth centuries.[4] The second was through the continued conceptualization of the economic relations of household production as patriarchal and familial—an understanding that was actually stressed in this period. The third was through the creation, in villages and towns, of a variety of institutions that relied on the concept of kinship for their form and appeal and that performed many of the tasks that had belonged to the extended family. Through fictive kin relations such as godparenthood and the various fraternal forms of association, kinship remained not just a powerful ideal, but a practical mode of organiza-

---

[3] Rayna R. Reiter, "Men and Women in the South of France: Public and Private Domains," in Reiter, *Toward an Anthropology of Women*, pp. 252–82, offers a theoretical discussion of this process, and Stone, "Nuclear Family," gives a particular example.

[4] John Bossy, "The Counter-Reformation and the People of Catholic Europe," *Past and Present*, no. 47 (May, 1970): pp. 51–70; Bloch, *Feudal Society*, pp. 123–42; and Stone, "Nuclear Family," pp. 14–21.

tion rooted in the realities of social, economic, and religious life. Godparenthood allows the best insight into the character of such relationships because even today we recognize it as a substitute kin relation entailing obligations on the part of the godparent to the child. But the modern concept of godparenthood sees only the relation between godparent and godchild; it ignores the ways in which the relation involves all the family members. What the anthropologist Esther Goody calls "pro-parenthood" is also an "effective way of forging links between adults. . . . Where the sharing of parental roles is institutionalized, as in the giving of foster children and ritual sponsorship, such links are systematically created. To understand these as simply ways of coping with crisis situations or of arranging to cope with them should they occur, is to fail to recognize the way in which many societies make use of the bonds between parent and child."[5] In late medieval and early modern society, baptism and the resulting godparental relationship was just such a form of ritual sponsorship, which functioned to intensify existing kin relations and to create new ones. Its ritual constructed a "formal state of friendship" that "somewhat resembles that of blood brotherhood or of fraternity in general."[6]

Just as baptism signified that one entered the church as a member of a kin group, so fraternal institutions like the confraternity, the guild, the société joyeuse, and the many youth societies indicate that people also structured their religious practice, their work, and their celebrations around relationships conceptualized as familial. Fraternal association provided the ritualized means by which their members could

[5] Esther N. Goody, "Forms of Pro-Parenthood: The Sharing and Substitution of Parental Roles," in Jack Goody, ed., *Kinship, Selected Readings* (1971), quoted in Herbert G. Gutman, *The Black Family in Slavery and Freedom, 1750–1925* (New York: Pantheon, 1976), pp. 220–21.

[6] Bossy, "Blood and Baptism," pp. 133–34; see also Bossy, "Counter-Reformation," p. 58; and A. N. Galpern, *The Religions of The People in Sixteenth Century Champagne*, (Cambridge: Harvard University Press, 1976), pp. 45, 78–80.

define one another as brothers; biologically unrelated individuals thus used kinship to construct the solidarity necessary to accomplish a variety of tasks. Despite the contraction of the extended family, the larger ideal of kinship remained "the idiom of social interaction" and "the model of all effective social relations."[7]

Once this is understood, we can see how the assumptions that underlay kin relations extended into the activities structured by fraternal association and permeated the fabric of everyday life. The model of society as family envisions people not as isolated individuals, but as occupants of specific social roles defined by their inherent relationships to one another. It envisions society not as a collection of individuals, but as a corporate entity that has meaning prior to and greater than the life and interest of any single person. In accord with such a concept of social life, fraternal institutions stressed an ethos of mutual obligation and collective responsibility for the well-being of others. At the same time, fraternal association, like the family system that was its implicit model, assumed the legitimacy of hierarchy and the givenness of age and gender inequality. An understanding of early modern fraternalism is thus necessarily predicated upon an understanding of the patriarchal family system to which it was so closely linked.

KINSHIP WITHIN THE PATRIARCHAL HOUSEHOLD

Patriarchy is a concept frequently used by contemporary feminists; in some cases it refers to any system of male dominance, in others it is defined more narrowly as any system

[7] Rubin, "Traffic in Women," p. 169; and Bossy, "Blood and Baptism," p. 135. In "Counter-Reformation," Bossy argues that a central aspect of the Counter-Reformation was the church's attempt to destroy a popular Catholicism that was dominated by kin imperatives and served as a counter to the power of the institutional church. In Bossy's view, the hierarchy was successful in breaking the power of kinship, but at the price of a Catholicism stripped of its popular appeal.

in which male power is derived principally from the rule of men in their roles as husbands and fathers. But in early modern Europe, patriarchy does not simply refer to the rule of men over women. Historians use the very similar term "patriarchalism" to describe the basic authority relation that governed production in a society in which production took place primarily within the household. It was thus an authority that included not only the householder's biological family, but also the servants and apprentices who lived as members of the family.[8]

Patriarchalism found its definition in the relationship between the father/head of household and the children, servants, and apprentices who were both his dependents and his workers. The proper relationship between master and servant was believed to be that of a father and child. Servants owed their master respect and filial obedience as well as labor, while he in return owed them religious education, moral governance, and education in a trade, as well as their keep. As a popular book on household government in Stuart England stated: "The householder is called Pater Familias, that is, a father of a familie, because he should have a fatherly care over his servants, as if they were his children. [All] godly servants . . . may in a few words learne what dutie they owe their masters, mistresses, and dames: namely to love them, and to be affectionated towards them, as a dutifull child is towards his father."[9]

However moralistic or ideological it might be, this interpretation of the patriarchal relation was rooted in social conditions that rendered it plausible. The small scale of production, combined with the practice of living in, meant that the head of the household "was in direct personal contact with those who worked side by side with him under his orders.

---

[8] Peter Laslett, *The World We Have Lost*, 2d ed., rev. (New York: Charles Scribner's Sons, 1973).

[9] John Dod and Robert Cleaver, *A Godly Form of Household Government*, quoted in Gordon J. Schocket, "Patriarchalism, Politics and Mass Attitudes in Stuart England," *The Historical Journal* 12 (1969): p. 415.

He knew them and could hardly help feeling some responsibility both for their physical and for their spiritual welfare."[10] The shared experiences of daily life worked to define the relationship as a familial one.

Equally important was a concept of the family that saw biological members as productive workers on whose labor the family depended.[11] Daughters and sons of the family routinely worked alongside servants or were themselves sent out to other households to work. Servants were typically young unmarried people, often children. The categories of child and worker were overlapping rather than distinct, because families viewed their biological children as workers, as well as their workers as family members.

Thus, the family in a system of household production was not congruent with the nuclear unit of mother, father, and children. The obligations, expectations, and authority relations that bound household members, including servants and apprentices, were not determined by either biological or contractual considerations. Instead, the relations of masters and servants in the patriarchal household of early modern Europe were placed within the rubric of kin relations.

The special situation of young people within this patriarchal household has been seen as one major source of early modern fraternalism.[12] In a society dominated by household production, which did not yet identify wage laborers as a

[10] Christopher Hill, *Society and Puritanism in Pre-Revolutionary England* (New York: Schocken Books, 1967), p. 449.

[11] Laslett, *World We Have Lost*, p. 3; Joan W. Scott and Louise A. Tilly, "Women's Work and the Family in Nineteenth Century Europe," *Comparative Studies in Society and History* 17 (January, 1975): pp. 41, 44–45.

[12] John R. Gillis, *Youth and History: Tradition and Change in European Age Relations, 1770–Present* (New York: Academic Press, 1974). His concentration on the history of youth sensitized Gillis to the significance of fraternalism, but it also led him to identify it exclusively in terms of the dilemmas of youth in the patriarchal family and to neglect its important adult manifestations. This limits his understanding of fraternalism, as does his failure to see that the history of "youth" as he describes it is essentially a history of young males. But his contribution to my thinking has been crucial.

permanent category (or was only beginning to), adulthood, proprietorship, and the right to marry were inextricably linked. On the one hand, a man could not hope to survive, as farmer or craftsman, on the basis of his own labor power; he needed a family or a household of dependents to work for him. On the other hand, the ability to have a family depended on proprietorship, possession of some means of production, given the absence of wage labor as an alternative source of income. So despite the fact that servants and apprentices left their parents, earned their keep, and contributed to the productive capacity of the household, they were in no sense independent or adult. Subordinate to the household head, unable to marry, unable to live or work on their own, "they were constantly reminded of their semidependence by their inferior economic, social, and legal status in a society in which full rights were reserved mainly to the heads of families and other 'masters' of the craft and corporate hierarchies."[13]

The duration of this semidependent state must be stressed, as it often lasted into the late twenties. In France, for example, journeymen, not just apprentices, were legally minors until just prior to the Revolution.[14] And while its ultimate tendency would be to replace semidependency with wage labor, early capitalist development often had the reverse effect of prolonging youthful dependency and exacerbating its contradictions. As craft production was subtly altered by the demands of the market, the progression from journeyman to master ceased to be automatic; accession to mastership was increasingly reserved for the sons of masters or for those who could afford to pay the requisite fees. In rural areas, population pressures and attempts by large landowners to rationalize agriculture combined to deny many

[13] Gillis, *Youth and History*, p. 9.
[14] Emanuel Chill, "The Seventeenth Century Compagnonnage," paper presented at the Society for French Historical Studies, 2 April 1965, pp. 22–23.

young men the chance to own land and to delay the possibility for many more.[15]

Thus, young people typically faced a long period of dependency and subordination, even when their age and skills qualified them for adulthood. A potential for conflict was built into the patriarchal household. How did masters cope with restive young people and how did they in turn endure the long period of subordination?

They may, of course, have shared the values of patriarchalism that so permeated the entire society. The patriarchal relationship was not confined to the household; rather, it was used in the early modern period as an overarching metaphor that explained and justified other forms of authority, including that of the king over his people.[16] The fact that patriarchalism was tied into the culture's larger system of authority, and not just limited to specific relationships within the household, must have greatly increased its power. This was especially true when linked to the expectation that one would oneself some day succeed to some form of patriarchal authority.

But the existence of associations of young people separate from the family suggests that whatever value consensus did exist was not sufficient, or at least that it had to be mediated through semi-autonomous forms of interaction, rather than directly through the family. Separate traditions of youth, "horizontal bondings of young single persons," occurred throughout society, from the associations of young craftsmen to the social groupings of rural youth. These fraternal institutions have been viewed as an integral part of the system of patriarchal social control, functioning to sustain youth during the long period of apprenticeship, formal or

---

[15] Cynthia M. Truant, "Independent and Insolent: Journeymen and Their 'Rites' in the Old Regime Workplace," in Stephen Laurence Kaplan and Cynthia J. Koepp, eds., *Work in France: Representations, Meaning, Organization, and Practice* (Ithaca, N.Y.: Cornell University Press, 1986), pp. 137–38; and Gillis, *Youth and History*, pp. 12–14, 31.

[16] Schocket, "Patriarchalism," p. 424.

otherwise. But while this was surely the case, the study of fraternal youth institutions reveals that they also provided their participants with institutionalized ways to intervene in the patriarchal system in defense of their own interests. The fraternal forms of early modern youth must be seen as social relationships that both articulated patriarchal assumptions and values and asserted the interests of the semi-autonomous young against particular manifestations of patriarchal power.

Associations of journeymen, known as compagnonnages in France and *Gesellenverbande* in Germany, arose from the traditional practice of journeymen going out on the road after finishing their formal apprenticeship, but before themselves becoming masters. Usually understood as a way for craftsmen to gain additional experience in their trade, it was also a method of lengthening the period of apprenticeship at a time when the progression from journeyman to master was becoming problematic. The journeymen's associations helped to make this growing period of travel meaningful by upholding "the ideal of continence and the delay of marriage, relying on an elaborate imagery and ritual of 'brotherhood' to solidify the social and moral bonds within their group."[17] This was done through a constant invocation of the imagery and authority of the family, which makes the connections between patriarchalism and fraternalism especially clear.

The three compagnonnages were titled the Children of Father Soubise, the Children of Master Jacques, and the Children of Solomon. Their familial character was made immediately explicit in their elaborate initiation ritual, a "baptism" in which the initiate became a member of a symbolic family. During this ceremony he renounced his original family name, received a nickname known only to his brother journeymen, and was "baptized" with wine by a "priest" in the presence of a "godfather" and "godmother," all of whom

17 Gillis, *Youth and History*, p. 22.

were fellow journeymen.[18] These compagnons clearly viewed baptism in the tradition of medieval popular religion, as an event celebrating and affirming the individual's entrance into a kinship group. The direct appropriation of the baptismal rite as the initiation rite for the group shows the extent to which these journeymen's associations were conceived of as substitute kin groups.

Journeymen were, as the name implies, among the most geographically mobile people in their society, and they were also among the few to be physically removed from direct patriarchal supervision within the household. The compagnonnage, with its elaborate rituals, can be seen as a direct response to the particular and rather unusual situation that journeymen faced. It provided a "highly institutionalized arrangement by which members of the trades were cared for and protected while on the road," a ritualized and structured social life to make up for the absence of actual physical supervision in the household.[19]

For these reasons, fraternal rituals and traditions were most elaborately developed among craftsmen. Youth in other strata experienced different needs, yet almost all of them faced the common dilemma of a prolonged period of celibacy and subordination. Rural youth comprised by far the largest group, because 85 percent of the population lived on the land during this period. These young people lived under the much more direct supervision of father or master and were much more tightly bound into the network of patriarchal control. They had far less need to affirm and re-

[18] E. J. Hobsbawm, *Primitive Rebels* (New York: W. W. Norton, 1965), pp. 155–56; Gillis, *Youth and History*, p. 23; Daniel Roche, "Work, Fellowship and Some Economic Realities of Eighteenth Century France," and Truant, "Independent and Insolent," both in Kaplan and Koepp, *Work in France*, pp. 66, 144.

[19] Gillis, *Youth and History*, p. 23. See Rose Laub Coser, "Stay Home Little Sheba: On Placement, Displacement, and Social Change," *Social Problems* 22 (1975), for ritualistic role enactment as a way of minimizing the potentially disruptive effects of travel.

create the structures of patriarchal authority within their associations because they were constantly encountering it within the household. Their activities were more concerned with the celebration of whatever moments of free time they had and with the articulation of a separate youthful identity. Yet their concerns remained focused on the power of the patriarchal household and the period of enforced celibacy that shaped their existence. These concerns were expressed by the youth abbeys, the associations of village youth, and by their most characteristic weapon, the charivari—the noisy, masked demonstration and procession which attacked its victims through ridicule and public humiliation.

The chief activity of village youth groups was "the regulation of communal sexuality, particularly the access to marriage."[20] Their goal was to protect the pool of young unmarried women during the period when young men were unable to marry because of their dependent status. The charivari's most common target in rural areas was the rich, elderly widower who had remarried and thus taken one of the village girls out of the pool of eligibles. In such cases, the aged newlywed would find himself awakened by a crowd outside his window, as effigies of his dead wife and of himself sitting backwards on an ass were paraded through the streets for all to see. Although these young people were theoretically powerless to override the authority of elders, in fact they could influence communal standards and to some extent affect particular parental decisions through this aggressive system of social pressure and ridicule. This was far from an empty conflict. "Parents were naturally concerned with marriage as a means of improving the family's holdings and status in the community, and it was not uncommon for well-to-do peasants to withhold their daughters from peer group activity in order to protect this vital interest."[21]

[20] Gillis, *Youth and History*, p. 29.
[21] Ibid., pp. 30–31. See also Natalie Z. Davis, "The Reasons of Misrule: Youth Groups and Charivaris in Sixteenth Century France," *Past and Present*, no. 50 (February, 1971): pp. 50–54.

When village youths challenged a family's choice of a mate for its daughter, they were in fact challenging a critical prerogative of parental authority. Yet the challenge remained, as Natalie Z. Davis has pointed out, a highly ritualized one, embedded in a complex set of rituals and traditions whose major effect was to sustain and incorporate them into the village community. "They gave the youth rituals to help control their sexual instincts and also allowed them some limited sphere of jurisdiction or 'autonomy' in the interval before they were married. They socialized them to the conscience of the community by making them the raucous voice of that conscience." Like the compagnonnages, the abbeys and Brudderschaften provided the young with emotional support, moral standards, and a social role that helped them to remain content with their dependent status and their prolonged inability to marry and set up their own households. They created, as Davis comments, not just "a rule which youth had over others," but a "brotherhood existing among themselves."[22]

Fraternalism among Adults

Fraternalism was just as basic to the organization of the adult world, if not more so. Trade corporations or guilds, for example, were the principle means by which craft production was organized in the cities of the early modern period.[23] As organizations of master craftsmen, they regulated apprenticeship, set the conditions for admission into the trade, controlled prices and enforced standards of quality

[22] Davis, "Reasons of Misrule," pp. 55, 54.
[23] I use the term trade corporation rather than guild because it is more inclusive. The precise organization of the trades varied from city to city. "But whether organized as métiers jurés, as municipally regulated trades, as confraternities, or as simple customary communities, corporations everywhere had the same essential characteristics"—William H. Sewell, Jr., *Work and Revolution in France: The Language of Labor from the Old Regime to 1848* (Cambridge: Cambridge University Press, 1980), p. 39.

33

through periodic inspections. In addition, trade associations functioned as organs of urban government with responsibility for civic defense, policing, and public ceremonial as well as for the organization of production. But, in an important sense, these activities were infused with meaning through the trade association's constitution of itself as a fraternity, a religious society that arranged special devotions, buried and prayed for deceased members, and distributed charity to needy living members. United by solemn religious oath, the trade association was thus "a wide-ranging and deep-reaching moral community . . . a sworn spiritual brotherhood." So deeply felt was this bond, Sylvia Thrupp has commented, that "the religious and fraternal sanction was the source of the guild's deepest solidarity."[24]

In this regard, the trade association was one variant of a much more widespread form of association, the religious fraternity or confraternity, in which groups of lay people organized to pray for the souls of deceased members. Because the length of time someone spent in purgatory could be reduced by the prayers of the living, people in all ranks of society devoted considerable effort to this end, as evidence from wills, bequests, church windows, and popular devotions attests.[25] The religious fraternity was a practical solution to the problem of life after death for the large sectors of the populace who could not afford, as the wealthy did, to leave bequests to ensure that they would be prayed for after death. Instead, common people pooled their efforts pledging to pray for one another and contribute stipulated amounts for funerals and masses. Just as nineteenth-century workers joined fraternal benefit societies to pay for funerals and provide for their families, so sixteenth- and seventeenth-century city dwellers joined religious fraternities to provide for their souls.

[24] Ibid., pp. 34–35; Sylvia L. Thrupp, "The Guilds," in M. M. Postan, E. E. Rich, and Edward Miller, eds., *The Cambridge Economic History*, vol. 3, (Cambridge University Press, 1963), p. 238.
[25] Galpern, *Religions of the People*, p. 7.

Praying for the dead was the central activity of the fraternity, but aside from this unvarying function, its most notable characteristic was a multiplicity of purpose. "Any group that had religious objectives and included laypeople could be styled a confraternity." Thus the world of confraternaties included political factions, groups to perform mystery plays, groups to build cathedrals, as well as more commonplace guilds and pious fraternities.[26] The purposes of the confraternity were notably similar to the traditional activities of the extended family, in their inclusion of "mutual aid, burial and commemoration, fellowship and feasting, drama and ceremonial sponsorship."[27] Banquets and celebrations were the source of a conviviality that constantly threatened to emerge as the dominant theme of fraternal life, and the elaborate processions with which they celebrated their patron saints' feast days were an important source of public entertainment. Indeed, between them the guilds and the confraternities bore the primary responsibility for creating the elaborate public ceremonial events that were so central to the collective life of late medieval and early modern cities.

Seasonal festivities and public ceremonial events of a more frivolous kind were the special province of the fraternal organizations called sociétés joyeuses or Abbeys of Misrule. Found throughout Europe from the late Middle Ages and closely linked to the seasonal religious calendar, their festival activities included "masking, costuming, hiding, charivaris . . . farces, parades and floats, collecting money and sweets and distributing money and sweets, dancing, music-making, the lighting of fires, reciting of poetry, gaming and athletic contests."[28] Like other fraternal activities, the Abbeys of Misrule were popular, initiated and controlled by laymen. Sometimes they were put on by groups of families, friends, and neighbors, sometimes by craft guilds or confra-

[26] Ibid., p. 52.
[27] Jack C. Ross, *An Assembly of Good Fellows: Voluntary Associations in History* (Westport, Conn.: Greenwood Press, 1976), p. 141.
[28] Davis, "Reasons of Misrule," p. 42.

CHAPTER ONE

ternities, and sometimes by societies organized for that purpose alone.

Its origin in the activities of guilds and confraternities is not the only factor that locates the société joyeuse in the complex of fraternal associations. It was also connected to the traditions of rural youth, in that it represents an extension and transformation of elements taken from the village youth culture. The continuity is visible in their common use of the term "abbey" or "Abbey of Misrule." Most significant is the central use that both made of the charivari, the noisy, masked procession that used ridicule and public humiliation to punish wrongdoers. Urban charivaris were much more complex and sophisticated than their rural counterparts, with primitive effigies replaced by elaborately produced floats and the simple charivari song often developing into a full-fledged play that was sometimes even printed.[29] But the form remains identifiable, in spite of the elaboration, as does the central theme, which remains that of a status reversal in which those of lower rank claim to rule over their superiors, deny their subordination, and turn the social structure upside down.[30]

Like that of youth, the fraternalism of urban adults addressed particular needs, especially those created by the disintegration of large extended families and cohesive village societies and the more complex economic and political demands of urban life. It is significant that the chief activity of the confraternity was burial and commemoration of the dead, a duty that traditionally belonged to the family in rural society, but was transferred to an "artificial" kin group in the cities. In a similar way, the public events—religious processions, festival celebrations, and convivial gatherings—put on by confraternities, guilds, and sociétés joy-

[29] Ibid., p. 50.
[30] Ibid., pp. 43–44, 54; also Charles Phythian-Adams, "Ceremony and the Citizen: The Communal Year at Coventry 1450–1500," in Peter Clark and Paul Slack, eds., *Crisis and Order in English Towns, 1550–1700* (London: Routledge and Kegan Paul, 1972), pp. 66–69, 75.

euses represent urban elaborations of traditional holidays and celebrations centered around the parish and village community.

The urban charivari also retained the traditional interest in marital and domestic relations, although its ridicule was increasingly focused on a different target, that of dominant wives and those husbands who permitted or acquiesced in such relationships. These offenses were graphically portrayed; frequently the husband himself would be led through the streets backwards on an ass. More elaborate demonstrations are illustrated by the 1566 festival in Lyons, which included "seven floats in which husbands identified by street and occupation were being beaten variously with tripe, wooden sticks, knives, forks, spoons, frying pans, trenchers and water posts; having stones thrown at them; their beards pulled; and being kicked in the genitals—each, as the printed description said, representing the actual 'martyr' of the quarter."[31] Thus the charivari retained its consistent preoccupation with family, marriage, and proper relations between husband and wife. In this way, the abbeys and fraternities, which often staged these public performances, continued to play a kin-like role, for they claimed the right to interfere in the internal affairs of the nuclear family as the extended family might have done in another setting. They reveal a world in which the conjugal unit was still enmeshed in more extensive social networks, answerable to a broader public that considered itself fully entitled to criticize and influence relations within the family. Through them, the community asserted its jurisdiction over matters that are today characterized as 'private' concerns.

This persistent attention to conjugal relations is another indication of how fraternal institutions functioned as part of a larger kinship system. Fraternalism's role was a supplementary but important one. As we have seen, a kinship model served as a vehicle for the organization of many activ-

[31] Davis, "Reasons of Misrule," p. 45.

3 7

ities outside the household unit. At the same time, fraternalism provided young people with semi-autonomous modes of association that represented their interests without challenging the overarching framework of patriarchal authority. Despite the varied uses to which they were put, fraternal modes of organization revealed four characteristics: (1) the use of a "corporate" idiom, (2) the construction of solidary ties through ritual and public ceremony, (3) proprietorship or the anticipation of proprietorship as a qualification for participation, and (4) the assertion of masculine privilege and authority. Together, these interconnected elements comprise the social relationship that may be defined as fraternal, a relationship that maintains a remarkable continuity from the popular institutions of early modern Europe to the fraternal orders of nineteenth- and twentieth-century America.

CORPORATISM

Basic to the fraternal relation, as to kin relations generally, is the use of what William Sewell, Jr. has identified as the "corporate idiom." Corporatism explains social relations through the metaphor of the body, a consistent theme of medieval society, expressed most frequently in the concept of the church as the Mystical Body of Christ. The corporate metaphor expresses not just the mechanical interdependence of people but the indissolubility of human ties. It sees social institutions as being like bodies, "made of a single internally differentiated but inter-connected substance," so that "harm inflicted on any member was felt by the whole."[32] A corporate concept of society assumes that groups, not individuals, are the basic units of society, and that people act, not primarily as individuals, but as members

[32] Sewell, *Work and Revolution*, pp. 36–37. The formulation of corporatism presented here follows Sewell's work closely; see especially chapters two, three, and eight.

of collectivities. It assumes, moreover, that social institutions are governed not only collectively, but hierarchically. Corporatism is the social metaphor that most forcefully asserts that unity of interest is compatible with hierarchy and inequality.

What did corporatism mean in practice? First, the assertion of social and collective modes of governance over and above the will of the individual. We have already seen how both the rural and urban Abbeys of Misrule asserted the rights of the community to overrule the decisions of individuals in favor of communal norms of domestic life. In a similar, albeit more institutionalized way, trade associations asserted their control over individual masters. This exercise of authority was based, as Sewell points out, on a concept of property that did not recognize individual rights in property as absolute; the master's capital was not simply subject to his private decision, for "his mastership was not, strictly speaking, an individual property at all but a share in the privileges that were the collective property of the entire corporation—a fictitious person that embraced masters, journeymen, and apprentices alike.[33] The trade corporation was a structure of collective governance, controlling the apprenticeship system, the methods of work, the standards to be met, and the prices to be charged. Because the privileges of the craft were granted by civic authorities, the trade corporation was held responsible to the public good and was to be governed accordingly. This did not mean that handicraft manufacture operated as a free public service nor that relations between masters and workers were in any way egalitarian, much less idyllic. But it does mean that the organization of production was based upon traditional beliefs about fair practice and moral obligation, beliefs that motivated both the legalistic regulation of the trade and the detail of customary workshop practice.

The depth of this attachment to corporate assumptions

---

[33] Ibid., p. 139; Truant, "Independent and Insolent," p. 138.

and values is most clearly demonstrated in the practices of the compagnonnages and journeymen's confraternities that emerged in the sixteenth, seventeenth, and eighteenth centuries. The products of an increasingly capitalistic organization of production, these associations, "comprehensible only in the context of continuing tensions with masters," were formed and structured precisely to institutionalize the practice of resistance.[34] Through the weapon of the interdict, by which they withheld the labor of their members from a particular master or even from an entire town, compagnons prevented the masters from hiring unskilled labor. If necessary, they could set up as independent artisans and work illicitly during these periods of interdiction.[35] In doing this, the compagnons implicitly recognized that their status of wage laborer was a permanent one and that they must regard themselves as adult, independent actors whose interests diverged in significant ways from those of the masters. Thus they denied one of the most fundamental precepts of corporatism and patriarchalism.

Despite this implicit contradiction, journeymen displayed a deep attachment to the concept of the trade as a corporate body. Their relationships to one another continued to be defined in terms derived from the patriarchal household. In each city on their customary tour de France, journeymen stopped at a designated inn where they were given food, shelter, and assistance in finding work. Both inn and innkeeper were commonly called "mother" by the compagnons, while the masters continued to be referred to as father and the journeymen as their good sons. As a group of journeymen printers in Lyon themselves characterized "this interlocking system of fraternal and patriarchal authority . . . , 'Masters and journeymen are and ought to be one body together, like a family and fraternity.' "[36]

[34] Ibid., p. 59.
[35] Sewell, *Work and Revolution*, p. 49; Chill, "The Seventeenth Century Compagnonnage," pp. 10–11.
[36] Gillis, *Youth and History*, p. 23. For the importance of inn and innkeeper,

This continued assertion of mutual interest was sustained in some degree by the cooperation that continued to occur between masters and journeymen, even punctuated, as it now was, by bitter disputes. Without implicit recognition and cooperation from the masters, the compagnonnages could not have succeeded in placing traveling journeymen. In practice, masters relied on the associations' contribution to the organization, training, and disciplining of the workforce, sometimes even bargaining with them to establish standard wage scales. Despite frequent conflicts, masters still recognized the possibility of a reciprocal relationship with their workers. Journeymen, in turn, continued to acknowledge the importance of mastership in defining the meaning of the craft. However great their antagonisms, it is clear that masters and journeymen were united in their rejection of individualism and in their attachment to corporate forms of production and governance.[37]

Closely related to the vision of a collectively governed community was the practice of mutuality. The religious confraternities engaged in prayer as a cooperative activity, a pooling of spiritual resources that made them the religious equivalent of a mutual benefit society. The compagnonnage patterned itself after the traditional trade corporation, reproducing mutualistic activities such as assistance to needy members and visits to the sick, while the informal social life of compagnons revolved around the custom of "treating rounds" of drinks and the constant exchange of gifts and loans in a "perpetual fraternal potlatch that reinforce[d] the common feeling of solidarity."[38] In all cases, these activities

---

see Truant, "Independent and Insolent," p. 143, and Michael Sonenscher, "Journeymen's Migrations and Workshop Organization in Eighteenth-Century France," also in Kaplan and Koepp, *Work in France*, pp. 89–93.

[37] See Steven Laurence Kaplan, "Social Classification and Representation in the Corporate World of Eighteenth Century France: Turgot's 'Carnival,' " for the masters, and Daniel Roche, "Work, Fellowship," for the journeymen, both in Kaplan and Koepp, *Work in France*, pp. 193–95; 68–69.

[38] Ibid., p. 69.

were motivated by a sense of corporate and reciprocal obligation, such as that owed to family members, rather than by a sense of charity, which has as its goal the practice of independent virtue rather than interdependent exchange.

RITUAL

Like all forms of fraternal association, the early modern guilds, corporations, and festival societies relied on ritual to create kin-like relations and thus to constitute themselves as corporate bodies. In the case of the compagnonnages, two factors made ritual especially important: first, the national, not local, character of the compagnonnage and the consequent need to establish working relations among strangers, as journeymen traversed the countryside. Second, their status as proscribed bodies, vulnerable to repression by the church and the state, as well as to the actions of the masters. The compagnonnages developed a highly elaborate ritual that incorporated many of the traditional practices of the trade corporation but went considerably beyond them. The "baptism" was the compagnonnage's most important innovation; the fact that it reached outside specific craft traditions to appropriate an actual sacrament revealed the grave significance that compagnons attached to their initiation. As Sewell notes, the compagnonnages had to emphasize their own ritual forms because, as oppositional organizations, they could not rely on the reinforcing effects of larger authority systems.

Other kinds of fraternal bodies could conduct themselves in a more public fashion; indeed, the public role of the guilds and confraternities stood at the heart of their identity. For religious confraternities, whether independent or linked to trade associations, the patron's feast day and the funeral were the chief ritual occasions. Trade associations typically paid for the funerals of members, but all confraternities enjoined their members to attendance as the most solemn of duties. This emphasis on the funeral as a corporate event served to define in precise terms the significance of the fraternal relation: "the passage from this life to the hereafter was a matter for corporations—rather than simply for the family or the parish. . . . To borrow from the language of another religious oath that created another permanent moral body, the corporate funeral demonstrated and reiterated to the members of the community that they were bound to one another 'until death do us part.' "[39]

The celebration of the patron's feast day was another declaration of fraternal solidarity. The members marched in procession through the town, carrying candles and torches, sometimes adorned with special insignias or even dressed in costumes representing the saints. Their procession ended at the church, where a high mass was celebrated.[40] The mass, and the banquet that often followed it, served, like the funeral, to bind the members into a unitary whole, while the procession displayed their public identity as a corporate body existing within a larger urban community.

Two aspects of early modern fraternal ritual should be noted: its dramatic character and its reliance on the processional as a ritual form. The charivari was both a pantomime and a procession, relatively crude in rural areas but readily transformed into an actual play in the more sophisticated environment of urban centers. Feast-day celebrations by confraternities also had the character of a pageant, and could, in some cases, develop into theatrical set-pieces with costumed confreres acting out the roles of priests, saints, and biblical figures.[41]

The dramatic potential of such events was most fully realized in the pageants presented by guilds in major urban centers. In England, for example, the city of York was especially famous for its Corpus Christi celebration, produced by the drama companies of twenty-four separate craft and

[39] Sewell, *Work and Revolution*, p. 36.
[40] Galpern, *Religions of the People*, pp. 55–56; Sewell, *Work and Revolution*, p. 34.
[41] Galpern, *Religions of the People*, pp. 57–8.

CHAPTER ONE

trade organizations. As many as fifty-seven separate tableaus depicted Old Testament scenes such as the creation, Noah's ark, Moses before Pharoah, plus scenes from the life of Christ. Pageants could be elaborate and graphic in their portrayals, as the following list of properties from a Corpus Christi guild of Lincoln indicates: "hell mouth with a nether chap, a prison with a coveryng, Sara's chambre, a great idoll with a clubbe, a tombe with a coveryng, the city of Jerusalem with towers and pynacles . . . a firmament with a fierye clowde and a duble clowde."[42]

An even more sophisticated development was the mystery play, which was often commissioned by a confraternity and portrayed by the members. The mystery play was an extension of fraternal guild ceremonials that "fully realized the latent theatrical possibilities in mimed confraternity processions." Growing out of the institutions of collective public life, it was "a genuinely popular art form, which could satisfy the tastes of men and women of all social ranks without exceeding the capacities of any."[43]

If the theatricality of fraternal ritual satisfied the public appetite for entertainment, its use of the processional form reflected the society's preoccupation with the visual articulation of social boundaries.[44] The charivari was, as E. P. Thompson has pointed out, an anti-processional, "in the sense that the horse-men, drums, lantern-bearers, effigies drawn in carts, etc., turn to ridicule the ceremonial processions of the army, the courts, the Church."[45] Fraternal institutions frequently displayed such an oppositional thrust, from the compagnonnage's militant defense of journeymen's

[42] Ross, *Assembly*, p. 195; H. F. Westlake, *The Parish Gilds of Medieval England* (New York: Macmillan, 1919), p. 51.

[43] Galpern, *Religions of the People*, pp. 78–80.

[44] Natalie Zemon Davis, "The Sacred and the Body Social in Sixteenth-Century Lyon," *Past and Present*, no. 90 (February, 1981): pp. 40–70; Phythian-Adams, "Ceremony and the Citizen."

[45] Edward P. Thompson, " 'Rough Music': Le Charivari Anglais," *Annales Economies Societes Civilisation* 27 (March–April, 1972): p. 282 (my translation).

interests to the Abbeys of Misrules' use of the charivari as a vehicle for the expression of popular discontent and antagonism toward rulers and clergy.

The solemn processions of the trade corporations and confraternities, on the other hand, identified these bodies as part of that larger authority structure: "When all masters and journeymen annually processed in their respective companies at Corpus Christi-tide and on the eves of Midsummer and St. Peter, therefore, the community in its entirety was literally defining itself for all to see."[46] From this use of processional to symbolically constitute the civic community, we may discern the boundaries of that community. When we look at the participants in the public ritual of early modern fraternal institutions, what most clearly emerges are the connections that it draws between proprietorship, social adulthood, and masculine identity.

FRATERNALISM AND PATRIARCHALISM: MASCULINITY AND PROPRIETORSHIP

As much as by its corporate or by its ritual character, fraternalism was defined by masculinity. It was a brotherhood, a type of association "between and among men" that was as much a part of the social relations of male dominance as the more recognized complex of male-female interchange. But it was a historically specific form, in which masculine identity and proprietorship were closely intertwined. In the early modern period, patriarchalism, as a social relation grounded in household production, specified much of the content of masculine identity, and thus of fraternalism.

Early modern patriarchalism was an authority relation rooted in the two-fold character of the household, a unit that organized production as well as reproduction. Because the household was the basic productive unit as well as the site of domestic relations, the householder was simultaneously

<hr />

[46] Phythian-Adams, "Ceremony and the Citizen," p. 58.

the father of the family and the director of production. In such a setting, the two kinds of authority—that of father and that of master or employer—are conceptually and actually one, in a relationship grounded in the social reality of both family relations and productive activity. Structurally external to the household, early modern fraternalism is nevertheless a product of this world in which masculine identity was defined in terms of patriarchal authority.

The conceptual link between fraternal association and the masculine ideal of proprietorship is suggested by the identity of the participants. Trade associations were by definition composed of master craftsmen, proprietors heading their own enterprises. Although confraternities and sociétés joyeuses had a somewhat more diverse composition, often including wealthy merchants and government functionaries as well as artisans and smaller tradesmen, membership was drawn most heavily from among proprietors. The rural youth abbeys included the sons of poor peasants as well as rich ones, with no involvement by the sons of nobles or large landholders. But while sons of landless peasants were included in the abbeys, where they existed, the evidence suggests that where divisions between landed and landless were most advanced, as in England, the youth abbey as a corporate form failed to survive.[47] Like other fraternal institutions, it was preeminently an institution of artisan and peasant-proprietor communities.

As such, fraternalism publicly affirmed the values of a patriarchal society in which social adulthood, proprietorship, and masculinity were inextricably linked. This was most clearly revealed in the official fraternal bodies of the adult world, where the categories of people excluded from guilds and confraternities were precisely those people who were denied recognition as juridical adults because of their semidependent status—unskilled workers, servants, and

[47] Galpern, *Religions of the People*, p. 62; Davis, "Reasons of Misrule," p. 64; Gillis, *Youth and History*, p. 31.

women. When guilds and fraternities engaged in the great civic and religious displays that were so much a part of their identity, they were constituting themselves as a civil community that was synonymous with the society of adult male proprietors. Fraternalism thus served as one way in which the connections were drawn between proprietorship and social adulthood, through its exclusion of all those who had not attained this dual status.

Youth abbeys and journeymen's societies emerged in response to this exclusion. But they did not represent a repudiation of patriarchalism, either as an individual aspiration or an overarching system of authority. Fraternal youth institutions developed only among those groups who could either anticipate an eventual succession to patriarchal authority or assert their moral right to it. Fraternal association was *not* found among servants, casual laborers, or young women, only among journeymen and peasants. They used the cultural materials of patriarchalism—the metaphors of domestic life and the assertion of masculine privilege—to create institutions that were detached from the structure of the patriarchal household but grounded in its social assumptions and concerned with its dilemmas.

As servants or apprentices, young men occupied a position in the family roughly similar to that of women—both were subject to the adult male head of household. Moreover, there might be female servants within the house, since girls as well as boys were routinely sent away to work as servants. The presence of young female servants in a household would tend to emphasize that women's subordination in such a society was not based exclusively on their personal relationship as wife or daughter, but was part of a larger system of authority to which at least some males were also subject. But although both young women and men were subject to the authority of the head of household, their positions were not equivalent, for young men were only temporarily dependent and subordinate. Fraternal youth institutions can be seen as

47

an attempt to distinguish between young men and young women, to express the fact of eventual male authority.

For some young males, this distinction was already made by the institutions of adult society. Formal apprenticeship made the separation between women and men quite clear for craft workers because girls were in most cases specifically barred from learning a craft (and from experiencing the geographical mobility and broadening of social intercourse that went with being a journeyman). For students, knowledge of Latin served in a similar way to isolate boys from the world of women, who knew only the vernacular. Studying Latin became a test, a way of achieving masculinity, and the knowledge of Latin, like the signs and rituals of the journeyman, became "the tongue of an exclusive all-male society."[48]

In rural households, where both boys and girls were present as agricultural and domestic servants, the distinction was harder to maintain. Because gender differentiation was not sufficiently expressed within the structure of their training, as it was for craft apprentices and students, rural youth sought to create their own institutions outside the household, which would express their identity as males and their potential authority over women. The fraternal complex provided them with a set of sex-segregated activities to affirm their status as men at a time when it was obscured within the family due to their subordinate status there.

The way in which the separate and subordinate status of girls was enforced can be seen in the contrasting treatment of male and female sexual activity. Younger boys who violated sexual norms were taken aside and dealt with privately by older boys, but allegedly promiscuous girls of the same age were pressured into proper behavior by the decoration of their doorways with "the obscene symbol of the gorse bush."[49] Girls were thus treated as outsiders to be controlled

[48] Phythian-Adams, "Ceremony and the Citizen," pp. 58–59; Gillis, *Youth and History*, p. 25.

[49] Gillis, *Youth and History*, pp. 29–30.

by the shame of public ridicule in the same way as were elderly widowers and strangers to the village, while boys were subject only to private chastisement within the male brotherhood. A clear line was drawn between masculine and feminine prerogatives.

Indeed, the attacks on what was defined for girls as promiscuity can be seen as an attack on the right of girls to bestow themselves sexually rather than to have their sexual activity governed by males. For the primary activity of these youth abbeys was to regulate courtship and especially "to exercise tight control over the eligible females in their villages . . . even influencing the choice of mates."[50]

Such activities reveal the importance of relationships among males in the assertion of masculine hegemony. The claim of the charivari was not simply an anticipation of the authority of the man within the family, which stems from his position as head of household. Rather, it was an attempt to invoke an authority that is specifically male, even before its participants had attained either the control over material resources or the position of adult householder that typically legitimated such authority. By forming an exclusively masculine relationship with one another, members of youth abbeys asserted a generalized male authority over women that went beyond the patriarchal relations of the family.

The formation of such male relations of dominance over women has consequences reaching beyond the attempt to dominate any particular woman. As Rubin has noted, "As long as the relations specify that men exchange women, it is men who are the beneficiaries of the product of such exchanges—social organization."[51] There are few institutionalized roles for women outside the family—"Women, as wives, mothers, or sisters, gain respect, power, and status

---

[50] Ibid., p. 30.

[51] Rubin, "Traffic in Women," p. 174. See also Heidi Hartmann, "Capitalism, Partriarchy, and Job Segregation by Sex," in Zillah Eisenstein, ed., *Capitalist Patriarchy and the Case for Socialist Feminism* (New York: Monthly Review Press, 1978), for the significance of masculine organization.

through their personal relations with men." Men, on the other hand, act and are judged in terms of formal roles within male hierarchies that are outside the family and exist precisely to make such evaluations and express such gradations.[52]

In the patriarchal society of early modern Europe, these extra-familial ties existed in a reciprocal relationship to the sources of masculine power within the household. The possession or anticipation of power within the family provided a basis for the generalized authority claimed by male groups outside the family. But at the same time, masculine participation in a world outside the family—a world that excluded women while it created and defined the social order—meant that the man came to the family as an emissary from the outside world, the public domain, carrying with him something of the moral and political force of the entire society. His power in the family was legitimated, in a way that a woman's could not be, through his participation in male social networks. Moreover, his involvement in male networks provided him with a source of concrete power in the form of a group that was always ready to intervene in cases in which the individual man was unable to maintain his authority within the family.

This analysis of masculine forms of association and their rewards illuminates the specifically masculine character of fraternal associations in early modern Europe. The rural youth abbeys represent attempts by young men to detach

[52] Michelle Zimbalist Rosaldo, "Woman, Culture and Society: A Theoretical Overview," in Michelle Zimbalist and Louise Lamphere, eds., *Woman, Culture and Society* (Stanford: Stanford University Press, 1974), p. 26. Rosaldo points out that access to this masculine world is problematic for young men, who must find a way to detach themselves from childhood roles within the family and prove themselves. She relates this to the hierarchical character of masculine social organization: "If 'becoming a man' is, developmentally, an achievement, social groups elaborate the criteria for the achievement and create the hierarchies and institutions we associate with an articulate social order" (p. 28). See also Nancy Chodorow, "Family Structure and Feminine Personality," in Rosaldo and Lamphere, *Woman, Culture and Society.*

themselves from their subordinate position within the family, to form independent masculine relations, and to use these to establish superiority over their female age peers. The guilds united in political and ritual association men who would have been isolated in the household by the nature of economic organization; in this way the guilds established a network of masculine hierarchies to which households were subordinate. The uses of such networks are revealed in the activities of the urban charivaris, in which submissive husbands of dominant or unfaithful wives were publicly ridiculed. Here, a generalized male solidarity intervened to pressure those individuals who failed to uphold masculine authority within the household. Such activities served to punish those who had failed and to warn those who might be tempted to falter. Finally, the journeymen's organizations such as the compagnonnage present us with a vivid example of a male association that incorporates into its ritual in explicit and literal ways the functions that Michelle Zimbalist Rosaldo has ascribed to the male social order. In the ceremony of "baptism," the compagnon symbolically rejected his family of origin and took on a new identity in an exclusively masculine world. He went through an initiation that was intended to test his courage and loyalty, and through the system of degrees, he ascended a complicated hierarchy in which he could learn to give deference to superiors and exercise authority over subordinates. Self-conscious dissociation from women and the family, the rituals of initiation and testing, and the articulation of a hierarchical social order were not simply a latent part of the compagnonnage's organizational existence; rather, they were verbalized and acted out in elaborate detail. In all these ways, fraternal association provided an institutional means by which men, as agents between households, were able to dominate the religious, political, economic, and social networks that were understood to define the culture and unify society.

A corporatist impulse, a fascination with dramatic ritual, and an attachment to the inter-connected identities of proprietorship and masculinity characterize early modern fraternalism and its nineteenth century counterparts. This continuity is what allows us to see them both as "fraternal." But this does not represent and cannot be explained as the simple and unproblematic survival of an earlier social form. The values we recognize from earlier fraternal institutions—a paternalism based on the moral authority of the independent proprietor, a positive evaluation of work and skill, a belief in kinship as a significant social bond, and the use of masculine solidarity to strengthen that bond—were all profoundly congenial to American society. Their articulation in the nineteenth century lodge was the product of a dynamic and selective historical process. Institutionally, this occurred through the medium of the Ancient and Accepted Society of Freemasons, an organization that appropriated, reinterpreted, and transformed selected aspects of early modern fraternalism. Important in its own right as the largest, most prestigious, and most vital of modern fraternal organizations, Freemasonry provided the recognized model for the complex of nineteenth-century associations that are the substantive focus of this book. Any serious attempt to understand fraternalism must inevitably confront and make sense of Freemasonry.

TWO

The Craftsman as Hero

BEGINNING in the mid-seventeenth century, British gentlemen began to request admission into the lodges of practicing stone masons, and then to form their own "accepted" lodges. The question immediately arises: why? What motivated gentlemen, even members of the nobility, to seek honorary acceptance into organizations of craftsmen? The answer to this question underlies an understanding of Freemasonry's significance as a social institution that drew upon the popular traditions of an earlier fraternalism, particularly those of craft workers, to create its own unique blend of tradition and modernity. Consistent with its origins, "accepted" Masonry displayed all the elements that comprise fraternalism as I have defined it: the centrality of kin and corporate idiom, the use of ritual to create solidarity, and the twin themes of proprietorship and masculinity. Freemasonry transformed these traditional elements into a new form of voluntary association, one that promoted a bourgeois sociability and expressed the values of an emerging capitalist order in a way that proved appealing to a wide range of men.

WHY MASONRY?

Masonic lodges arose spontaneously throughout Britain without benefit of any central structure until 1717, when the Grand Lodge of England was formed by four London lodges in an effort to establish a national structure of governance and thus to assert control over the burgeoning movement. The Grand Lodge's consolidation of power and expansion beyond London by 1730 was undoubtedly facilitated by the 1723 publication of the Reverend James Anderson's *Constitution of the Free-Masons*, a document that represented the Grand Lodge's first attempt to define its organizational character and construct a meaningful history for itself.[1] This redefinition and codification of Masonic principles established and publicized regular methods for already existing lodges to put themselves under the authority of the Grand Lodge as well as outlined the procedure for the creation of new ones. But its greatest importance was as a statement of principles which infused Freemasonry with the ideas of popular Newtonianism. The development and dissemination of such a propaganda piece allowed Freemasonry to begin to extend its influence beyond Britain and its colonies, so that by the mid-eighteenth century, Masonic lodges could be found in France, Germany, Austria, the Netherlands, and Italy.

Arising in the era of the club and the coffee house, Freemasonry was part of a general movement toward voluntary association and informal conviviality. Like the club, the early Masonic gatherings were largely devoted to socializing, and like most clubs, Masonic lodges usually met in taverns, coffee houses, and chocolate houses.[2] Clubs and coffee houses, J. M. Roberts has written, were "the inventions of men making new demands on society and discovering new capacities in themselves which could not be given expression within the historic unities of look, locality, religion, occupation and legal subordination." They were part of a general turning away "from the hope of building community on

[1] Douglas Knoop and G. P. Jones, *The Genesis of Freemasonry—An Account of the Rise and Development of Freemasonry in Its Operative, Accepted, and Early Speculative Phases* (Manchester: Manchester University Press, 1947), provide the most scholarly account of Masonic origins, but see also Robert Freke Gould, *History of Freemasonry throughout the World*, revised by Dudley Wright (New York: Charles Scribner's Sons, 1939). Anderson's *Constitution* is reprinted in Margaret C. Jacob, *The Radical Enlightenment: Pantheists, Freemasons and Republicans* (London: Allen and Unwin, 1981), pp. 279–87.

[2] Bernard E. Jones, *Freemason's Guide and Compendium* (New York: Macoy Publishing and Masonic Supply Company, 1950), p. 167.

inherited subordination or confessional unity" and toward the ideal of a "secular and voluntary community which would be a true community." This seventeenth- and eighteenth-century concern to devise new social relations that could bridge divisions of religion, class, and inherited position is clearly reflected in the Masonic characterization of itself as "the Means of conciliating true Friendship among Persons that must else have remain'd at a perpetual Distance."[3]

But to analyze the Masonic lodge as a type of club is to disregard much that is crucial. With its emphasis on personal interaction and the pleasures of spontaneous but cultivated conversation, the club was an institution that self-consciously rejected a predetermined content for itself. In contrast, those who became Masons involved themselves in the remnants of a tradition-laden medieval institution whose elaborate rituals and mythical accounts of ancient origin remained centrally important to Accepted Masonry's definition of itself. This affiliation to the institutions and traditions of an ongoing, if declining, trade, laid the basis for many of Freemasonry's lasting characteristics: its existence as a secret brotherhood, the sense of consistent Masonic identity from one lodge to another, the centrality of ritual, initiation, and myths of origin, and the explicit connection to an artisanal culture. In contradiction to the club, the meaning of Masonic participation resided not in the spontaneous interaction of its members, but in a content that was in large measure given. Central to this content was the idea that in becoming a Mason, a gentleman symbolically assumed the identity of a craft worker, a manual worker, albeit a highly skilled one.

The answer to why so many English gentlemen should have wished to do this, an answer that is central to an un-

[3] J. M. Roberts, *The Mythology of the Secret Societies* (London: Secker & Warburg, 1972), pp. 17–18; Anderson, *Constitution*, in Jacob, *Radical Enlightenment*, p. 280.

derstanding of Freemasonry's ideological significance both in Britain and America, rests on a consideration of two tendencies existing in British society: first, the widespread European interest in magic and esoteric brotherhood that was a significant element of Renaissance science, and second, the more specifically British tradition of collaboration between gentlemen scientists and skilled artisans. In both the Baconianism of the seventeenth century and the Newtonianism of the eighteenth, British philosophy sought to link such collaborations to the progress of science and the well-being of the nation. Once located within this tradition, early Masonry can be understood in terms of its role in a society increasingly committed to commercial expansion and increasingly sensitive to the value of productive activity.

SCIENCE AND CRAFT

The Masonic historians Knoop and Jones have suggested that the earliest Accepted Masons may have been motivated by the Renaissance interest in architecture. Concretely, this interest was expressed by the activities of many Renaissance gentlemen, who not only patronized architects but even made their own attempts to design buildings or supervise their construction.[4] Behind this gentlemanly pastime rested a view of architecture as the queen of all the sciences. It had been designated as such by the classical Roman architect Vitruvius, who argued that it was in architecture that all the other arts and sciences were practically united. The true architect, according to Vitruvius, needed to know geometry, proportion, perspective, and mechanics, as well as the mathematically grounded arts of music and painting.[5] At the same time, Renaissance thought identified architecture with the articulation of moral values, in the sense that buildings

[4] Knoop and Jones, *Genesis*, pp. 136, 138–40.
[5] Frances Yates, *The Rosicrucian Enlightenment* (London: Routledge and Kegan Paul, 1972), pp. 11–12.

give concrete expression to society's ideas about how people ought to live, how social life should be constructed. Architecture was thus the perfect activity for the cultivated and humane Renaissance gentleman.

The connections between architecture and Masonry were clearly perceived by the earliest Masons. Much of Anderson's *Constitution of the Free-Masons*, the formative document of the early Grand Lodge of England, is a "history" of architecture, beginning with "Adam, our first parent, created after the Image of God, the great Architect of the Universe." The "great *Vitruvius*, the father of all true Architects to this day," appears as the creator of the classical style that was destroyed by the barbarians and only recovered in the works of Renaissance architects such as Palladio and Inigo Jones, "our great Master-Mason." In this view architecture symbolizes what is most godly and thus most human, for Adam, created as he was in the image of the Great Architect, "must have had the Liberal Sciences, particularly Geometry, written on his Heart, for ever since the Fall, we find the principles of it in the Hearts of his offspring."[6]

Why, then, were the Masons not an organization of symbolic architects, rather than of craftsmen? Some, of course, may have perceived that master masons were in fact the designers of most medieval buildings, rather than the scholars and professional architects who had begun to replace them during the Renaissance. But probably most important was the fascination with esoteric brotherhoods and secret societies that characterized Renaissance science. This was a world in which the boundaries between science and magic had not yet been drawn, the distinctions between pseudosciences such as alchemy and astrology and "genuine" sciences such as chemistry and mathematics not yet recognized.

Magic and science are similar to one another and distinct

---

[6] Anderson, "Constitution," quoted in Jacob, *Radical Enlightenment*, pp. 213–14.

from religion in that the former both attempt to understand the natural world so as to alter or control it. This understanding of magic and science as essentially the same enterprise explains the frequent involvement of Renaissance and Elizabethan scientific thinkers in the practice of alchemy, astrology, and conjuring. As Christopher Hill has noted, the tendency to focus on those scientific activities that later generations pronounce legitimate and to ignore the rest is to impose a false clarity upon the origins and motivation of early scientific practice, to risk "forgetting that the eminent mathematician John Dee was an astrologer and that Robert Boyle was to transmute alchemy into chemistry; forgetting that there were Fellows of the Royal Society who believed in witches; forgetting that both Napier and Newton attached more importance to their researches into the Apocalypse than to logarithms or the law of gravitation."[7]

When early scientific practitioners were attacked as magicians and witches, they frequently responded not by denying the charge altogether, but by defining and thus defending science and mathematics as "*good* magic." As the seventeenth-century alchemist Robert Fludd explained, there are good and bad kinds of magic; if the good kind is condemned or driven underground, then "we take away all natural philosophy," that is, science.[8] Science and magic were distinguished, then, by the uses to which they were put, rather than by any fundamental difference in method or efficacy.

From this close identification of magic and science comes the interest in secret brotherhoods, including craft organizations, of which the Masonic lodge represented a variant. Craft associations were perceived as repositories of esoteric knowledge, and this was significant in two ways. First, the so-called "mysteries" of a craft were believed to include the

[7] Christopher Hill, *Intellectual Origins of the English Revolution* (London: Oxford University Press, 1965), p. 7. See Yates, *Rosicrucian Enlightenment*, for a detailed exposition of this point in Elizabethan England.

[8] Quoted in Yates, *Rosicrucian Enlightenment*, p. 76.

secrets of the trade, some of which might be useful to scientific or magical practitioners. In part, this belief was based in the more general association between magic and secrecy, but it was also stimulated by an awareness that the accumulated knowledge of craft practice was in fact a principle source of knowledge about the material world.

Second, craft organizations like guilds claimed to inculcate devotion and morality in their members as well as technical knowledge and thus suggested a way of dealing with the concern over the dangerous potential of scientific knowledge. The view that the new science had a "diabolic" as well as an "angelic" side led to a concern that science be developed within the context of a beneficent and reformed society where its power would be used only for good. Thus the character of craft orders as moral organizations spoke to a concern that scientific work should only be undertaken within and by morally responsible communities committed to social betterment.[9]

For many, these themes were most clearly articulated in the phenomenon of Rosicrucianism. Early in the seventeenth century, in Germany and Bohemia, a series of tracts appeared describing a supposed Rosicrucian brotherhood, a fraternity of learned men possessing both magical powers and scientific knowledge and sworn to use them in the interests of a general reform of society. Rosicrucian writings enjoyed a wide circulation throughout Europe; many people believed the Rosicrucian brotherhood to be a genuine organization, which they sought to locate and join. Among them was the English antiquarian Elias Ashmole, who was also a charter member of the Royal Society and one of the first two gentlemen recorded as being initiated into a Masonic lodge.[10]

The Rosicrucian brotherhood never existed as an organization, yet the widespread belief in its existence was, as the

[9] Ibid., pp. 76, 191, 233.
[10] Ibid., p. 193.

Renaissance historian Frances Yates argued, an important social fact. The presence of Rosicrucian symbolism within Masonic ritual suggests that it was a significant part of the social and intellectual materials that early Freemasonry drew upon.[11]

The concept of a brotherhood as the moral guarantor of scientific knowledge and as the institutional framework for scientific work was itself a logical outgrowth of the earlier European reliance upon corporate forms for the organization of a variety of tasks and activities. Esoteric brotherhoods such as the Rosicrucians were appealing in European society because they seemed to offer the means to organize an emerging complex of new ideas and activities in a traditional, and thus emotionally resonant, way. In Britain, however, the Rosicrucian model, while influential, was inserted into the context of an ongoing tradition of practical collaboration between scientists and artisans. It was thus assimilated to an intellectual synthesis that united the advancement of learning, the recognition of craft labor, and the commercial development of the British nation. Recognition of this specifically British context allows us to understand why Freemasonry flourished when other esoteric brotherhoods failed to survive.

BEGINNING in the Elizabethan period, that is, well before the emergence of accepted Masonry, British society was distinguished by an active process of interaction and collaboration between scientifically educated gentlemen and artisans. This originated in the movement for popular education in science and technology that emerged in London during the late sixteenth and early seventeenth centuries. Existing scientific works were translated for the first time from Latin into English, and important mathematicians such as John Dee, Robert Recorde, "the founder of the

---

[11] Albert C. Stevens, *The Cyclopaedia of Fraternities* (New York: E. B. Treat & Company, 1907; Detroit: Gale Research Company, 1966), p. 87.

English school of mathematics," and Thomas Digges, the first English Copernican, began to write only in English. The effect was to extend the audience for such works beyond the university-educated by making them accessible to those literate in English but not Latin. Indeed, such works were specifically directed at an audience of merchants, artisans, seamen, gunners, and surveyors, for whom these early scientists frequently wrote textbooks and almanacs to assist them in their work.[12] As John Dee wrote in his 1570 preface to the first translation of Euclid into English, he had made the translation for the benefit of the many "common artificers" who, by virtue of "their own skill and experience already had, will be able by these good helps and informations to find out and devise new works, strange engines and instruments: for sundry purposes in the commonwealth."[13]

Several factors encouraged this commitment to popular education. First, the early mathematicians and scientists lacked an institutional base in the universities, where mathematical and scientific subjects were not even taught until the 1600s, and even then only in the form of commentaries on classical texts—Ptolemy, Hippocrates, and others. Many scientists had to make their livings by giving popular lectures; in this way they developed close ties with the largely self-educated tradesmen, artisans, and mechanics who comprised their primary audience. The need to tailor their presentations to the practical concerns of such an audience fit well with the scientists' own commitment to the idea of science as useful learning.[14]

But this movement represented something more fundamental than a well-meaning desire to popularize scientific learning or the recognition that scientists could use their knowledge to help further the growth of commerce. Beyond these concerns lay a strong sense that further scientific de-

---

[12] Hill, *Intellectual Origins*, pp. 16–18; the quote, from D. E. Smith's *A History of Mathematics* (1923), appears in Hill.

[13] Quoted in ibid., p. 18.

[14] Ibid., pp. 54–55; 34–36.

velopment was actually dependent upon, would necessitate, collaboration between scholars and artisans. This was the case in two ways. First, and most immediately, a genuinely experimental science was dependent upon the skills of craftsmen, since they were the only ones who could devise and construct the instruments and processes necessary for accurate observation and measurement. "Experimental science had to master certain techniques: distillation, lens-grinding, glass-blowing, even turning and metal-working and the art of assay," and these techniques were initially drawn from a variety of crafts, including clock-making, surveying, building trades, distilling, pharmacy, metal-smelting, and instrument-making.[15] This meant that theoretically educated men who wanted to do scientific work had to obtain some familiarity with craft skills, at least enough to be able to communicate their needs, while craftsmen had to become more knowledgeable and skilled in order to understand and meet the demands of scientists for more precise and sophisticated instruments and procedures.[16]

Secondly, and perhaps more fundamentally, collaboration between scientists and artisans was advocated because of the recognition that the understanding of material processes that had been accumulated in the practice of various crafts constituted a massive source of knowledge for scientists who wanted to learn about the physical world. It was apparent that the rule-of-thumb shop practices of navigators, watch-makers, instrument-makers, and builders made effective use of physical and mathematical principles that had not yet been explained theoretically. This awareness served as a great stimulus to would-be scientists, as did their interest in the alchemical trades of surgeons, apothecaries, and metal-workers. Conceptual advance itself was to be derived from the knowledge of the physical world residing in that body of

[15] A. P. Hall, "Engineering and the Scientific Revolution," quoted in A. E. Musson and Eric Robinson, *Science and Technology in the Industrial Revolution* (Manchester: Manchester University Press, 1969), p. 340.

[16] Ibid., pp. 18, 25; Hill, *Intellectual Origins*, p. 40.

unsystematized knowledge that had been developed by craft workers in the course of their labors. And this sense of craft practices as developing bodies of knowledge was intensified because of the visible improvements in standards and the introduction of new processes and techniques in so many trades—including clock-making, metallurgy, glass-making, and instrument-making—during the seventeenth and eighteenth centuries.

Frances Bacon was the leading advocate of this reciprocal relationship between craft knowledge and scientific advance. The recognition that craft practice constituted the greatest existing accumulation of empirical knowledge was at the heart of Bacon's experimentalism. Pointing to the fact that great inventions such as printing, gunpowder, and the compass had been discovered by craftsmen in the course of their work, Bacon argued that still greater advances could be made if their methods and empirical knowledge could be systematized and assimilated into a system of planned, directed observation and experimentation. What Bacon planned was "the true and lawful marriage of the empirical and rational faculties, the unkind and ill-starred separation of which has thrown into confusion all the affairs of the human family."[17]

But Baconianism is something more than a call for experimentalism and collaboration between artisans and natural philosophers; for at the same time, Bacon drew explicit connections between the growth of science and technology and the development of commerce, manufacture, and exploration. Again, note that what Bacon does is to argue for the value of an already existing set of practical relationships. The great advances in navigational techniques that were the crowning achievement of the London mathematicians were clearly stimulated by and in turn facilitated the English entrance into exploration and colonial expansion that occurred

[17] Hill, *Intellectual Origins*, pp. 86–87; Bacon, quoted in Hill, *Intellectual Origins*, p. 74.

in the Elizabethan and early Stuart periods. Similarly, the development of more accurate land-surveying methods was related to the increased interest in "drainage, mining, water-supplies, and a host of other industrial activities," that arose out of large landowners' attempts to exploit their holdings more rationally and profitably through both agricultural enclosure and nonagricultural uses such as mining and canal-building.[18] Bacon's contribution was to infuse such developments with a sense of higher purpose, that of national expansion via commercial development, arguing that it was "part of God's plan that 'the opening of the world by navigation and commerce, and the further discovering of knowledge, should meet in one time.' "[19]

By identifying scientific development with the public good, Bacon gave a sense of common purpose to merchants, artisans, and scientists. By explicitly tying the development of science to its ability to make contact with and learn from artisans, he enormously enhanced the prestige of craft labor. While such collaboration had been practically established in certain sectors of English society for a generation or more, Bacon's theoretical justification of its worth had the effect of raising its prestige and extending its influence far beyond its original audience. By the 1650s it was considered not only appropriate but fashionable for the well-to-do to interest themselves in the latest scientific developments, an interest that extended to teachers, government officials, and professionals as well as to the artisans who still comprised a major audience for scientific popularization.[20]

It was the recognized value of scientific interchange between gentlemen and artisans that led to the development of institutions in which such associations could occur. By the end of the seventeenth century numerous scientific societies and societies for the promotion of useful knowledge had

[18] Ibid., pp. 18, 34–41, 87; Musson and Robinson, *Science and Technology*, p. 15.
[19] Hill, *Intellectual Origins*, p. 87.
[20] Musson and Robinson, *Science and Technology*, pp. 21–24.

THE CRAFTSMAN AS HERO

been formed to promote interaction among scientists, artisans, and all those who were interested in science and technology. Such societies clearly followed in the tradition of the earlier popularizing lectures, but with significant differences. The change from the lecture format to that of the scientific society placed the participants on a more equal footing, at least in a formal sense: rather than scientists lecturing to artisans, all were members of the same organization. Moreover, the frequent use of the coffee house as a meeting place changed the terms of the encounter to foster a relationship that was convivial as well as intellectual.[21]

Set within the context of such associations, the emergence of Masonry becomes more comprehensible. Although similar to the learned societies, Freemasonry emphasized conviviality rather than scientific expertise and thus enlarged its pool of potential members. It replicated the social experience of the learned societies, thus allowing for symbolic participation in the project of scientific and technical development by those who were sympathetic to its aims but incapable of more substantive involvement. The creation of Masonry served to express in a particularly vivid and accessible way the broader social importance of craft labor, which contributed to scientific advance as well as to commercial and manufactured wealth.

THE GRAND LODGE AND LATITUDINARIANISM

With the establishment of the Grand Lodge of England in 1717, one tendency within Freemasonry made its bid to impose organizational coherence and its own vision of the craft upon a previously diverse and inchoate movement. By the early eighteenth century, Newtonianism had emerged as a central intellectual influence, developed by its popularizers into a political and religious perspective as well as a scientific system. The Grand Lodge of England was an organization

---

[21] Ibid., p. 59.

dominated by this popular Newtonianism. Although it is generally seen as a decisive repudiation of Baconian inductionism, the two systems shared a common estimation of the value of productive labor and a commitment to practical applications of scientific knowledge. This continuity is visible in the Grand Lodge, which continued the tradition of collaboration among the socially disparate that early Masonry seems to have expressed both symbolically and, to some degree, in practice.

The Newtonian flavor of Masonic rhetoric, with its frequent references to God as the Universal Architect, has often been noted and Freemasonry seen as an institution permeated with the values of the early Enlightenment. With the aid of Margaret C. Jacob's work on political and religious interpretations of Newtonianism, it becomes possible to locate the intellectual and political origins of Grand Lodge Masonry more precisely, to see it as the project of a particular religious-political grouping within English society known as the latitudinarians.[22]

Latitudinarianism was a political-religious tendency within the Church of England in the late seventeenth and early eighteenth centuries, a time when religious and political positions implied one another. Theologically, the latitudinarians were moderate Protestants whose chief concern was to steer a middle course between Catholicism on the one hand and varieties of thought subversive of public order and Anglican authority (radical Protestantism, later atheism) on the other. Initially this was to be done through the medium of a doctrinally permissive Anglican Church, one that accorded a wide latitude in matters of ritual and belief as long as it was combined with a basic acceptance of the Church's authority. After the Revolution of 1688–1689, the Toleration Act established a limited form of religious pluralism for the Protestant churches. The hope of a united Church of

---

[22] Margaret C. Jacob, *The Newtonians and the English Revolution 1689–1720* (Ithaca, N.Y.: Cornell University Press, 1976).

England that would include all Protestant groups now rendered impractical, the latitudinarians attempted to establish their authority on the basis of moral and intellectual leadership rather than through institutional unification. This was to be done through the cultivation of what was called natural religion. "The preaching of natural religion based on solid and verifiable natural philosophy assumed critical importance; the only form of Protestant unification possible seemed to rely on the widespread acceptance of a liberal Christianity, not on an amalgamation of the Churches."[23]

The means selected to achieve this goal was the development and dissemination of a popularized Newtonianism, which provided scientific validation for a model of religion and society midway between Catholicism at one extreme and atheism or religious indifference at the other. This latitudinarian elaboration of the Newtonian model of the universe may be summarized as follows:

The fundamental tenet was that rational argumentation and scientific knowledge, rather than faith and revelation, should be the foundation of religious explanation and Christian belief. It was this position, combined with an assumption of congruence between the natural world and the social world, which led them to the realm of natural philosophy in the first place.[24] Newton described the natural world as harmonious, orderly, and regular, working through the natural laws that God had set in motion. This allowed the latitudinarians to retain a concept of the world as a place in which the hand of God was at work, while rejecting the traditional view of divine intervention in particular cases, and thus affirming the concept of natural law.

The idea of a world governed by natural law and shaped by an underlying purpose and harmony was understood by the latitudinarians to apply to the social world as well as the physical. Politically, this analogy to the physical world made

[23] Ibid., p. 141.
[24] Ibid., pp. 34–35.

67

possible the acceptance of an emerging market society. Just as matter in Newton's terms seemed to operate independently but was actually moved and governed by God and his law to produce a harmonious universe, so men might act in their own individual interests yet produce a social and economic world that was a harmonious totality conforming to certain underlying regularities.[25] "The Newtonian definition of the relationship between man and matter gives a philosophical sanction to the pursuit of material ends, to using the things of this world to one's advantage, in effect, to bargain, to sell, to engage in worldly affairs with the knowledge that this activity is a God-given right. Man's power to acquire material possessions is an extension of his right to change the very course of nature, to control 'brute and stupid' matter."[26] So that while the general tendency of latitudinarianism was to justify the emerging capitalist order, seen as a natural one, it also expressed the more egalitarian impulses of capitalism in its imputation of worth to the transformation of matter, that is to manual labor, which became analogous to God's own activity in the world.

Moreover, the latitudinarians, while they generally supported the emerging order, were troubled by the greed and unbridled expression of a self-interest which they saw accompanying the new society and constantly, in their view, threatening to destroy it. Their response was not, like their Tory contemporaries Swift and Gay, a complete moral rejection; rather, it involved an attempt to modify such excesses by showing that an enlightened and somewhat restrained self-interest was in the end the most effective course to follow. This enlightened rationality was to be cultivated in two ways, through the study and contemplation of nature as a way to curb antisocial impulses and through the use of institutional religion as a social cement and bulwark against

[25] Ibid., pp. 18, 59.
[26] Ibid., p. 189.

instability.[27] Reflection upon God's plan in the natural world could be used as a guide to God's plan for the moral world, or at the very least as an assurance that such a plan did exist. Especially, contemplation of the physical order could reveal the importance of social order and harmony. Equally important as an aid to social harmony was religion, now conceived not primarily as a medium of private devotion but as a public institution that could inculcate practical virtue and bring people together socially in ways that would minimize an unreasonable individualism.

This understanding of the political agenda of popular Newtonianism permits us to move beyond the common observation that the early Grand Lodge reflected Newtonian assumptions and to see it as a political and religious expression of latitudinarian aims. We see this confirmed by looking at the identities of early leaders such as John Beal, a member of the Royal Society; John, second Duke of Montague, a noted Newtonian and also member of the Royal Society; and above all, John Theophile Desaguliers, whose rule as Grand Master and later as Deputy Grand Master initiated the revitalization of the Grand Lodge through the attraction of aristocratic members, the articulation of a new program, and the energetic centralization of the movement.

In the person of Desaguliers, the central figure in the early Grand Lodge, are united the scientific and political themes that constitute the materials of an emerging Freemasonry. Following in the earlier English traditions of scientific collaboration, Desaguliers was perhaps the most important scientific popularizer of his day, lecturing to public audiences in London, and, significantly, to private audiences of gentry and nobility, including George I, George II, and other members of the royal family. Beginning in 1713, when he left Oxford, his lectures on science and technology emphasized the need to unite theory and practice through the exchange of knowledge between artisans and natural philoso-

[27] Ibid., pp. 195, 181.

phers. "To have a compleat Theory," he wrote, "[t]he Undertaker must understand Bricklayer's Work, Mason's Work, Mill-Wright's Work, Smith's Work, and Carpenter's Work; the Strength, Duration, and Coherence of Bodies; and must be able to draw not only a general scheme of the whole Machine, but of every particular part."[28] He was, moreover, strongly committed to the cultivation of useful knowledge, and to this end, expressed the hope that scientists "wou'd not think it below them to direct Workmen, and consider Engines a little more than they do, which wou'd render their Speculations more useful to Mankind."[29] In accord with this belief, Desaguliers himself engaged in various attempts at practical inventions such as pumps, sounding devices, and engines. Though his own efforts did not meet with spectacular success, his active involvement allowed him to be well informed about the most advanced industrial and engineering ventures. His ability to describe new inventions and demonstrate the principles of their operation was one of the keys to his popularity. At the same time he was highly regarded within the scientific community; his position as the Royal Society's official curator and demonstrator reflecting the esteem in which he was held by Sir Isaac Newton, then president of the Society.

On the basis of these activities, we can locate Desaguliers squarely within the earlier British scientific tradition of experimentalism, popularization, collaboration between scientists and artisans, and commitment to practical applications of scientific knowledge. Not himself a great innovator, Desaguliers played an important role in the diffusion of knowledge to crucial publics by popularizing the development of scientific knowledge among craftsmen and by informing the upper classes about remarkable technological advances in the sphere of production. This is significant in

[28] Quoted in Musson and Robinson, *Science and Technology*, p. 39.
[29] Quoted in Bernard Fay, *Revolution and Freemasonry 1600–1800* (Boston: Little, Brown, and Company, 1935), p. 106.

terms of early capitalist development, since the engineering innovations that Desaguliers was especially interested in—mines, pumps, bridges, water supplies, engines—provided the technical basis and the infrastructure for later technological development and required large infusions of capital for their implementation.

Desaguliers was at the same time an important member of a younger generation of latitudinarians. His place in history rests primarily on his work as a scientific lecturer and popularizer of Newton. But within the political context of Stuart and Hanoverian England, such a scientific role implied a particular political and religious position as well. While this would have been true had Desaguliers done nothing more than deliver his scientific talks, he did at times reveal his latitudinarian views in more explicit terms, arguing, for example, that it was the task of theologians to encourage the contemplation of creation, which was the proof of God's existence, rather than engaging in technical disputes. In his 1728 work, "The Newtonian System of the World, the Best Model of Government: an Allegorical Poem," he defended the legitimacy of the Hanoverian monarchy by arguing that the British form of a limited monarchy was the system of government that most closely conformed to the Newtonian model of the universe. "I have considered GOVERNMENT as a Phenomenon, and look'd upon that Form of it to be most perfect which did nearly resemble the Natural Government of our System according to the laws settled by the All-wise and All-mighty Architect of the Universe."[30] Clearly Desaguliers's simultaneous involvements in scientific popularizing, political-religious discourse, and the nascent Grand Lodge of England represent facets of a coherent and consistent latitudinarian position, just as the Grand Lodge expressed in institutional form a whole range of latitudinarian concerns.

Freemasonry embodies the latitudinarian view of religion

[30] Quoted in ibid., p. 95.

as a social cement, as an institution that brings order and harmony to society. In its rejection of religious and political disputes and its espousal of "that Religion in which all Men agree," the Grand Lodge proposed to unite men within a wide latitude of doctrinal difference. This was a role that the latitudinarians had once seen for the Anglican church but was now set aside as unrealistic.

Freemasonry also promoted that contemplation of nature that the latitudinarians saw as so important. Many lodges of the early eighteenth century featured regular lectures on geometry and architecture.[31] The Masonic references to God as the Supreme Architect reflect and call to mind, as we have seen, a specifically Newtonian understanding of a harmonious and ordered universe. The proper awareness of nature's harmony would act as a corrective to the individualism and greed that threatened the social and political order. Freemasonry also attempted to check the growth of an unrestricted pursuit of self-interest through its concept of itself as a brotherhood, an institution that promoted loyalty and benevolence and emphasized the ties binding Masons to one another, ties that specifically included a responsibility to help any brother Mason who was in trouble.

But at the same time as it was an institution that attempted to moderate the excesses of an emerging capitalist system, Freemasonry affirmed the basic worth of productive activity. It did this not just indirectly, through the latitudinarian analogy between God as the transformer of matter in the universe and man as the shaper of matter in the human world, but most strikingly and graphically, through the institution's descent from an order of craft workers, and its explicit identification of itself with that tradition.

In their attempt to centralize and direct the Masonic movement through the vehicle of the Grand Lodge, the latitudinarians moved beyond their role as articulators of a particular religious and political position within the Church

[31] Knoop and Jones, *Genesis*, p. 6.

of England, or even within the wider political discourse of the time. Instead, they became key participants in the creation of a social and cultural institution of much broader applicability. As a social paradigm, Freemasonry offered a complex of values and assumptions that can be characterized as those of an emergent bourgeoisie—a detachment from inherited social identities, a belief in social mobility, an acceptance of market relations and property-based authority, and a positive evaluation of science, technology, and productive labor. As a paradigm, it acquired a greater accessibility and emotional resonance through its assimilation to a social institution that could express its values symbolically, in the rituals of craft workers, and interactionally, through the promotion of social relations between Anglicans and nonconformists, aristocrats, gentry, wealthy bourgeois and middling tradesmen. At the same time, Freemasonry incorporated this paradigm into the traditional context of a fraternal association, using a corporate idiom to soften the harsher outlines of the social vision it presented.

THE MASONIC PARADIGM: DIVERSITY AND INDIVIDUALISM

"GENTLEMEN, mechanics, porters, parsons, ragmen, hucksters, divines, tinkers, knights . . .": thus were the Masons portrayed in a satiric speech made in Dublin in the year 1688.[32] It was in fact unlikely, though not impossible, for ragpickers or porters to become Masons. Nonetheless, Masonic social inclusiveness proved startling to many who inhabited the hierarchical and circumscribed social worlds of the eighteenth century.

Freemasonry was in its origins a venture in boundary-crossing, as gentlemen sought to affiliate themselves with lodges of practicing stone masons. In the Scottish lodges, the Accepted Masons continued to participate in the opera-

[32] Ibid., p. 152.

CHAPTER TWO

tive lodges for some time. Evidence from the Lodge of Aberdeen suggests that operative masons, members of a declining trade, were outnumbered by 1670, but that the lodge retained a remarkable diversity, with a membership of four noblemen, three gentlemen, eight professional men, nine merchants, and twenty-five craftsmen or tradesmen, ten of whom were actually stone masons. Most of the craftsmen were presumably well-to-do masters, who themselves no longer worked with their hands. But as individuals who had begun their working lives as craft laborers, they constituted a tangible link to the lodge's craft origins at a time when being "in trade" represented a grave social disqualification.

In England, Accepted Masons quickly gravitated to their own separate lodges. But the available evidence indicates that the craft retained substantial membership among small merchants, tradesmen, master craftsmen, and even journeymen artisans. Of the Four Old Lodges (that is, the lodges that joined forces to form the Grand Lodge of England), one had a predominantly aristocratic membership, while the others seem to have had significant numbers of artisanal masters. Of the first ten Grand Wardens of the early Grand Lodge, two were identified as carpenters, two as stonecutters, one as a mason, and one as a blacksmith.[33] The fact that the office of Grand Warden was apparently reserved for a representative of this artisanal element suggests a concern on the part of the Grand Lodge's aristocratic leadership to allow for regularized symbolic participation in leadership by those of lower social standing.

As the case of the Four Old Lodges suggests, lodges varied in the social composition of their membership and, at least initially, in the character of their rituals. Lodges with stronger artisanal bases tended to retain the kind of horseplay traditionally associated with initiations in guilds and journeymen's societies. In a Masonic catechism of 1723, for

[33] Ibid., information on the Lodge of Aberdeen, p. 144; on the Four Old Lodges, p. 198.

74

example, an initiate is called upon to " 'behold a thousand different Postures and Grimaces, all of which he must exactly imitate, or undergo the Discipline til he does,' " a ceremony strongly reminiscent of traditional journeymen's initiations.[34] The maintenance of a degree of class segregation at local levels facilitated the heterogeneity of the movement as a whole. Yet the project was not without its tensions. The Grand Lodge periodically tried to narrow its recruitment base by raising initiation fees and banning public processions that might attract public attention. The Grand Lodge even took measures to eliminate the tricks and levity that characterized lodges with stronger operative traditions, as when Desaguliers recommended to a Norwich lodge a by-law specifying that "no ridiculous trick be played with any person when he is admitted."[35]

The formation of the Grand Lodge of the Ancients, a rival Grand Lodge that arose in 1751, was most probably a response to the Grand Lodge of England's efforts to enforce decorum, restrict membership, and in general distance the organization from its craft origins. The Ancients drew upon a lower social stratum of mechanics and shopkeepers for the bulk of their membership; indeed, Laurence Dermott, the Ancients' Grand Secretary and driving force for more than thirty years, was a journeyman painter of Irish birth. Yet in spite of these more plebeian origins, the Ancients succeeded in their goal of gaining aristocratic and ultimately royal patronage; by 1813, the two rival Grand Lodges were reunited on terms of equality, each with a royal duke at its head.[36] It is true that the older and more elite Grand Lodge was constantly tempted to retreat toward more restrictive

[34] Quoted in ibid., pp. 208–9; E. J. Hobsbawm, *Primitive Rebels* (New York: W. W. Norton, 1959), p. 157.

[35] B. Jones, *Freemason's Guide*, p. 196; Desaguliers is quoted in Knoop and Jones, *Genesis*, p. 209.

[36] Wayne A. Huss, *The Master Builders: A History of the Grand Lodge of Free and Accepted Masons of Pennsylvania*, vol. 1, *1731–1873* (Philadelphia: Grand Lodge F. & A.M. of Pennsylvania, 1986), pp. 12, 15.

practices. Nonetheless, it never wholly abandoned its character as an institutionalized meeting place for men from various social strata.

The point here is not simply that men of different ranks, classes, and religions were enabled to interact with one another, but rather the terms in which Freemasonry interpreted such meetings. In contrast to the vertical and deferential relationships of medieval and early modern society, Masonry encouraged the construction of horizontal social ties. The Masonic initiation is a rite of leveling, in which the candidate enters the lodge divested of money and jewelry and stripped of all but shirt and pants, thus symbolically detached from his worldly standing. Since the rite creates a fraternal bond predicated upon the formal equality of members, even the most socially restrictive lodges engaged in a symbolic repudiation of distinctions of rank and class.

Distance, of course, could equally be derived from religious difference, and here too Freemasonry asserted the possibility that men could divest themselves of traditional identities for the purpose of fellowship. In keeping with the latitudinarian concern to overcome sectarianism, the 1723 "Constitution" required only that Masons follow "that religion in which all Men agree, leaving their particular opinions to themselves." As the wording of this passage reveals, this was more than a plea for toleration. Rather it asserted that men could enter the order, and relate to one another, as individuals, without reference to their identities as members of confessional communities. Protestants, Catholics, and even Jews could become Masons and be bound together as brothers through a ritual process that claimed to override their sectarian loyalties. Freemasonry explicitly claimed that morality itself, the capacity to be and do good, was not conditioned by religious belief, that Masons were to be "good Men and true, or Men of Honour and Honesty, by *whatever* Denomination or Persuasion they may be distinguished." In other words, Freemasonry expressed an ideal of secularism in its reduction of religion to the level of an individual "Persuasion" that could be conveniently ignored in most situations, having lost its power to define identity in any absolute sense.

Freemasonry thus promoted a cosmopolitanism that was one significant part of its appeal. Just as the ritual and institutions of the compagnonnage had enabled journeymen to travel, to work in a variety of settings, and to view at least some strangers as "brothers," so the Masonic secrets facilitated mobility, both spatial and social, in a world in which the growth of national and international markets and of nation-states made an intense particularism increasingly problematic. Benjamin Franklin, a Masonic enthusiast, revealed a sophisticated awareness of the functions served by the ritual when he wrote of his brother Masons:

> They speak a universal language, and act as a passport to the attention and support of the initiated in all parts of the world. . . . On the field of battles, in the solitude of the uncultivated forests, or in the busy haunts of the crowded city, they have made men of the most hostile feelings, and most distant religions, and the most diversified conditions, rush to the aid of each other, and feel social joy and satisfaction that they have been able to afford relief to a brother Mason.[37]

Through its novel proclamation that within the lodge all men were brothers, Freemasonry taught its members to view themselves as such, putting aside, at least temporarily and symbolically, the distinctions of rank and belief. In its assertion that ascribed characteristics are irrelevant in the fact of individual merit, Freemasonry proclaimed an individualist philosophy. But interestingly, it promoted its individualism through the creation of a new collectivity, based in turn upon the ritual assumption of a new symbolic identity:

[37] Quoted in Stevens, *Cyclopaedia*, p. 17; Jews were admitted to London lodges as early as 1732. The inclusion of prayers for the use of Jewish Freemasons in a Masonic handbook of 1756 suggests that Jews were present in significant numbers.

77

CHAPTER TWO

that of artisanal master, an identity that proclaimed a further Masonic agenda.

THE MASONIC PARADIGM: TECHNOLOGY AND CRAFTSMANSHIP

In the words of its ritual, Freemasonry is a "system of morality veiled in allegory and illustrated by symbols." What is striking is that the objects used to illustrate the Masonic morality are the tools of working stone masons. The square admonishes the Mason to be honest and straightforward, the level represents equality, and the plumb line justice and uprightness. The twenty-four-inch gauge represents the twenty-four hours of the day, symbolizing "the passage of time, and in particular, of time well spent."[38] Note both the character of the virtues portrayed, which are the idealized characteristics of the hard-working artisan, and the identification of the tools, the instruments of manual labor, as the symbols of this morality.

When men became Accepted Masons, they symbolically became craft workers. The assumption of this identity was signified by the use of the operative tools as ritual objects and above all by the wearing of the leather apron as the central symbol of Masonic identity. Freemasonry thus expressed a new awareness of craft labor's contributions to both scientific advance and the success of commerce and manufacture. When the eighteenth-century Mason donned his leather apron, he implicitly acknowledged the moral worth of economically productive activity, including manual labor, since the leather apron was the universally recognized uniform of the artisan in a society that used dress as an explicit, almost theatrical statement of rank and position.[39]

These meanings were clearly recognized by Freemason-

[38] B. Jones, *Freemason's Guide*, pp. 432, 442, 430.
[39] Eric Foner, *Tom Paine and Revolutionary America* (New York: Oxford University Press, 1976), p. 37; Richard Sennett, *The Fall of Public Man* (New York: Alfred A. Knopf, 1977), pp. 66–68.

ry's eighteenth-century participants, as we can see from various attempts to redefine or reject the original Masonic identity. In Britain, anti-craft sentiments were expressed through the fashion of wearing the apron upside down. As Laurence Dermott, the plebeian Grand Secretary of the Grand Lodge of the Ancients pointed out, the wearing of aprons was disliked by many of the "young architects," precisely because it "made the gentlemen look like so many mechanicks." Initially they had proposed to dispense with the aprons altogether, but when this was rejected, suggested that "they should be turned upside down, in order to avoid appearing mechanical." In this way, Dermott noted, "the bib and strings hung downwards, dangling in such a manner as might convince the spectators that there was not a working mason among them."[40] To Dermott, a working journeyman painter, this was clear snobbery and a betrayal of everything that made Freemasonry so appealing to people like himself.

In Europe, reaction against Masonry's operative origins was articulated most forcefully in the development of Templarism, or Scottish Masonry. In each of its national manifestations, such as the German Rite of the Strict Observance or the French Rite of Perfection, Templaric Freemasonry involved the multiplication of degrees, the creation of a Masonic world beyond the three traditional levels of Entered Apprentice, Fellow Craft, and Master Mason.[41] The chapters, directories, consistories, and commanderies of higher degree holders created more exclusive and hierarchical subgroups within Masonry. This tended to deny the egalitarian impulses symbolized by the original ritual, as well as to pose financial barriers to participation by the less affluent. But most significantly, Templarism involved a reinterpre-

[40] Quoted in Gould, *History of Freemasonry*, p. 155.

[41] Information about Templaric Masonry appears in Gould, *History of Freemasonry*; Roberts, *Mythology of the Secret Societies*; Stevens, *Cyclopaedia*; Fay, *Revolution and Freemasonry*; and Klaus Epstein, *The Genesis of German Conservatism* (Princeton, N.J.: Princeton University Press, 1966).

CHAPTER TWO

tation of Masonic origins. While the details of the story varied from country to country, all the new versions agreed that Masonry was not descended from the lodges of operative stone masons, but from the orders of Crusader knights such as the Knights Templar. The higher degrees thus organized their ritual around the trappings of knighthood—the wearing of armor, the carrying of swords. The connection to Masonry was located in the claim that the Crusaders had to learn to be masons so they could rebuild the Holy Sepulchre. Templarism constructed an alternative identity for Freemasonry, an aristocratic identity that denied any craft or commercial origins and thus decisively repudiated the value that British Masonry had accorded to productive labor and its practitioners.

The changes that occurred in Freemasonry as it spread to the continent illustrate how its significance as an institution could be contested, reinterpreted, and transformed. In creating the Grand Lodge of England, the latitudinarians had made a relatively self-conscious political and ideological statement, yet the character of that statement would be periodically altered as different groups sought to redefine it and as larger social and political contexts framed the terms within which it was understood. Templarism, for example, originated as an aristocratic and anti-capitalist version of Freemasonry in France, where it survived as one of a number of tendencies. But it achieved its most thorough dominance in Germany, where it developed as part of a wider reaction against the rationalistic values of the Enlightenment.[42]

In Britain, as we have seen, there were also currents of opposition to the craft version of Masonic identity. But the Grand Lodge of England remained the central arbiter of the movement in Britain. And while it periodically tried to place practical limitations on the range of participants, it never attempted to repudiate either its historical roots or its sym-

[42] Epstein, *German Conservatism*, pp. 86–87.

80

bolic identity in operative Masonry. In large part this must reflect British society's more advanced degree of capitalist development and its greater commitment to market relations. Within this context, the Masonic ideals and the lodge's role in promoting the social integration of gentlemen and entrepreneurs gave Freemasonry a valuable role to play in the development of England as a society committed to bourgeois values.

This commitment included not just a generalized approval of economically productive activity, but a clear statement about the social arrangements that were to govern production. This is most forcefully articulated in the rite of the Third Degree, the Making of the Master Mason, usually considered the dramatic centerpiece of Masonic ritual. In this ceremony the initiate assumes the role of Hiram Abif, in Masonic legend the heroic architect and grand master mason of King Solomon's Temple, who was slain by jealous apprentices for his refusal to betray the secrets of the craft. The candidate is blindfolded, the secrets are demanded from him, and when he resists answering, his attackers (the jealous apprentices) pretend to abuse and then to murder him. After an enactment of the discovery of the body and execution of the killers, the initiate is "raised" from his grave by the lodge Master, an action that symbolizes his resurrection from a "figurative death" to a new way of life as a Master Mason.[43]

The values articulated here are of a paternalistic early capitalism. The casting of a master craftsman as the hero of a morality play clearly affirms the dignity of labor and craft knowledge. Yet the authority of the master as *master*, and his right to sole possession of the secrets of his craft, are upheld; his heroism consists precisely in his willingness to die rather than give them over to his apprentices. The independent organization of apprentices and journeymen is con-

[43] James Dewar, *The Unlocked Secret: Freemasonry Examined* (London: William Kimber and Company, 1966), pp. 98–100.

81

demned; their relationship to craft tradition in the person of the master persists only so long as they accept his right to private property and his authority over them. If they accept these, they may themselves hope to rise in the hierarchy of the trade.

The Masonic paradigm presents a defense of capitalist relations as encapsulated within the heroic figure of the craftsman. The system of degrees indicates the possibilities for individual mobility in such a society, possibilities available to anyone possessing the requisite skills and commitment to hard work. Yet the implicit analogy is a flawed and distorted one because mobility within the lodge is available to everyone. Each member begins symbolically at the bottom with nothing, and then rises at will through a ritualized and regularized procedure. Thus to the extent that the Masonic degrees represent a model of social structure, they present a distinctly partial and optimistic view of mobility and equality in capitalist society.

Similarly, the Hiramic legend presents an idealized defense of individual private property. In this portrayal, property is represented by the artisan's skill, which is acquired by the individual in the course of his labor. Yet the defense of property extends implicitly to all private property, including the manufacturer's capital and the aristocrat's landed wealth as well as the painstakingly earned competency of the craft worker. The selection of the hard-working artisanal producer as the emblematic figure of capitalist society thus capitalizes on what Wilentz has called the "duality in the social relations of the [artisanal] workshop."[44]

The Masonic ritual thus presents an idealized version of capitalist production and market relations. Yet its portrayal is more complex and thus more appealing than might initially appear, for its fraternal form allows an implicit recog-

[44] Sean Wilentz, *Chants Democratic: New York City and the Rise of the American Working Class 1788–1850* (New York: Oxford University Press, 1984), p. 4.

nition of the tensions and dilemmas that such relations might produce. Its use of a corporate organization and idiom meant that it continued to articulate an ethos of mutuality. The Masonic institution asserted that voluntary association outside the sphere of production could alleviate the social dislocations caused by individualistic, market-oriented economic relations. While the degree structure proclaimed the inevitability of success for all, the enunciation of the fraternal obligation to assist needy brothers implicitly conceded that some would fail. Freemasonry thus maintained that the moral community that had been banished from the workplace could be successfully reconstructed in civil society and effectively used to alleviate the worst failures of the new social system. It was precisely the contradictory character of its message that gave Freemasonry its appeal as it entered the nineteenth century.

PART TWO
*
AMERICAN
TRANSFORMATIONS

THREE

Was the Lodge a Working-Class
Institution?

AT approximately the same time as it was spreading throughout Europe, Freemasonry reached North America, where the first lodge was formed in Philadelphia in 1730. Masonry established itself early in American culture and its influence was exercised not simply though the growth of the craft itself, but through its role in shaping the character of the countless other fraternal orders that would be founded during the nineteenth century. Belleville, Illinois, for example, a midwestern town of fifteen thousand in 1884, possessed numerous voluntary associations, including organizations like the Pecan Club, the Liederkranz Society, and the Widows and Orphans Mutual Aid Society. By far the most common organization of a single kind, however, was the fraternal order, a form of association that seemed to hold a uniquely strong appeal to nineteen-century American men. In Belleville, for example, lodges such as "Pride of the West, No. 650, International Order of Odd Fellows," and "Cavalier Lodge, No. 49, Knights of Pythias," comprised thirty-five of the fifty-five organizations listed in the city directory of that year. At about the same time a much larger industrial city, Buffalo, New York, had seventeen local lodges of the Knights of Pythias alone, with more than 1,500 members.[1]

---

[1] *Belleville City Directory* (Urbana, Ill.: D. McKenzie, 1884). *Buffalo Street Guide and Knights of Pythias Lodge Directory* (Buffalo, New York: Albert J. Kuebler and Fred Kroebel, 1894). In 1900, the two largest organizations, the Masons and Odd Fellows, had one million members each out of a total male population of thirty-nine million. At least four other orders had more than 500,000 members. Albert C. Stevens, *The Cyclopaedia of Fraternities* (New

CHAPTER THREE

Historians have increasingly recognized the fraternal order as a numerically massive and widely distributed presence in late nineteenth-century America, with special relevance for the study of social relations, institutionalized friendship patterns, and the formation of community and subgroup identities.[2] The fraternal order's rhetoric of equality and its often proclaimed disregard for social and economic position reveal an institutional preoccupation with issues of class and identify the lodge as a significant resource for the study of nineteenth-century class relations.[3] But while the importance of the lodge as a social institution is acknowledged, there is little consensus and even less theoretical clarity about its role in the construction of class identities in this period.

Some scholars, such as Roy Rosenzweig and Lynn Dumenil, argue that the fraternal order was primarily an organ of lower-middle-class respectability, while others see it as an institution that was significant in the development of working-class solidarity.[4] John Cumbler, for example, in his book *Working-Class Community in Industrial America*, de-

York: E. B. Treat and Company, 1907; Detroit: Gale Research Company, 1966), pp. 43, 254, 113–14.

[2] See, for example, John Cumbler, *Working Class Community in Industrial America: Work, Leisure and Struggle in Two Industrial Cities—1880–1930* (Westport, Conn.: Greenwood Press, 1979); Alan Dawley, *Class and Community: The Industrial Revolution in Lynn* (Cambridge, Mass.: Harvard University Press, 1976); Brian Greenberg, "Worker and Community: Fraternal Orders in Albany, New York, 1845–1885," *Maryland Historian* 8:2 (1977): pp. 38–53; Charles Stephenson, "A Gathering of Strangers? Mobility, Social Structure and Political Participation in the Formation of Nineteenth Century American Working Class Culture," in Milton Cantor, ed., *American Working Class Culture: Explorations in American Labor and Social History* (Westport, Conn.: Greenwood Press, 1979); Daniel Walkowitz, *Workers' City, Company Town* (Urbana, Ill.: University of Illinois Press, 1978).

[3] See Roy Rosenzweig, "Boston Masons, 1900–1935: The Lower Middle Class in a Divided Society," *Journal of Voluntary Action Research* 6:3–4 (1977), for egalitarian rhetoric within Freemasonry.

[4] Rosenzweig, "Boston Masons;" and Lynn Dumenil, "Brotherhood and Respectability: Freemasonry and American Culture, 1880–1930." Ph.D. diss., University of California, Berkeley, 1981.

scribes the role of the Lynn, Massachusetts, Odd Fellows lodge in providing its largely working-class membership with opportunities for social expression and political comradeship, as well as material resources such as sickness and death benefits. The lodge, writes Cumbler, was an important part of that complex of "working-class community institutions, both formal and informal . . . [that] acted to maintain strong class solidarity as well as contribute to collective action." David Montgomery is in basic agreement with this characterization. While he recognizes that fraternal orders "tended to group people along religious or ethnic lines" rather than restricting their membership to wage workers, they were nonetheless the characteristic workers' institutions of the Gilded Age: "During these decades, workers created a wide variety of institutions, all of them infused with a spirit of mutuality. Through their fraternal orders, cooperatives, reform clubs, political parties, and trade unions, American workers shaped a collectivist counter-culture in the midst of the growing factory system."[5]

In contrast, I argue that the meaning of fraternalism in class relations was more complex than either of these characterizations can encompass. Large numbers of American working-class men did participate in fraternal orders in the late nineteenth and early twentieth centuries. But this did not lead to the consolidation of lodges as organs of working-class solidarity. The reasons for this lie in the complex symbolic and institutional realities of fraternalism that are the primary focus of this book.

THE WORKING-CLASS LODGE AS AN ORGANIZATIONAL RESOURCE

The idea that the lodge and the social relations embodied in it constituted one of the key resources of American working-

[5] Cumbler, *Working Class Community*, pp. 44–45; David Montgomery, "Labor in the Industrial Era," in Richard B. Morris, ed., *The United States Department of Labor History of the American Worker* (Washington, D.C.: U.S. Government Printing Office, 1976) p. 121.

class communities can be theoretically grounded in a re-source mobilization approach to the study of collective be-havior and social movements.[6] Such a perspective, as exem-plified by the work of Charles Tilly, begins with the perception that structural position is in itself insufficient to explain collective mobilization. Groups that share a com-mon interest and location in the social structure may act in quite different ways; some may never engage in visible col-lective action while others are militant. In the effort to spec-ify the particular circumstances influencing the emergence of collective action, the resource mobilization perspective identifies the presence of already-existing social ties as a key variable. When such ties link people into solidary units, they are then available to facilitate communication and action and to serve as the organizational basis for more explicitly polit-ical acts of mobilization, resistance, and struggle.[7]

Although their work is applicable to a variety of social movements, resource mobilization theorists such as Tilly make a special contribution to the analysis of class forma-tion, addressing the question, in Marxist terms, of why "the carriers of economic relations (do or) do not act politically as class members."[8] Increasingly the nature of social net-works has emerged as one key variable.[9]

[6] This account makes primary use of Charles Tilly's *From Mobilization to Revolution* (Reading, Massachusetts: Addison-Wesley, 1978), but see as well Anthony Oberschall, *Social Conflict and Social Movements* (Englewood Cliffs, N.J.: Prentice-Hall, 1973).

[7] While this perspective focuses equally on how externally imposed costs structure collective action, that part of the argument is not pertinent to the analysis of social fraternalism, which has not existed in the United States as a conflictually oriented movement.

[8] Adam Przeworski, "Proletariat into Class: The Process of Class Formation from Karl Kautsky's *The Class Struggle* to Recent Controversies," *Politics and Society* 7:4 (1977): p. 384.

[9] The recent historical literature on class formation begins with E. P. Thompson's *The Making of the English Working Class*. A very partial selection of subsequent work would include Herbert Gutman, *Work, Culture, and Soci-ety in Industrializing America* (New York: Alfred A. Knopf, 1976); Alan Daw-ley, *Class and Community*; and John Foster, *Class Struggle and the Industrial Revolution* (New York: St. Martin's Press, 1974).

Theorists and historians continue to focus upon the relational character of class in Marxist thought. But they now extend this insight beyond the usual recognition that classes exist and are constituted in opposition to one another, giving an equivalent importance to relations within structurally-defined classes. As David Stark has written, "the capacity for class organization" is directly related to "the degree and forms of connectedness within a class . . . the extent to which intra- or inter-ethnic, racial, etc., relations facilitate or inhibit the communication of ideas and the co-ordination of activities within particular historical settings."[10] The value of this perspective lies in its ability to conceptualize and make available for analysis the vast terrain between determinism and voluntarism, between structural location and consciousness, which is central to the issue of class formation. It identifies an intermediate and historically specifiable range of social relations that can serve as the basis for the organization of class capacity. Tilly's concept of a "catnet" is especially pertinent.

Following Harrison White, Tilly distinguishes between categories and networks. Categories are sets "of people who share some characteristic"—all women, all Baptists, all brown-eyed people, all those who share a common relation to the means of production. They refer to attributes possessed by individuals. Networks refer to social relations; they are comprised of "people who are linked to each other, directly or indirectly, by a specific kind of interpersonal

---

Class formation as a theoretical issue in Marxism is discussed in Przeworski, "Proletariat into Class;" David Stark, "Class Struggle and the Transformation of the Labor Process," *Theory and Society* 9 (January, 1980); and Ira Katznelson, *City Trenches: Urban Politics and the Patterning of Class in the United States* (Chicago: University of Chicago Press, 1981). Craig Calhoun, "The Radicalism of Tradition: Community Strength or Venerable Disguise and Borrowed Language," *American Journal of Sociology* 88:5 (1983): pp. 886–914, is an interesting critique of Marxist approaches.

[10] Stark, "Class Struggle and the Transformation of the Labor Process," p. 97.

CHAPTER THREE

bond." On the basis of this distinction, Tilly defines a "cat-net" as "a set of individuals comprising both a category and a network." A catnet is otherwise known as a group and it is this quality of "groupness" that generates organizational capacity. "The more extensive its common identity and internal network, the more organized the group" and the more capable of articulating a common interest and mobilizing in pursuit of it.[11]

Such a perspective reveals the importance of institutions and relationships that may previously have been dismissed as apolitical, "merely" expressive, and generally irrelevant to issues of class or other power relations. In explaining class formation, it posits the development of class-based institutions that create social networks and overcome divisions within the structurally defined class while at the same time reducing social ties to members of other class groups. This is a model in which working-class development depends not only on common economic position but also on the formation of dense and extensive networks, working-class institutions that unite and organize myriad individuals into a group, a community with the organizational capacity to act in its own behalf.

Institutions that approximate such a model of class formation may be identified in nineteenth-century European society. Ronald Aminzade's studies of nineteenth-century Toulouse provide one powerful example.[12] Toulousain artisans entered the 1830s enmeshed in a variety of hierarchical, vertical relationships with the aristocracy and its mediary the Church. In the 1840s, as capitalist development altered the local economy and eroded patronage relationships of economic dependence, Toulousain workers began to with-

[11] Tilly, *Mobilization*, pp. 62–63.
[12] Ronald Aminzade, "Breaking the Chains of Dependency: From Patronage to Class Politics, Toulouse, France, 1830–1872," *Journal of Urban History* 3:4 (1977): pp. 485–505; and "The Transformation of Social Solidarities in Nineteenth Century Toulouse" in John Merriam, ed., *Consciousness and Class Experience in Nineteenth Century Europe* (New York: Holmes and Meier, 1979).

92

draw from the networks created by traditional institutions such as the religious confraternity and to form independent institutions such as secular mutual benefit societies.[13] These societies severed connections with the aristocracy and the bourgeoisie while they created new social networks within the working class by including workers from a variety of trades. Moreover, the new type of workers' organizations stood in pronounced contrast to the traditional organization of artisans in compagnonnages, with their emphasis on trade rivalries and hierarchies.

The growth of such autonomous working-class institutions in Toulouse was crucial to the development of class solidarity and a militant working-class politics, most obviously through the concrete resources that they were able to offer their members. The existence of an already functioning organizational structure facilitated the organization of strikes and political actions, while their class homogeneity enabled them to use benefit funds for strike payments, something that would have been impossible in traditional benefit societies, with their ties to dominant groups. But beyond these practical and observable consequences lie the much looser, more intangible areas of sociability, of structures of communication and sentiment that are themselves resources for collective action. Finally, their autonomy and homogeneity encouraged the development of alternative organizational and interactional modes: "Cafes, taverns, social clubs, mutual benefit societies and labor associations became centers of new regularized patterns of interaction which fostered and sustained new sets of social and political values. These autonomous counter-institutions offered areas of sociability where a spirit of camaraderie and brotherhood, not

[13] See Foster, *Class Struggle*, and Frank Beckhoffer and Brian Elliott, "An Approach to the Study of Small Shopkeepers and the Class Structure," *European Journal of Sociology* 9 (1968): pp. 180–202, for accounts of working-class withdrawal from cross-class institutions in England, and Donald H. Bell, "Worker Culture and Worker Politics: The Experience of an Italian Town, 1880–1915," *Social History* 3:1 (1978): pp. 1–21, for an Italian case.

hierarchy and domination, prevailed."[14] The horizontal, egalitarian character of the networks created within working-class social institutions provided a contrast to the hierarchical social relations of the workplace and civil society, and through this contrast, an implicit critique.

Is it possible to find similar processes at work in the nineteenth-century United States, and was the fraternal order, as has been suggested, a principal site for their working out? The fraternal order was the voluntary association that most consistently mobilized large numbers of American workers, and except for the trade union, the lodge was the organizational form most available to them.[15] Membership and involvement in a lodge involves by definition the creation of a network, of a particular, and in this case highly institutionalized, social bond. To the extent that the members of a lodge, the participants in the network, are also drawn from a category, such as class, we may say that the fraternal order could further the creation of groupness in Tilly's sense and thus the development of class organizational capacities.

In their emphasis on mutuality, benefit functions, and male camaraderie, European mutual benefit societies and American fraternal orders seem to have functioned in very similar ways. The European institutions conform in significant ways to Tilly's concept of a catnet, by increasing horizontal ties within the working class and progressively decreasing vertical ties between workers and members of the clergy, aristocracy, bourgeoisie, and petite bourgeoisie. It is reasonable to ask whether American fraternal orders developed in similar ways.

This implies a series of questions about the class composition of the American movement. Was there significant working-class participation in fraternal orders? And if so,

---

[14] Aminzade, "Breaking the Chains," p. 502.

[15] One indication of its availability and appeal is the fact that so many early unions were originally organized fraternally.

what was the nature of this participation? Was it concentrated in organizations that were homogeneous in their membership, or were American fraternal orders the multiclass institutions that their rhetoric proclaimed?

Much of what is known about the social composition of fraternal orders comes from studies of Masonic lodges. On the basis of this data, summarized in Table 3–1, scholars such as Roy Rosenzweig, Lynn Dumenil, and John Gilkeson have characterized the Masons, and by implication the entire fraternal movement, as a predominantly lower-middle-class phenomenon. They show that during the late nineteenth and early twentieth centuries, about 75 percent of the members of Masonic lodges examined were white-collar workers, a finding that seems to contravene the alternative view of the lodge as an institution of working-class solidarity.

But this finding is of limited use: conclusions that are ac-

TABLE 3–1. Social Composition of Masonic Lodges

Location/Lodge	Date	White-Collar (percent)	Blue-Collar (percent)	Number
Providence*	1874	68	32	N = 284
Oakland†				
(Live Oak)	1890	79	20	N = 169
Providence*				
(Orpheus)	1898	82	18	N = 105
Boston‡				
John's	1899	96	4	N = 70
Webb	1901	84	16	N = 96
Mt. Lebanon	1901	73	27	N = 99
Oakland†				
Oakland	1912	78	22	N = 494
Brooklyn	1912	70	30	N = 291
Alcatraz	1912	44	56	N = 355

* Gilkeson, pp. 121–22, Tables 9 and 10.
† Dumenil, Table B–1, p. 395; Table B–4, p. 398.
‡ Rosenzweig, Table 1.

curate for Masonry may not be valid when applied to the entire fraternal movement. The Freemasons were the accepted elite of the fraternal world, priding themselves on their venerable traditions, their greater selectivity, and their resistance to the recruiting practices employed by other orders. A focus on the Masons as the representative group may lead to an underestimation of working-class participation in the movement as a whole. It overlooks the importance of orders such as the Ancient Order of United Workmen, Improved Order of Red Men, Knights of Pythias, Modern Woodmen of America, and Independent Order of Odd Fellows, all of which flourished during the period from 1875 to 1920. These organizations, although generally patterned after the Masons, engaged in open, and presumably more inclusive, recruiting and should be included in any analysis that seeks to understand the class character of fraternal membership. Therefore, we need to examine the available evidence about the social composition of orders other than the Masons.

WORKING-CLASS PARTICIPATION IN FRATERNAL ORDERS

Table 3–2 summarizes available data concerning the social composition of non-Masonic fraternal lodges. In Lynn, Massachusetts, Cumbler found Odd Fellows lodges with an overwhelmingly working-class membership, as we might expect given Lynn's history as a highly industrialized city with a rich tradition of labor militancy and indigenous working-class institutions.[16] Gilkeson's study of Providence, Rhode Island, shows more moderate levels of working-class membership, ranging from 30 to 53 percent, which nonetheless supports the idea that these other orders such as the Odd Fellows, Knights of Pythias, and Red Men

---

[16] For information on Lynn, see Dawley, *Class and Community*, as well as Cumbler, *Working Class Community*.

TABLE 3–2. Social Composition of Non-Masonic Fraternal Lodges

Location/Order	Date	White-Collar (percent)	Blue-Collar (percent)	Number
Providence*				
Red Men	1872	47	53	N = 40
Knights of Pythias	1875	70	30	N = 79
I.O.O.F.	1877	54	46	N = 107
I.O.O.F.	1896	58	42	N = 99
Lynn†				
I.O.O.F.	1908	25	74	N = 229
I.O.O.F.	1914	20	80	N = 261

* Gilkeson, Tables 9 and 10, pp. 121–22.
† Cumbler, Table 5, p. 46.

did show higher rates of working-class participation than did the Masons.

My research on Knights of Pythias membership, based on a much greater number of lodges, confirms the view that the non-Masonic orders were more receptive to working-class participation. Table 3–3 shows membership figures for Pythian lodges in two cities, Belleville, Illinois, and Buffalo, New York.[17] In each one, the Knights of Pythias attracted approximately as many blue-collar as white-collar members. Moreover, the composition of the blue-collar membership is surprisingly similar—about 60 percent skilled, one-third semiskilled and service workers, and a small number of unskilled laborers. Obviously these organizations did not constitute a representative sample of the population, skewed as

[17] The Belleville data comprise an aggregation of charter members from the town's three Pythian lodges, established from 1874 to 1881, while the Buffalo data come from the *Buffalo Street Guide and Knights of Pythias Lodge Directory* (Buffalo, New York: Albert J. Kuebler and Fred Kroebel, 1894), which listed members' names, addresses, and occupations. In both cases I have classified members according to the categories presented in Stephen Thernstrom, *The Other Bostonians: Poverty and Progress in the American City* (Cambridge, Mass.: Harvard University Press, 1973) Appendix B, pp. 289–92, and used by Rosenzweig and Dumenil in their Masonic studies as well.

TABLE 3–3. Social Composition of Knights of
Pythias Members (percent)

Occupation	Belleville, Ill. 1874–1881	Buffalo, N.Y. 1891
White-Collar	47.8	50.2
upper	12.0	6.3
lower	35.9	44.0
Blue-Collar	52.2	49.8
skilled	31.5	28.3
semiskilled	17.4	16.6
unskilled	3.3	4.9
Number identified	$N = 92$	$N = 1003$
Number not identified	$N = 12$	$N = 337$

Sources: Buffalo: Buffalo Street Guide and Knights of Pythias Directory; Buffalo City Directory.

Belleville: original membership lists, in possession of Grand Secretary of Illinois Knights of Pythias; photocopies in author's possession; plus information from city directories and newspapers.

they were in favor of white-collar participants. Nonetheless they attracted a large enough number of blue-collar workers to ensure that they were not, as institutions, numerically *dominated* by business-class men, and thus possessed a marked heterogeneity.

But local lodges may have been almost exclusively white-collar or blue-collar in composition. An examination of the disaggregated data is needed, since the city-wide heterogeneity may conceal significant variations among individual lodges. In the cases of both Belleville and Buffalo, such an examination does reveal a tendency toward greater class homogeneity on the level of the local lodge, but this tendency is limited and subject to important exceptions.

WITHIN a period of seven years, from 1874 to 1881, three Knights of Pythias lodges were established in Belleville, a town of 15,000 located about fifteen miles from St. Louis,

Missouri. With an industrial base in coal mining and metal working, Belleville had a vigorous tradition of labor activity, including the formation by local miners of the American Miners Association, the country's first attempt to establish a national union of coal miners.[18] Belleville was also the seat of county government, a commercial center, and a center of pre–Civil War settlement for educated German immigrants who had organized many of its cultural activities, including the library, the *turnverein* (gymnastics society), philharmonic, and various bands and singing societies. Despite this pre-existing structure of voluntary associations, Belleville participated fully in the explosive national growth of fraternal orders after the Civil War. The 1868 City Directory showed only the Masons and Odd Fellows; by 1884 the fifty-five listed voluntary associations included thirty-five lodges of sixteen different secret societies, among them the three Knights of Pythias lodges examined here.

Two of the three Pythian lodges shown in Table 3–4 delineate homogeneous social worlds based upon common occupational and ethnic identities. While the small German-language Lessing Lodge seems relatively diverse, with its 60 percent white-collar and 40 percent blue-collar membership, it was composed almost completely of artisans, only some of whom had achieved self-employment at the time of its 1877 founding but almost all of whom would at some later point. Not all these small proprietors were successful in their business ventures; some would find themselves reduced to the position of paid employee, but it is fair to say that Lessing Lodge brothers were concentrated in occupations such as butcher or watchmaker, in which the ideal of proprietorship remained a reasonable one.

This was not the case for the members of Cavalier Lodge, which was overwhelmingly composed of waged manual

---

[18] Edward A. Wieck, *The American Miners' Association* (New York: Russell Sage Foundation, 1940), p. 9; Andrew A. Roy, *A History of the Coal Miners of the United States* (Columbus, Ohio: Trauger Printing Company, 1903; Westport, Conn.: Greenwood Press, 1970), pp. 62–67.

TABLE 3–4. Social Composition of Belleville Knights of
Pythias Members by Lodge (percent)

Occupation	Cavalier	Lessing	Garfield
White-Collar	21	60	56.6
upper	—	—	20.8
lower	21	60	35.8
Blue-Collar	79	40	43.4
skilled	37.5	26	30.2
semiskilled	29.1	13	13.2
unskilled	12.5	—	—
Number identified	$N=24$	$N=15$	$N=53$
Number not identified	$N=12$	$N=60$	$N=0$

Sources: Same as for Belleville data in Table 3–3.

workers.[19] Its membership included boilers, nailers, coal
miners, and laborers, many of whom were employed at the
Belleville Nail Mill, one of the city's largest employers. Even
its small group of so-called white-collar workers tended to
be marginal proprietors engaged in saloon-keeping or artisanal trades. Cavalier's location in a working-class milieu is
further established by the identification of William E.
Owen as a member. A leader in the American Miners Association and its successor, the Miners' National Association, Owen was one of "the key figures in the early development of the state's mine-safety legislation, holder of office,
and simultaneously director of the miners' trade union."
Owen's active participation in fraternal affairs, as a member
and officer of the Knights of Honor, the Temple of Honor,
and the Odd Fellows, as well as the Pythians, suggests the

[19] Indeed, the lodge's 79 percent blue-collar membership is probably an un-
derstatement, since the Cavalier charter, unlike the other two, did not list occupations, and the occupations of only twenty-three of the thirty-five could be
identified. Individuals with blue-collar occupations tend to be underrepre-
sented in city directories and other published sources, so it is likely that the
twelve unidentified members included an even higher proportion of such occupations.

intimate connections between working-class leadership and fraternal activity.[20]

The larger Garfield Lodge, the last to be organized, presents a distinct contrast to the homogeneity of the two smaller groups. Its inclusiveness of membership, at a time of marked labor tensions in the Belleville area, gives the lodge a representative character that is so systematic as to seem calculated. About a third of its members were lower-level white-collar—retail merchants, small proprietors, clerks. Almost a third were skilled blue-collar workers, with some semiskilled workers in addition. The blue-collar workers included cigar makers and significant numbers of the town's most important blue-collar occupations: seven miners, nine metal and foundry workers.

Most remarkable, however, is the Garfield Lodge's inclusion of key members of the town's business elite: Frederic Scheel, a lawyer, editor, and well-connected member of Belleville's German elite; James M. Hay, lawyer and co-owner of a nail mill employing nine hundred men, who missed the first meeting but enrolled the following week;[21] and Edward L. Thomas, an important figure in legal and business circles. Although he was an attorney, Thomas's influence was based heavily on his role as an entrepreneur. In addition to controlling several coal mines, he was responsible for the incorporation and construction of the all-important railroad lines that tapped his own and other mines and transported the coal to the St. Louis markets.

The presence of such a range of members cannot be taken

[20] David Montgomery, *Beyond Equality: Labor and the Radical Republicans, 1862–1872* (New York: Vintage, 1967), p. 218; *Belleville Advocate*, February 2, July 30, 1877; January 15, 1878.

[21] Frederic Scheel was the nephew of Gustave Koerner, a German immigrant who was Belleville's most illustrious citizen, having served as Lieutenant Governor of Illinois and U.S. minister to Spain under President Lincoln. For information about Scheel, see *Belleville Advocate*, June 14, 1872; October 26, 1877; March 5, 1880; November 17, 1899. For Hay see *Belleville Advocate*, August 10, 1883, and *Belleville Daily Advocate*, April 12, 1926.

to indicate a simple lack of class consciousness. As the following incident will reveal, Thomas was an ardent and activist defender of his class interests, which he perceived to be threatened by the workers' movement, while others in the lodge supported that movement.

In 1881, the same year as the creation of the Garfield Lodge, a group of Belleville miners had organized a cooperative mining company. The formation of cooperatives was a popular strategy of resistance to the "wage system" among American workers of the Gilded Age. Having successfully leased and equipped a mine, the miners ran into trouble when they attempted to contract for the ten railroad cars a day that were needed to transport the coal to markets in nearby St. Louis.

The Southern Railway Company, which Edward L. Thomas controlled, refused to furnish the cars, on the grounds that the members of the cooperative had previously engaged in strikes. The miners appealed to the governor, who responded by sending his representative to investigate the matter. But before the governor's representative could reach Belleville, the Southern Railway Company had torn up the switch leading to the mine. The attorney general of the state subsequently ruled that it would require a civil suit by the miners to force the railroad company to replace the switch. Since the miners had neither the time nor the money to do this, they were forced to abandon their effort and return to work as wage laborers.[22]

Thomas's role in the co-op mine incident, and his nearly simultaneous involvement in the formation of the socially inclusive Garfield Lodge, suggests the contradictory character of the social relations inherent in American fraternalism. Thomas was an aggressive leader in the struggle against the miners; his activities ranged from admonishing striking

[22] Information about Thomas is derived from his obituary, *Belleville Daily Advocate*, July 6, 1911. The cooperative mine incident is described in Roy, *History of the Coal Miners*, pp. 73–74.

miners to practice moderation and observance of the law to engaging in his own acts of class violence, as in the case of the torn-up railroad spur. What then, did it mean that seven miners were charter members of an organization in which Thomas played a leading role? We cannot simply assume that these miners were quiescent collaborators with the town's business interests, for at least two of them had been involved in miners' actions. George King, originally a miner and then a saloon keeper, was an organizer of another co-operative mining venture, and Fred Beinicke had been arrested and fined for "intimidating blacklegs," or scabs.[23]

Belleville's tradition of mine workers' agitation went back to the 1860s, when the American Miners Association was formed. Yet within this context of militant struggle and ongoing tensions between employers and workers, the Garfield Lodge existed as an institution in which individuals clearly committed to opposing sides could unite as brothers and term themselves the modern-day counterparts of Damon and Pythias. Its creation suggests that, at least in smaller populations, the lodge could be a vehicle for the promotion of cross-class social relations as well as the organizational expression of more homogeneous social groupings. But the Garfield Lodge was not unique in this respect, as data from the much larger city of Buffalo indicates.

In Buffalo, with a population of 255,000 in 1890, the Knights of Pythias numbered more than 1,500 in seventeen local lodges. In 1891 the Buffalo Pythians, following a national trend, published a directory of members. Occupations were listed in 75 percent of cases, and such information is included for at least 50 percent of the members in each lodge. This data offers one of the most extensive bodies of non-Masonic data yet examined, containing as it does the members of all the Pythian lodges in Buffalo in a single year, rather than from a selected few lodges that happen to have preserved their records.

---

[23] *Belleville Advocate*, July 21, 1881; November 16, 1883.

Table 3–5 presents this information on a lodge-by-lodge basis. It lists the lodges in order of their proportion of white-collar members, and divides the seventeen lodges into three groups, based on natural breaks in the data. In Buffalo as in Belleville, working-class men constituted a significant proportion of Knights of Pythias membership, far more than the analysis of Masonic data would have suggested.[24] Of seventeen lodges, ten had white-collar majorities while seven had blue-collar majorities. But total membership was almost evenly divided (499 blue-collar and 504 white-collar), since the white-collar lodges were, on average, slightly smaller.

If the white-collar/blue-collar distinction is made central, few of these lodges were completely homogeneous; only three of the seventeen drew more than 75 percent of their members from one or the other group. The most homogeneity is to be found when we combine the two modal subcategories of proprietor and skilled worker, which together make up the majority of lodge membership in all but one case. But while they remain a consistent core (53 percent of Group I, 61 percent of Groups II and III), they never reach more than 68 percent of the total in any lodge. There always remain substantial minorities of semiskilled and unskilled workers or of managers, professionals, and clerical workers.

Thus in Buffalo as in Belleville, a high degree of working-class participation was accompanied by variation in the composition of individual lodges. In some instances, blue-collar workers constituted the majority of a lodge's membership. In others they represented a substantial minority in local lodges that were numerically dominated by proprietors and other white-collar workers. The data from the Buffalo Pythians indicates that even in large industrial cities sub-

[24] In those cases where an artisanal title could imply either a proprietor or a wage worker, I classified as proprietors those who could be located in the business and commercial section of the 1894 *Buffalo City Directory*. See Thomas Smith, "Reconstructing Occupational Structures: The Case of the Ambiguous Artisan," *Historical Methods Newsletter* 8:3 (1975): pp. 134–46, and Thernstrom, *Other Bostonians*, p. 292, for discussions of this classification problem.

TABLE 3–5. Social Composition of Buffalo Knights of Pythias Members by Lodge, 1891 (percent)

Lodge	Total White-Collar	Proprietors	Other White-Collar	Total Blue-Collar	Skilled	Semiskilled	Unskilled	Number identified	Number not identified
GROUP I									
Eagle	77.8	25.0	52.8	22.8	13.9	8.3	—	36	24
International	74.0	37.0	37.0	26.0	18.5	7.4	—	27	27
Fidelity	73.3	46.7	26.7	26.7	10.0	13.3	3.3	30	21
Queen City	70.0	40.0	30.0	30.0	20.0	6.7	3.3	30	15
Columbus	67.2	32.8	34.5	32.8	20.7	10.3	1.7	58	0
GROUP II									
Ragau	65.5	29.3	36.2	34.5	32.8	1.7	—	58	2
Custer	64.1	46.1	17.9	35.9	11.5	7.7	16.7	78	6
Bison	62.5	43.8	18.8	37.5	12.5	21.8	3.1	32	1
Fillmore	60.3	33.6	26.7	39.7	26.7	10.7	2.3	131	80
Triangle	59.1	47.7	11.4	40.9	20.5	18.2	2.3	44	18
GROUP III									
Amherst	46.8	36.1	10.6	53.2	31.9	19.1	2.1	47	20
Hydraulic	42.6	29.6	13.0	57.4	33.3	16.6	7.4	54	21
Dowdall	40.4	33.3	7.0	59.6	22.8	26.3	10.5	57	37
Buffalo	35.7	17.9	17.9	64.2	45.2	14.3	4.8	84	23
Selkirk	34.4	24.6	9.8	65.6	32.8	29.5	3.3	122	17
East Buffalo	21.6	13.5	8.1	78.4	40.5	37.8	—	37	2
Lake Erie	16.6	15.3	1.3	83.4	48.7	23.0	11.5	78	23

Sources: Same as for Buffalo data in Table 3–3.

stantial numbers of working-class men were tied into networks of personal acquaintance with proprietors, professionals, and salaried white-collar workers through the aegis of the fraternal order. It is likely that few of the American fraternal organizations were class homogeneous on a national or state level and that a mixed-class membership was to be found among a substantial number of local lodges. What then is the meaning of this extensive working-class participation in the multi-class social institutions characteristic of the American fraternal movement?

In the fraternal order, large numbers of working-class men were involved in social relations with non-working-class men, relations that were both institutionalized and discretionary, that represented personal choices by all concerned about how and with whom to spend leisure time. It may be plausibly argued that this is no more than reflective of the larger contrasts between European and American societies. In Europe, workers' tendency to withdraw from cross-class relationships and to form their own organizations reflected their relative class consciousness, while American workers' continued affiliation with cross-class fraternal orders was consistent with a generally less developed conception of themselves as a separate and oppositional class.[25] This argument sees American working-class participation in fraternal orders as an indicator of the differences between class relations in the United States and Europe, differences that have been explained in terms of a supposed "American exceptionalism."

The concept of organizational capacity, on the other hand, gives a more active role to multi-class social institutions such as the fraternal order, demanding their recognition as something more than the expression of independently operating, almost innate social and cultural

[25] John Laslett and Seymour Martin Lipset, eds., *Failure of a Dream?* (Garden City, N.J.: Doubleday Anchor, 1974) contains a variety of positions on "American exceptionalism."

differences. At the level of individual relationships, the mixed-class composition of many local lodges presumably facilitated the maintenance of personal loyalties and a potential solidarity across rather than within class boundaries. At the level of the institution as a resource, it meant that blue-collar workers in mixed-class lodges were directing their personal energies into the construction of organizations that could not be used to further class, as opposed to individual, interest. To the extent that the fraternal order incorporated working-class men into networks that undercut class as a category, the potential for working-class organization was diminished.[26]

BEYOND THE LODGE AS AN ORGANIZATIONAL RESOURCE

The evidence from the Buffalo Knights of Pythias and from Cumbler's study of Lynn shows that there were, however, local lodges that were very heavily working-class in composition. In Buffalo, for example, almost two-thirds (63.7 percent) of the Knights of Pythias's blue-collar membership was located in lodges with a blue-collar majority, and almost half (45.7 percent) was in lodges where the majority reached two-thirds. Almost one-fifth (18.8 percent) of the blue-collar members were in lodges that were approximately 80 per cent blue-collar, and in those lodges the white-collar members tended to be proprietors, many of whom probably served working-class neighborhoods and

[26] In "Against Exceptionalism: Class Consciousness and the American Labor Movement," *International Labor and Working Class History* 26 (Fall, 1984): pp. 1–24, Sean Wilentz justly criticizes the essentialist notions of class that underlie exceptionalist arguments as well as their tendency to emphasize differences in American and European working-class history while ignoring important parallels. While accepting these criticisms, I believe that the American multi-class fraternal order, with its large membership and popularity among male wage-earners, represents a phenomenon for which there is no exact equivalent in European societies.

had family ties to manual workers, if not personal histories as manual workers themselves. (See Table 3–5.)[27] Thus, even with quite restrictive criteria, roughly one-fifth of Buffalo blue-collar workers who were Pythians were members of what we may call working-class lodges, institutions that could have served as a base for class mobilization. To what extent could such a potential be realized?

At this point scholars lack evidence about how such lodges functioned, and in that sense alone, it may be premature to characterize the lodge as an institution that functioned to construct working-class community. Moreover, despite its crucial insights, the resource mobilization perspective that underlies such a view is itself open to question, limited by its failure to see the development of group identity as problematic. It assumes that a consistent class composition will translate into a consistent class perspective, which will then be reflected in the values and actions of the organization. It thus fails to recognize that class is itself a socially constructed category, rather than a preordained identity deriving from a given structural position.

The understanding of category as a given must be replaced by one that takes account of the role played by culture and communication in determining what a category is, or what people select as a significant category from the many potentially available to them. It must recognize that the cultural configurations, the cognitive maps, that people bring

---

[27] Twentieth-century biographical connections between workers and small proprietors are revealed in C. Wright Mills, "The Middle Class in Middle Sized Cities," in Paul K. Hall and Albert Reiss, Jr., eds., *Cities and Society*, 2d ed. (Glencoe, Ill.: Free Press, 1957), and in Seymour Martin Lipset and Reinhard Bendix, *Social Mobility in Industrial Society* (Berkeley, Ca.: University of California Press, 1967). Herbert G. Gutman explores solidary relations between workers and local small businesses in nineteenth-century communities in *Work, Culture, and Society*, chapter 5, "Class, Status, and Community Power in Nineteenth-Century American Industrial Cities," and in "The Worker's Search for Power: Labor in the Gilded Age" in H. Wayne Morgan, ed., *The Gilded Age: A Reappraisal* (Syracuse, N.Y.: University of Syracuse Press, 1963).

to their struggles are crucial in their understanding of who they are and what they want. Class formation then becomes an interactive process that includes structural position, the development of organizational capacities, and the creation of a class culture that interprets class experiences and thus contributes to the construction of class as a perceived category.

In this conceptualization, the importance of fraternalism resides not only in the networks it created or ratified, but equally in the meanings it articulated—that is, in its role in the social construction of categories. The point can well be made about the implicit models of society portrayed by any social institution, but it is especially pertinent to the American fraternal order, with its ritual character and its origins in the rich traditions of Freemasonry. Even those local lodges that were predominantly, or even totally, working class in membership existed not as socially and culturally autonomous working-class institutions but as subordinate units of much larger national organizations that were themselves part of a more general culture of fraternalism. The rest of this book attempts to suggest some of the consequences of this fact.

The national fraternal order was by definition an organizational means for creating symbolic networks. Its initiation rituals bound the entrant not only to the members of a local lodge, that is, to people immediately available to him, but also to a symbolic union with Pythians, Odd Fellows, or Masons throughout the reaches of a complex and highly stratified society. Moreover, the fraternal order not only created cross-class relationships, it idealized them. Fraternal orders prized and publicized their illustrious members, who added to the luster of the organization and the prestige it could impart to its members.[28] At the same time, they proscribed and thus rendered dishonorable certain other kinds

[28] Jno. Van Valkenberg, *The Knights of Pythias Complete Manual and Textbook* (Canton, Ohio: Memento Publishing Company, 1887); Theodore A. Ross, *Odd Fellowship: Its History and Manual* (New York: M. W. Hazen Co., 1888).

of relationships, as between men and women, blacks and whites.

In class terms, American fraternal orders seem to have been quite representative of the population they took for their own: white men of British and Northern European descent. Theirs was an egalitarianism made possible by the exclusion of women, blacks, and ethnic minorities from the relevant social universe, a universe whose boundaries fraternal institutions helped to demarcate and guard. American fraternalism thus heightened the already great social and cultural distinctiveness of those white male workers who were also the most highly skilled and privileged segment of the wage-earning work force. The fraternal order was not, in other words, a neutral social arena in which some people happened, in random fashion, to unite as brothers. Rather, it was a form of association with a particular history and content, based on deeply grounded social and cultural assumptions.

FOUR

Fraternal Orders in Nineteenth-Century America

THE last third of the nineteenth century was American fraternalism's golden age. Membership grew exponentially and every year saw the creation of at least one new order. But the period prior to the Civil War established the basic framework within which fraternalism would develop.

Two types of fraternal association had emerged in the United States in the early nineteenth century. First, many organizations developed around the workplace. Some were trade associations, which included both masters and journeymen, while others were organizations of either masters or journeymen. Journeymen's associations might evolve into trade unions, or they could continue to function primarily as fraternal benefit societies that dispensed mutual aid and organized social activities, distinguished from the traditional trade association only by their exclusion of employers. In all cases, work-based fraternal associations were local in character, making no attempt to extend their organizations beyond their home cities. Their identity was based upon craft.[1]

In contrast were organizations existing within the Masonic model, of which the most important were the Red Men, the Odd Fellows, and the Masons themselves. In practical terms, they differed from trade associations in their purpose, which was primarily social, and in their character as regional or national organizations with expansionary ten-

[1] Sean Wilentz, *Chants Democratic: New York City and the Rise of the American Working Class, 1788–1850* (New York: Oxford University Press, 1984), pp. 56–58; Bruce Laurie, *Working People of Philadelphia, 1800–1850* (Philadelphia: Temple University Press, 1980).

dencies; there were Masonic lodges, for example, distributed throughout the colonies well before the Revolutionary War. But the Masonic model may be defined more precisely in terms of three characteristics. First, the ritual was organized around degrees or levels of membership, which were to be ascended one by one. Second, all the orders operating within this model shared to a greater or lesser extent the Masonic concept of the order as a moral system directed toward the edification of the individual member. Third, these organizations did not confine themselves to any particular trade or occupation. Not only were they not workplace-based, but they claimed to disregard and reject an identity based upon class or occupation.[2] Yet they retained clear links to the fraternal culture of the workshop, continuing to draw upon the traditional elements of corporatism, ritual, proprietorship, and masculinity for their organizational esprit.

Freemasonry was the earliest and most powerful appropriation of artisanal fraternalism. The paradigm that Freemasonry presented, with its egalitarian rhetoric and glorification of the artisanal master, would seem a highly congenial one to a society that defined itself as a republic of independent owner-producers. Yet the powerful resentments generated by the craft resulted in the growth of an anti-Masonic movement that threatened to destroy it. By the time of the Civil War, however, Masonry had regained its public legitimacy. It, along with the Odd Fellows, presented itself as the organizational model for the hundreds of fraternal associations that would be established in the 1860s, 1870s, and 1880s.

AMERICAN FRATERNALISM BEFORE THE CIVIL WAR: MASONS AND ODD FELLOWS

Freemasonry spread quickly throughout the colonies. The establishment of the first lodge was accompanied by the ap-

[2] Noel Gist, "Secret Societies: A Cultural Study of Fraternalism in the United States," *The University of Missouri Studies* 20:4 (1940): pp. 65–68.

pearance of the first American edition of Anderson's *Constitutions of the Free-Masons*, the order's basic document. It was published by Benjamin Franklin, who was himself made a Mason in 1730 and remained active throughout his life.[3] By 1733, when St. John's Lodge of Boston was established as a Grand Lodge, American Masonic lodges were organized within a structure of Provincial Grand Lodges, themselves operating under the authority of the Grand Lodge of England. American Masons were apparently eager for such organization; as Benjamin Franklin wrote in 1734, " 'the craft is like to come into disesteem among us unless the true Brethren are countenanced and distinguished by some such special authority.' "

Initially, American Freemasonry was, as Dorothy Lipson has pointed out, "part of a colonial culture," that derived some of its appeal from "the special ties it afforded with the fraternity at 'home.' " Early Masonic lodges tended to center on English trade routes and military posts and to attract a membership primarily composed of merchants, colonial officials, military officers, and other cosmopolitans, men who valued not only the ties to England but also the ready-made circle of acquaintances that a Masonic lodge could provide the newcomer.[4] But it is also true that Freemasonry's emphasis on universalism and rationalism enabled American Masonry to present itself as a part of America's Revolutionary heritage, detached from its colonial associations. This was facilitated by the strong and public presence of the craft within the Continental Army, where not only Washington but nearly all his generals were Masons.[5] Indeed, the promotion of the cult of Washington as Mason continued to be a significant part of the order's presentation of itself to an often suspicious American culture; the fact that Washington

[3] Albert C. Stevens, *The Cyclopaedia of Fraternities* (New York: E. B. Treat and Company, 1907; Detroit: Gale Research Company, 1966), p. 27.

[4] Dorothy Ann Lipson, *Freemasonry in Federal Connecticut* (Princeton, N.J.: Princeton University Press, 1977), pp. 48–49, 46.

[5] Stevens, *Cyclopaedia*, p. 27; Bernard Fay, *Revolution and Freemasonry 1660–1800* (Boston: Little, Brown and Company, 1935) p. 249.

had been a Mason was a perplexing problem that the later anti-Masonic movement would have difficulty explaining away.[6] During and after the Revolutionary War the American Provincial Grand Lodges, following the example of the larger political body, declared their independence from the Grand Lodge of England; they then faced the problem of how American Masonry was to be organized. A national Grand Lodge was the first solution proposed, but the most promising attempt to form such a body with George Washington as Supreme Grand Master failed when Washington proved unwilling to serve.[7] In the absence of a single national authority, Grand Lodges were organized within each state during the federalist era.

This was also the period when the two American versions of chivalric Freemasonry, with their elaborate structures of higher degrees, were established. The Ancient Accepted Scottish Rite was the elder of the two. Founded in 1801, its thirty-three degrees were based on the twenty-five-degree French system called the Rite of Protection, augmented by eight more, all of which tended toward the exotic and fanciful—for example, the Patriarch Noachite (twenty-first degree), the Knight of the Brazen Spirit (twenty-fifth), and the Sublime Prince of the Royal Secret (thirty-second). The rival chivalric body, known as the American Rite or as Masonic Knight Templary, conferred a group of thirteen degrees, most of them reworked versions of Scottish Rite ceremonies. American Rite Masons were organized into bodies called Encampments while Scottish Rite degrees were conferred in Councils, Chapters, and Consistories, depending on their level. In the early nineteenth century their membership was quite small—the Knights Templar have been esti-

[6] David Brion Davis, "Some Themes of Counter-Subversion: An Analysis of Anti-Masonic, Anti-Catholic, and Anti-Mormon Literature," *Mississippi Valley Historical Review* 27 (September, 1960): p. 215; Lipson, *Freemasonry*, pp. 316–18.

[7] Stevens, *Cyclopaedia*, p. 32; Lipson, *Freemasonry*, pp. 60–61.

mated at fewer than five hundred in 1816, the year the national Grand Encampment was organized—but they were important for two reasons. First, unlike the lower-degree lodges, chivalric Masonry was organized nationally and probably provided whatever national leadership existed in the Masonic world. Second, the exoticism of the higher degrees was to have a profound influence on the style and aspirations of subsequent American fraternal organizations.[8]

The decentralized character of American Freemasonry, coupled with the absence of effective record keeping in this period, makes it difficult to estimate the size of Masonic membership in the late eighteenth and early nineteenth centuries. It was estimated at three thousand in 1800 by one scholar, but the existence of forty-four subordinate lodges in Connecticut alone in 1800 suggests that figure is probably too low.[9] What is certain is that by the 1820s, the Masons had enough members distributed over a wide enough geographical area to have aroused the widespread resentments and antagonisms that gave birth to anti-Masonry as a significant political movement.

THE ANTI-MASONIC PERIOD

The anti-Masonic agitation began in 1826 when William Morgan of Batavia, New York, formerly a Mason, was allegedly harassed and kidnapped by a group of Masons in revenge for his attempts to publish a Masonic exposé, the *Illustration of Masonry*. The Masons claimed to have taken Morgan to Canada in a rowboat and released him there, but he was never seen again; it was charged and has been assumed that his abductors threw him overboard in Lake Ontario. The incident itself, coupled with the complicity of local legal authorities and newspaper editors in covering it up "confirmed the worst fear of Masons' neighbors about the

[8] Stevens, *Cyclopaedia*, pp. 41–42, 45, 53, xxiv.
[9] Gist, "Secret Societies," p. 40; Lipson, *Freemasonry*, p. 80.

secret power of Masonry to 'thwart the operation of democratic principles.' Their 'great moral shock' reverberated through-out the countryside, mobilized an indignant investigation of the 'fearful moral influence' of Masonry, and coalesced into a coherent movement to eliminate the fraternity."[10] Anti-Masonry quickly developed into a widespread social and political movement. There were, for example, 130 anti-Masonic periodicals in 1830. Anti-Masonic political parties were organized and ran candidates in a number of states, and the Anti-Masonic Party actually replaced the National Republicans as the only party opposing the Democrats in New York, Vermont, and Pennsylvania. The Anti-Masons even ran a candidate for president in 1832, but after this the political energies of the movement were largely dissipated and ultimately absorbed into the emerging Whig Party.[11]

Viewed as an incident in the history of Freemasonry, the Morgan episode is decidedly peculiar. Exposés were endemic to Masonic history, beginning in Britain with Prichard's *Masonry Dissected* in 1730. In the United States as well, Masonic exposés had been widely available: one of the most famous, *Jackin and Boaz: or, An Authentic Key to the Door of Freemasonry, Ancient and Modern, by a Gentleman Belonging to the Jerusalem Lodge*, went through sixteen editions in England and twelve in America from 1762 to 1825.[12] Not only were they used by non-Masons to learn the ritual in order to pass themselves off as Masons without being initiated, they were commonly purchased by Masons

[10] Lipson, *Freemasonry*, p. 268; Whitney R. Cross, *The Burned-Over District: The Social and Intellectual History of Enthusiastic Religion in Western New York, 1800–1850* (New York: Harper and Row, 1965), pp. 114–15.

[11] Charles W. Ferguson, *Fifty Million Brothers* (New York: Farrar S. Rinehart, 1937) p. 24; Stevens, *Cyclopaedia*, pp. 13–14; Cross, *Burned-Over District*, p. 116.

[12] James Dewar, *The Unlocked Secret: Freemasonry Examined* (London: William Kimber and Company, 1966), p. 38; Lipson, *Freemasonry*, pp. 361–62.

themselves as aids to memory. An illicit but recognized part of the Masonic world, exposés were viewed by the order's leaders as a nuisance, but certainly not as a threat. Therefore, the actions of these upstate New York Masons against Morgan fall outside the bounds of Masonic practice.

Similarly, the sources of the anti-Masonic reaction remain unclear. While the movement displayed an anti-elitist content in many areas, this was not a consistent theme, nor does there seem to have been a consistent class character to either its leaders or its participants. In cultural terms, anti-Masonry may have drawn upon the opposition of Calvinists. Dorothy Lipson reports a considerable base of social anti-Masonry even prior to 1826 in the New England states, where Freemasonry existed as a quasi-religious alternative to Calvinist mores. The tension between the two perspectives can be seen by comparing the funeral services of the two. The Masonic funeral, which was explicitly nondenominational and even non-Christian in content, emphasized the comforting hope that the deceased Mason would meet the "Supreme Grand Master" who reigned in the "celestial lodge," while the severe Calvinist funeral assumed that the deceased had already met his fate of probable damnation. In examining the records of one Connecticut lodge, Lipson found that even before the rise of the anti-Masonic movement, Masonic funeral ceremonies were being "either tacitly rejected or actively opposed" by survivors, often in opposition to the wishes of the deceased.[13]

Whatever the roots of the anti-Masonic movement, its effects on the fraternity are unquestioned; it was devastated. In New York, for example, membership fell from 30,000 to 300 and in Vermont and Illinois all lodges ceased to operate for a time. In those states where lodges continued to meet, they did so privately, circumspectly, and with greatly reduced attendance. While anti-Masonry as a political move-

[13] Lipson, *Freemasonry*, pp. 165–68, 170, 174.

ment was ineffective by 1834, its condemnation of Freemasonry continued to be felt socially, so that large-scale recovery of membership and resumption of normal activities began in earnest only after 1840.[14]

THE INDEPENDENT ORDER OF ODD FELLOWS

Like the Masons, the Odd Fellows had also originated in England, but they represented a distinctly different kind of fraternal organization. The Masons were a multi-class organization in which artisanal rites and customs had been used as the basis for a highly elaborated ritual and what came to be seen as a moral system. The Odd Fellows, on the other hand, began as a convivial society, a product of a working-class tavern culture, much closer to the traditional journeyman's society than to the Masonic model. But while it began as a working-class convivial society, American Odd Fellowship had transformed itself, by the 1840s, into something much closer to the Masonic model—a multi-class organization that espoused morality and the promotion of individual self-improvement.

The order originated in late eighteenth-century England, where convivial societies scattered around the country began to be called Odd Fellows lodges, despite their lack of any organized connection to one another. By the early nineteenth century, at least two associations had emerged: the Grand United Order and the Manchester Unity. American Odd Fellows lodges were established by English immigrants to the United States, artisans and mechanics attempting to recreate the social life of the plebeian communities they had left behind. The American order traces its official birth to the 1819 formation of a lodge in Baltimore, Maryland, by Thomas Wildey, a blacksmith and coach-spring maker, and four other members of the Grand United Order.

[14] Ferguson, *Fifty Million Brothers*, p. 24; Lipson, *Freemasonry*, p. 207; Stevenson, *Cyclopaedia*, p. 16.

In 1821, the Baltimore group affiliated with the Manchester Unity, which invested it with the power to grant charters under the title of Grand Lodge of Maryland. The Maryland lodge, established in 1821, was the institutional predecessor of the national Grand Lodge. But the existence of Odd Fellows organizations in Massachusetts, New York, and Pennsylvania in the 1820s indicated that lodges were being formed contemporaneously almost everywhere that significant concentrations of English workingmen were emigrating.[15]

The founders of the American Odd Fellows naturally sought to recreate the familiar practices of the English societies. While the Manchester Unity had begun to move in a quasi-Masonic direction by 1817, when it established a system of three degrees, both of the major English bodies primarily emphasized the practice of what was referred to as "conviviality," or group drinking. This was the conception of Odd Fellowship that the English immigrants brought with them to the United States. Here, as in England, the early lodges met in taverns, "hosted" by the tavern keeper, for whom the weekly meeting was a source of reliable business. The host "furnished the meeting-room, light and heat free of charge; and 'Proposition of Harmony' was the principle feature of the meetings, during recess from lodge and work, when the mug and pipe were in order, and mirth and merry-making held sway." Drinking, then, was the central ritual of the early Odd Fellows' meetings: "When any important event took place or the bickerings and unpleasantness of the times crept into the meetings, and when it looked stormy, the lodge 'proceeded to harmony'; when, after a brief session, quietness was restored."[16]

Beginning in the 1820s, however, the character of the Odd Fellows as a working-class convivial society began to

[15] Stevens, *Cyclopaedia*, pp. 244, 250, 257; Henry Stillson, *The History and Literature of Odd Fellowship, The Three-Link Fraternity* (Boston: Fraternity Publishing Co., 1897), pp. 79–80, 234, 276.

[16] Stillson, *Odd Fellowship*, pp. 227, 276.

be challenged. In each of the major state Grand Lodges, individuals with different goals entered the organization. The most important of these was James Ridgeley, a college-educated lawyer who, in his many years as Grand Secretary, guided the national organization through a series of transformations. But Ridgeley was only the most outstanding representative of a type of man entering the organization in every state, men characterized by their American birth, their higher social status, and their ambition for themselves and for the organization. Augustus Mathiot, in Maryland, and Daniel Hersey, in Massachusetts, were "the first Americans of prominence to join our order," while George P. Norris of New York was "a man of good address, well educated and ambitious."[17]

These men shared the goals of attracting higher-status members to the organization and transforming it into a vehicle of self-improvement. Like Ridgeley, they "endeavored to make the moral and the intellectual features predominate the merely social and beneficial," and like Ridgeley, they realized that if Odd Fellowship was to realize its "great possibilities . . . it must discard the mere rude and convivial features which formed a main attraction of the earlier lodges." That is, it must forbid drinking in the lodge room.[18]

The mobilization against drinking was, of course, a part of the wider interest in temperance that had emerged throughout American society in the 1820s. Like the larger movement, but more obviously, the attack on drinking within the Odd Fellows had a specific class content. First, the banning of drinking would increase the respectability of the organization and thus draw a better class of member. Ridgeley bemoaned the fact that "Odd Fellows were, originally, convivial men, and as such, were the subject of reproach in both hemispheres, for many years." Second, the promotion of temperance could contribute powerfully to the

[17] Ibid., pp. 276, 223.
[18] Ibid., p. 762.

project of individual self-improvement that the order now set for itself and its members. George P. Norris, the New York reformer, was drawn to the Odd Fellows because of "its admirable fitness to better the condition of the industrial classes, to raise their intellectual, social, and moral standard, to inculcate a greater respect for their personal character, and educate them in the principles of self reliance."[19]

The mobilization against drinking was paralleled by a new and narrower definition of the limits of fraternal obligation. It had been the custom, in the early lodges operating in the English convivial style, "to inquire of the host: 'Is there any tramp waiting?' meaning those who were seeking employment or aid to reach the next town." But many American lodges found this custom, so reminiscent of the compagnonnages and journeymen's societies of Europe, to be burdensome and distasteful. In the 1830s they went so far as to charge that English workingmen joined the Manchester Unity, or took out false membership, just before emigrating to the United States so they could take advantage of American largess, knowing that "they would be admitted to membership, assisted to procure employment, or furnished relief if needed."[20]

The American lodges responded with attempts to rationalize and systematize the practice of mutuality: by organizing district relief committees by compiling statistics, by district, of relief disbursed, and by urging local lodges to record their disbursements on the membership cards of those given aid so as to prevent the receipt of contributions from more than one lodge. The Independent Order of Odd Fellows continued to maintain, throughout the century, that the obligation of reciprocal relief was one of the order's defining characteristics, but its mode of practice tended to transform fraternal aid from a right (and a rite) to a kind of charity that would be afforded only to the deserving. By denying the

[19] Ibid., p. 43.
[20] Ibid., pp. 221, 254.

unconditional character of fraternal obligation, the Odd Fellows moved to distance themselves from the traditions of artisanal mutuality and to affirm instead that the individual was ultimately responsible for his own well-being.

The attack on conviviality and the reinterpretation of mutuality were accompanied by the elaboration of formal ritual. As previously noted, the Manchester Unity had in 1817 instituted a system of three degrees, White, Royal Blue and Scarlet, each to be conferred with "appropriate lectures." But American Odd Fellowship was consistently more focused upon the elaboration of the ritual component of its identity. To the three degrees of the Manchester Unity, the early Grand Lodge of Maryland added two more, the Covenant, and the Remembrance, in 1821. The Encampment, or higher degrees, were systematized by 1829 and began to achieve widespread popularity in the 1840s. Differences over ritual contributed to the tensions between the Grand Lodge of the United States and the Manchester Unity. The American ritual had been revised in 1835, but after the split from the English order, the Grand Lodge of the United States immediately undertook to devise a new ritual that would be "distinctively American." "The crude ceremonies of the earlier days, to be sure, had been improved at various periods, notably in 1835; but a comparison of the rituals of 1835, with those of 1845 and 1880, proves the assertion that it was left for American Odd Fellows to prepare their own American ritual."[21]

The emphasis on ritual served a number of related purposes. In practical terms, it gave the lodges an activity to take the place of the now proscribed practice of conviviality: the old ritual activity was replaced by a new one. Beyond that, it invested the order with the sense of decorum and moralism that the middle-class reformers were so eager to achieve. The ritual was a way of educating the workingmen who constituted the order's first constituency and of attract-

[21] Ibid., pp. 53, 68, 101.

ing the "lawyers, physicians, merchants, skilled mechanics and tradesmen, farmers and retired gentlemen" whom people like Ridgeley sought.[22]

In 1844, after at least ten years of mounting tensions, the American Odd Fellows severed all connections to their parent body, the Manchester Unity, to form the Independent Order of Odd Fellows (IOOF). By this time the order had essentially completed its transformation: the drive to attract a more diverse and prestigious membership served to distance it from its working-class origins and identity, while the newly emphasized and elaborated ritual appeared as a source of moral culture and the lodge itself as a medium of personal transformation. Although it continued to have a very high proportion of artisans and other manual workers as members, the IOOF had come to approximate the Masonic model in most significant respects.

FRATERNALISM AFTER THE CIVIL WAR

The Civil War represents a watershed in the history of American fraternalism. Before the war, fraternal growth meant primarily the growth of the Masons and Odd Fellows; their boundaries largely defined the boundaries of social fraternalism. In sharp contrast, the last third of the nineteenth century saw a different kind of expansion and vitality. Not only did membership of existing orders increase exponentially, but fraternal organizations seemed to proliferate with a kind of luxurious abandon. The *Cyclopaedia of Fraternities*, a systematic directory of fraternal secret societies compiled in 1897 and revised in 1907, identified some three hundred fraternal organizations as sufficiently important to be included. The twenty years from 1864 to 1884 were particularly important as the period when the majority of the new orders were established: the Knights of Pythias (1864), the Benevolent and Protective Order of Elks (1866), the

[22] James Ridgeley, quoted in ibid., p. 217.

Ancient Order of United Workmen (1868), the Ancient Arabic Order of the Nobles of the Mystic Shrine (Shriners, 1871), the Knights of Honor (1873), the Royal Arcanum (1877), the Knights of the Maccabees (1878), and the Modern Woodmen of America (1883).[23] For every one that survived and grew, countless others must have failed. Fraternalism was a project that captured the nation's imagination.

The war itself was undoubtedly important to this trend. War can offer men perhaps the ultimate experience of male bonding, and many must have been attracted by any peacetime attempt to recreate such feelings. Others were drawn by the fraternal order's approximation of military hierarchy and ceremony. In the twentieth century, after each of the World Wars, similar needs were met by the creation of organizations explicitly for veterans: the American Legion, the Veterans of Foreign Wars, and the like. The Grand Army of the Republic was established as a veterans organization after the Civil War (significantly, it too was organized as a fraternal order), but its appeal was limited. It was specifically for veterans of the Union Army and thus could not develop as a *national* veterans association; even in the North it was probably too closely linked to the Republican Party and the Union cause to unite the widest range of veterans in what had after all been a highly controversial conflict, both in its aims and its conduct.

The fraternal orders, on the other hand, could serve: their resolutely apolitical stance extended to the war. When, for example, the Odd Fellows met in national deliberation, their ties to their absent southern brethren were affirmed by the practice of leaving their chairs vacant. And they were welcomed back into the organization as soon as the war was over.[24] Moreover, the theme of the fraternal was especially telling as a response to the Civil War, a war whose ruling

[23] Stevens, *Cyclopaedia*, pp. v, 263, 229, 128, 2, 146, 186, 152, 157.
[24] Stillson, *Odd Fellowship*, p. 131.

metaphor was that of brother fighting against brother. The obsession with fraternalism, which extended to the formation of college fraternities, may have been motivated in part, as Arthur Stinchcombe has suggested, by the search for ritual and organizational means by which men could *become brothers* again, could recreate the fraternal relationship severed by the war.[25] Whatever its sources, this growth of fraternal orders occurred primarily within the framework of the already-existing Masonic model. As their rather grandiose titles suggest, the new organizations retained and indeed tried to improve upon the elaborate ritual and allegorical tendencies of the Masonic tradition. The Pythian ritual, based on the legend of Damon and Pythias, was intended to portray the nobility of friendship, as symbolized by the willingness of one friend to risk his life for the other. The Modern Woodmen of America, meeting in "camps" instead of lodges, enacted a ritual that mixed metaphors of woodcraft and classical Rome; the result, in the words of the ritual, was "a strange mixture of Roman dignity and forest freedom."[26] And, of course, the Shriners remain well known for their red fezzes, their exaggerated titles, (Most Illustrious Grand Potentate, and so on), extravagant costumes, and public theatricality.

Like the Masons and Odd Fellows, the newer orders organized their membership into ascending degrees or ranks, typically ranging in number from three to seven. But the links to Masonry were more than conceptual. As more and more were founded, fraternal orders competed ever more vigorously against one another for members (see Chapter Seven for their competitive strategies). Yet they viewed themselves as part of a single movement united by overlapping participation, judicious borrowing, and common

[25] Arthur L. Stinchcombe, "Social Structure and Organizations," in James G. March, ed. *Handbook of Organizations* (Chicago: Rand McNally, 1965), pp. 142–43.

[26] Ferguson, *Fifty Million Brothers*, pp. 137–38.

modes of interaction, as well as by the openly acknowledged influence of Freemasonry as a model. The Catholic Church often charged that Masonic influence pervaded the world of American fraternalism. When, in 1884, Pope Leo XIII reaffirmed the papal condemnation of Freemasonry, he at the same time extended the ban to the Odd Fellows and Knights of Pythias. In part, this was because the Odd Fellows and Pythians seemed to the Church to resemble the Masons in their espousal of natural religion, the view that the ability to lead a good and moral life is not contingent upon the receipt of divine revelation or the gift of grace. But, as the Archbishop of Cincinnati argued in 1895, the Odd Fellows and Pythians were also compromised by their social connection to Masonry: "Now, it is often seen that the active promoters of these societies, now condemned, are also zealous Masons; and if a Catholic is drawn into one of them, he is in continual and familiar association with the admirers of Masonry, and immediately exposed to imbibe their sentiments, consciously or unconsciously." Therefore, these societies show "a decided influence to lead Catholics toward Freemasonry, and Freemasonry is under the absolute condemnation and excommunication of the Church."[27]

The perception of Masonic influence was not simply a product of Roman Catholic paranoia; it was widely acknowledged throughout the fraternal world. The founders of most of the important orders were themselves Masons, including Justus H. Rathbone of the Knights of Pythias, John J. Upchurch of the Ancient Order of United Workmen, and Joseph Cullen Root of the Modern Woodmen of America.[28] As fraternal orders became more numerous, genealogies became more complicated and rituals often represented a pastiche of their founders' prior fraternal experience. The Knights of the Globe, for example, was organized

[27] Quoted in Stevens, *Cyclopaedia*, pp. 11, 10; see also Fergus MacDonald, *The Catholic Church and the Secret Societies in the United States* (New York: U.S. Catholic Historical Society, 1946).

[28] Stevens, *Cyclopaedia*, pp. 263, 128, 157.

by members of the Scottish Rite Masons, Odd Fellows, the Ancient Order of United Workmen, the Royal Arcanum, the American Legion of Honor, the Woodmen of the World, and the Grand Army of the Republic. Consequently, notes the *Cyclopaedia of Fraternities*, "the influence of the Workmen is seen in the uniform assessment rate, of the Freemasons and Odd Fellows in the degree work and emblems, and the Grand Army in its obligation that 'no other flag than the glorious Stars and Stripes shall ever float over our country.' "[29]

Membership was not viewed as exclusive; indeed, it seems to have been assumed that multiple fraternal membership, at least among the leadership, was not only typical but desirable. An 1887 Pythian handbook, for example, contains biographies of leading Pythians in which fraternal affiliations are not just mentioned, but described in detail. The Honorable Halvor Nelson, for example, Past Grand Commander and Supreme Representative of the District of Columbia, is reported to be a Mason "in good standing in the Blue Lodge, R.A. [Royal Arch] chapter, and Commandery. In the A.A.S.R. [Scottish Rite] he has obtained the 32nd degree, and at present is Secretary of Rose Croix Chapter No. 1, and Recorder of Robert de Bruce Council of Kadosh, etc." In another case the handbook describes the success of Past Supreme Chancellor Samuel Read, whose "exalted rank in Odd-Fellowship . . . aided materially in his advancement to the high position he now holds in our beloved Order."[30] Less prestigious orders thus attempted to validate themselves through their ties to the older organizations, and a successful career in one order could facilitate progress in another.

The fact that so many orders were established by Masons meant that the ritual of many orders was heavily reliant on the Masonic ritual. In some cases this could verge on whole-

---

[29] Stevens, *Cyclopaedia*, p. 148.

[30] Jno. Van Valkenberg, *The Knights of Pythias Complete Manual and Textbook* (Canton, Ohio: Memento Publishing Company, 1887), pp. 441, 437.

sale plagiarism. M. W. Sackett, leader and chronicler of the Ancient Order of United Workmen (AOUW), tells the story of Dr. James M. Bunn, who agreed to produce a new ritual for an early faction of the AOUW. At the last moment, Dr. Bunn's creative faculties deserted him. In desperation he presented the Masonic ritual for the use of the United Workmen. Since none of the delegates to the Grand Lodge had ever been Masons, the plagiarism was not detected until some time later, when a former Mason was being initiated. "He pulled off the apron with which he had been invested, threw it on the floor and exclaimed, 'What kind of an institution is this! thieves!! Give me my hat; I want nothing to do with people who appropriate what does not belong to them. Why, I can repeat that lecture a hundred times better than that man can read it.' " "It is needless to say," Sackett comments, "that at the next meeting of the Supreme Lodge a new ritual was adopted."[31]

The outright appropriation of an entire ritual was unacceptable, but it was considered perfectly proper to incorporate bits and pieces of Masonic symbolism into supposedly new rituals. This is clearly visible in the *Cyclopaedia of Fraternities*' descriptions of various rituals, many of which revealed Masonic influence. The early leaders of the Elks, for example, could "safely be classed as Freemasons: for the ceremony of the Elks, although it has been changed several times, still presents features familiar to workmen from the quarries" (that is, Masons), especially in its use of aprons, its office of Tyler, and the conduct of "Lodges of Sorrow." Even after the Ancient Order of United Workmen rid itself of its bogus Masonic ritual, it retained in Upchurch's alternative version many traces of Masonic symbolism, especially in the ritual objects, which included the square, the compass, the plumb, and the trowel.[32] The Odd Fellows higher

[31] M. W. Sackett, *Early History of Fraternal Beneficiary Societies in America* (Meadville, Pa.: Tribune Publishing Company, 1914), p. 108.
[32] Stevens, *Cyclopaedia*, p. 230.

or patriarchal degrees were greatly influenced by Masonic Knight Templarism, possibly as a result of an influx of Masons into the IOOF during the anti-Masonic period.

Indeed, such incorporations and borrowings seemed to give both legitimacy and an added soupçon of interest and appeal to the ritual of new orders. The Knights of the Golden Eagle, for example, an order founded in Pennsylvania in 1872, based its ritual heavily on the model of the Masonic Knights Templar. As the *Cyclopaedia* comments, "there is reason to believe their ritual is indebted to membership in the Order of those who had been brought to light and had been advanced in the parent of all modern secret societies. With such reed, the blossoms could not fail to be numerous and beautiful."[33] Those rituals that did not draw explicitly on the Masonic ritual still looked to Freemasonry as a source of legitimacy and the obvious standard of comparison. Joseph Cullen Root, for example, extolled the uniqueness of his Modern Woodman ritual but found it necessary to refer to the good opinion of Masons to establish its quality, describing it as an "original and pleasing Ritual, based upon ancient usage, but entirely different from any secret work now in use, pronounced by 32nd degree Masons as creditable to the author and fit to rank with the sublimest conceptions of ritual writers." Even someone like Root, who conceived his "Modern" order as a departure from the "pretentious and so-called 'Ancient' Associations now in existence," was forced to appeal to the standard of the Masonic model.[34]

EXCLUSIONARY TENDENCIES IN AMERICAN FRATERNALISM

In nineteenth-century America as elsewhere, the construction of fraternal solidarity was based as much upon a process

[33] Ibid., p. 149.
[34] Este Erwood Buffum, *Modern Woodmen of America: A History* (Rock Island, Ill.: Modern Woodmen Press, 1927), p. 8.

of exclusion as it was upon a ritual of unification. Women were not eligible to become Masons, and the exclusion of women and articulation of masculine identity remained a constant element in fraternal association. But British Freemasonry had largely refrained from other kinds of explicit categorical exclusion, assisted in this by the relative homogeneity of the ambient society. The much greater ethnic and racial diversity of the United States, coupled with its persistent racism and sporadic bouts of nativism, produced more complex patterns of differentiation.

Fraternal policy toward immigrants varied remarkably over the years. Groups like the Masons and Odd Fellows have often appeared to be strongholds of nativist sentiment; there is, for example, evidence to suggest that Masonic lodges served as recruiting grounds for the Ku Klux Klan during the 1920s. But evidence from an earlier period suggests a much greater degree of openness to cultural difference.

One significant factor affecting the incorporation of immigrants into the fraternal movement was the fact that Catholics were forbidden to join on pain of mortal sin. Nonetheless, many Catholics did join these orders. This is indicated by the Church's perennial concern over the issue, as expressed in the extension of the ban on the Masons to the Odd Fellows and Knights of Pythias and by the stream of pastoral letters and ecclesiastical pronouncements forbidding Catholic participation. The emergence of the Knights of Columbus, the Catholic Knights of America, and the Knights of Father Matthew represents attempts of varying success to create Catholic fraternal orders and benefit societies that could compete successfully with the forbidden bodies. The manifestation of such concern identifies Catholic participation in proscribed fraternal orders as a problem for the Church. Clearly there was some Catholic ethnic presence within the major orders, but this presence probably diminished in response to increased nativism on the one hand and the creation of viable Catholic alternatives on the other.

In the period immediately following the Civil War, the fraternal movement was characterized by a striking degree of cultural pluralism. From the 1860s through the 1880s most orders had not only accepted immigrants as members but allowed local lodges to operate in languages other than English and even provided foreign language versions of the ritual. When, for example, the Knights of Pythias revised their ritual in 1872, authority was quite automatically given to translate it into German, French, and other languages.[35] Not only were foreign language lodges tolerated, they were given an official standing by the national orders. By the 1890s this had changed. The upsurge of organized nativism in the 1880s, coinciding with the beginnings of large-scale immigration from Southern and Eastern Europe, marked the point at which fraternal orders retreated from their previous acceptance of ethnic diversity. The abolition of foreign language lodges, which was actually challenged in court, unsuccessfully, by German Pythians, was a response not only to the growth of a generalized anti-foreign sentiment, but to the direct competition posed by the explicitly nativist orders such as the Junior Order of United American Mechanics that experienced a resurgence in this period.[36] None of the major orders ever openly barred admission to members of any ethnic minority, but the changing character of immigration, the increasing articulation of nativist sentiment and the polarization created by the interaction of fraternal anti-Catholicism and Catholic anti-fraternalism led the fraternal movement to abandon the model of cultural pluralism that had characterized its earlier years.

Policies toward race were much more consistent; indeed, racial exclusion was a hallmark of mainstream American fra-

[35] L. H. Prescott, *History of the Criterion Lodge No. 68, Knights of Pythias* (Cleveland, Ohio: Imperial Press, 1889); see also J. J. Upchurch and A. T. Dewey, *Life and Times of Father Upchurch, Written by Himself* (San Francisco, 1887), p. 72, for similar policies in the AOUW.

[36] John Higham, *Strangers in the Land: Patterns of American Nativism, 1860–1925* (New Brunswick, N.J.: Rutgers University Press, 1955).

ternalism throughout its history. This was accomplished not simply on a de facto basis, but by formally requiring that prospective members *must be* white. The consequence was the emergence of a separate black fraternal movement. Some black organizations, like the Grand United Order of Galilean Fishermen and the Order of Twelve, originated completely within the black community, but many others directly paralleled established white orders, from which they drew their inspiration. These included the Knights of Pythias of North and South America, Europe, Asia, and Africa, the Grand United Order of Odd Fellows, the Improved Benevolent and Protective Order of Elks of the World, and the Prince Hall Masons. In southern states where blacks comprised a large proportion of the population, the Prince Hall Masons and the Grand United Order of Odd Fellows were large organizations; in both North and South Carolina, for example, the Grand United Order was the largest fraternal order in the state. By the end of the nineteenth century the black Odd Fellows organization had grown to a membership of nearly 70,000, and the Prince Hall Masons to 60,000.[37]

Unlike the ban on women, the exclusion of nonwhites was not an inherent part of the British Masonic tradition. In fact, the Prince Hall Masons had been formed when Prince Hall, a black artisan, and fourteen other black residents of Boston were made Master Masons by an English army lodge during the Revolutionary War. Their Masonic credentials were thus completely regular, but despite this, they were refused admission by the Grand Lodge of Massachusetts, after which they applied to the Grand Lodge of England, which recognized them as a legitimate Masonic lodge, African Lodge, No 454. In the early nineteenth century, the existing black Masonic lodges constituted themselves as the African

[37] Stevens, *Cyclopaedia*, pp. 119, 237, 72. See also William A. Muraskin, *Middle Class Blacks in a White Society: Prince Hall Masonry in America* (Berkeley, Ca.: University of California Press, 1975).

or Prince Hall Grand Lodge and declared independence from the Grand Lodge of England (as their white counterparts had done after the Revolution), but they continued to maintain fraternal relations with the English body. Similarly, the black Odd Fellows organization originated as a recognized branch of the English Grand United Order and maintained its affiliation throughout the nineteenth century.[38]

It is not, of course, surprising to learn that nineteenth-century fraternal orders were segregated, but our recognition of American racism should not blind us to the need for an analysis of how such a racial order is constituted. It might be argued that white fraternal organizations simply reflected the racist assumptions and practices of the society of which they were a part; integrated fraternal institutions could not have sustained themselves in a society predicated upon white supremacy. But that is to oversimplify. If racism is a social system, rather than the reflection of 100 million bigoted psyches, then it must be produced and reproduced. From this perspective, fraternal orders may be seen as an active, albeit relatively small, part of a social structure organized to construct and maintain racial separation and inequality.

The local lodge holds the power of admission, and the use of the blackball was a traditional part of the admission procedure in almost every order. This gave a small minority within each lodge the power to reject anyone whom they might find unacceptable and should have provided a simple mechanism by which orders could exclude members of stigmatized groups without publicly contradicting their rhetoric of equality and universality. Yet almost all the American orders considered it necessary to enact the exclusion of nonwhites in state and national bylaws, apparently believing they could not rely upon the de facto use of blackball to enforce racial purity. Such public statements served not only

[38] Stevens, *Cyclopaedia*, pp. 72–73, 235–37.

133

to articulate racial boundaries but to enforce them in situations where they might be breached. The Modern Woodmen of America (MWA) was perhaps the only major order that did not specify the exclusion of blacks in its original membership requirements. This became a matter of controversy very quickly. An MWA publication, the *"Echo* of August 1889 practically admitted that a colored man had been admitted to one of the Illinois Camps, and while no color line had then been drawn in the laws, the act was vigorously protested as tending to impair risks, as well as to create fraternal complications." What apparently pushed the issue to a quick resolution was the attack of rival orders on the MWA's failure to exclude blacks and the awareness that this could affect the order in the competition for members. Consequently, the order enacted a whites-only regulation in 1892.[39]

Controversy within the Masons revolved not around the unthinkable question of whether to admit a black man, but over the legitimacy of the Prince Hall Masons. Although the Prince Hall Masons could trace their origin back to the Grand Lodge of England, white Masons persisted in viewing them as an irregular or "clandestine" body that was not "genuinely" Masonic and thus fraudulent. In the late nineteenth century black Masons began to argue in a more vehement and scholarly fashion for the regularity of their order, a claim that was acknowledged as correct by some white Masonic authorities. But when the Grand Lodge of Washington suggested in 1898 that the Prince Hall Masons be recognized as a legitimate Masonic body, the response was quick and sharp. Grand Lodges of at least four other states severed their fraternal connections to the Washington Grand Lodge, simply for proposing such recognition.[40]

Such examples reveal how the public commitment of the national organizations to a racist policy functioned to exer-

[39] Buffum, *Modern Woodmen*, p. 105.
[40] Stevens, *Cyclopaedia*, p. 74.

cise strong control over local liberalizing elements. They did this by making loss of fraternal legitimacy the price for any attempt, however minimal, to breach or weaken the color line, and thus provided one institutional resource for an organized defense of a segregated society. But these structures were not simply attempts to maintain a social separation of the races. As the treatment of the Prince Hall Masons reveals, white Masons not only wished to bar individual blacks from participation in white Masonic institutions, but to deny the legitimacy of parallel black institutions. In refusing to recognize the Prince Hall Masons as a regularly constituted Masonic body (which in fact it was by any conceivable standard) the white American Masons made the implicit claim that a black could not legitimately *be* a Mason; it was a contradiction in terms. In a significant sense, the exclusion of blacks was parallel to the exclusion of women, despite the absence in the British tradition of racial discrimination. For within the context of American society, white racial identity was just as intrinsic to the concepts of proprietorship, republican citizenship, and social adulthood as was being male. Within American society, adult manhood, which Freemasonry served to ratify, was historically no more available to black men than it was to women of any race.

FRATERNALISM'S WIDER INFLUENCE

The tremendous growth of the social order only begins to suggest the kind of appeal that fraternalism held for men of the late nineteenth century. While the fraternal order's growth was part of a larger efflorescence of voluntary associations in the growing cities and towns of the United States, it was distinguished from other kinds of organizations by its particularity as a social and cultural form. The special appeal of this form is visible not just in the spread of the social order but in the wider use of fraternalism as a model of organization.

As in the earlier part of the century, social orders existed alongside more instrumental, work-based associations, such as unions and trade societies, many of which continued to be organized on a fraternal basis. This practice continued into the 1860s and 1870s, when many, if not most, of the important trade unions were established as fraternal orders. By this time, however, the prestige and popularity of the social orders was such that the balance between the two types of fraternal groups had shifted. Individuals wishing to organize on behalf of a variety of political and labor causes often had prior experience in social orders; they now made intentional use of the fraternal mode as an organizing device, a way to arouse interest and build solidarity.

The agricultural reform movement provides one example of this. The Patrons of Husbandry, commonly known as the Grange, was established in 1867 by a Mason, Oliver U. Kelley. As an organization of farmers, the Grange worked to eliminate middlemen, improve the technical expertise of farmers, and better their material and cultural lot. Growing rapidly to 268,000 by 1874, the Grange suffered severe membership losses in the 1880s because of competition from the more militant Farmers' Alliances. The Patrons of Husbandry was conceived as a fraternal order, its Masonic influence revealed in its elaborate ritual of seven degrees. In contrast, the Alliance began as a purely political and economic organization, designed to promote the interests of farmers. But it soon became apparent that the Alliance would have a hard time competing with the Grange without the drawing card of a ritual; thus state and local lodges were given the option of adopting a secret ritual and an initiation ceremony in order to provide a more attractive organizational life.[41] People actively sought the mixture of the instrumental and expressive that the fraternal form could provide.

The labor movement was the one most infused with fraternalism. Many trade unions revealed this in the mythic

[41] Stevens, *Cyclopaedia*, pp. 395–96, 385–86.

character of their titles, such as the Grand Forge of the United States, Sons of Vulcan, an early union of iron workers (1862), or the Knights of St. Crispin, the large and militant shoemakers' union founded in 1867. But even unions with less fanciful names, such as the Bricklayers and Masons International Union (1866), the Order of Railway Conductors (1866), the Brotherhood of Locomotive Engineers (1863), and the Order of United Machinists and Mechanical Engineers (later to become the International Association of Machinists), were organized as secret fraternal bodies with initiation rituals and ceremonial meetings. In the case of the Locomotive Engineers, for example, the *Cyclopaedia of Fraternities* noted "the visible evidence" in ritual and symbolism that suggested that "its founders, or some of their successors among its leaders, were affiliated with the mother of nearly all modern secret societies of good repute," that is, the Masons.[42]

The use of fraternal forms to further working-class goals extended beyond the trade unions to the groups known as labor reform associations, which were an important part of the labor movement of the late 1860s and early 1870s. The trade union was, in David Montgomery's words, "an organization of workers in a given occupation which sought through the establishment of work rules and standard wages to regulate the conditions under which its members worked." Labor reform associations, on the other hand, "were primarily educational and agitational in purpose, and they admitted to membership anyone who subscribed to their principles." They thus differed from trade unions and shared with fraternal social orders a potential character as multi-class institutions: many of them did indeed, according to Montgomery, bring "craftsmen together with legislators and professionals or propertied men."[43] Increasingly, how-

[42] Gist, "Secret Societies," p. 26; Stevens, *Cyclopaedia*, p. 382.
[43] David Montgomery, *Beyond Equality: Labor and the Radical Republicans, 1862–1872* (New York: Vintage, 1967), pp. 139, 135.

ever, the post–Civil War labor reform associations were dominated by skilled workers, and many of them, like the trade unions organized by skilled workers in this period, were conceived as fraternal orders.

During the Civil War, for example, the League of Friendship, Supreme Mechanical Order of the Sun, had been organized as "a secret society with an elaborate ritual and several degrees of membership." Apparently the largest labor reform society of the late 1860s, the League of Friendship is also one of the most obscure, because of its early demise. We do know that despite its fraternal embellishments, it was a fully accepted participant in labor reform politics, represented, for example, at the 1868 National Labor Congress by John J. Junis, who was also head of the Cigar Makers' International Union.[44]

The Knights of Labor was the most dynamic labor organization in this period, growing to a membership of 110,000 in 1885 and 711,000 in 1886 before an almost equally rapid decline. But at the time of its founding in 1869, the Knights of Labor was "simply another secret society of this type."[45] Like so many other fraternal founders, the Knights' creator, Uriah S. Stevens, had been a Mason. Impressed by the efficacy of Masonic ritual, Stevens saw in fraternal ritual the means to impose secrecy and create solidarity, uniting workers in an inviolable bond of loyalty and trust. In response to the anti-Masonic concerns of the Catholic Church, the order in 1878 abandoned total secrecy and simplified the ritual. It has often been assumed that this action represented the end of the Knights' existence as a fraternal body. The ritual, however, while simplified, was not abolished, and the papers of Terence Powderly, Stevens's successor as Grand Master Workman and himself a Catholic, reveal a continuing preoccupation with ritual procedures among the local leaders who wrote to Powderly for guidance.[46]

[44] Ibid., p. 137.
[45] Ibid., p. 137.
[46] *Knights of Labor Illustrated*, "*Adelphon Kruptos*," *The Full Illustrated Ritual* (Chicago: Ezra A. Cook, 1886); George Rawick, personal communication.

This preoccupation persisted throughout much of the labor movement. When William N. Sayer, Grand Secretary-Treasurer of the Brotherhood of Locomotive Firemen, visited the Vigo Lodge of Terre Haute, Indiana, in 1875, his address to the membership focused primarily on proper observance of ceremony and use of lodge regalia.[47] Union locals were typically called lodges, and it was standard practice "to refer to a fellow unionist as 'brother' and to sign labor correspondence with 'fraternally yours.' " Though interest in elaborate ritual undoubtedly lessened after the 1860s and 1870s, it is nonetheless the case that "the image of the union as fraternity" remained "one of the dominant models of nineteenth century trade unionism."[48]

Social orders, such as the Knights of Pythias, and work-based organizations, like trade unions and agricultural reform societies, represented two different and clearly distinguishable kinds of organization. Yet their common fraternal character worked to maintain a permeability between the two categories: social orders could be transformed into political organizations, as the case of the Ku Klux Klan in the 1920s reveals (see Chapter Seven), and labor and agricultural organizations could evolve into societies that were primarily social or beneficial in nature. The early history of the Ancient Order of United Workmen reveals the kinds of links that connected the fraternalism of the social orders with that of the labor movement.

In the late 1890s, the Ancient Order of United Workmen was the fifth largest fraternal order, with a membership of 357,000 and a reputation as the first order to offer a life insurance benefit to its members.[49] It seemed to be a fairly standard version of its type. But the AOUW originated within the tradition of 1860s labor reform, where it had been estab-

[47] Nick Salvatore, *Eugene V. Debs: Citizen and Socialist* (Urbana, Ill.: University of Illinois Press, 1982), pp. 26, 49.

[48] Warren R. VanTine, *The Making of the Labor Bureaucrat: Union Leadership in the United States, 1870–1920* (Amherst, Mass.: University of Massachusetts Press, 1975), pp. 34–35.

[49] Stevens, *Cyclopaedia*, p. 128.

lished as a recognizable, albeit conservative, version of a labor reform organization.

The founder of the order, John J. Upchurch, was a skilled craftsman whose frustrated attempts at entrepreneurial mobility led him to an obsessive geographic mobility. During his active adult life, Upchurch relocated some twenty-five times, moving back and forth from south to north and east to west and holding at least thirty-three different jobs. While perhaps half of these jobs were variations on his trade of master mechanic, usually in railroad machine shops, Upchurch consistently sought to be an entrepreneur, and his numerous and dismally unsuccessful ventures into self-employment found him running a temperance hotel, manufacturing cornshellers and barrows, superintending a flour mill and a planing mill, speculating in oil, running at least three distinct but ill-fated "provision stores," and working as a horse-tamer and an undertaker.[50]

By the time of the Civil War, Upchurch had conceived an antipathy to trade unions, which he perceived as placing unjustifiable strictures on the rights of workers to labor when and for whom they chose. His ideas were formed, he claimed, in the course of an 1864 railroad strike. When train hands of the Mine Hill & Schuykill Haven Railroad struck for higher wages, the federal government, justified in its actions by the Civil War, sent in replacement workers to break the strike, and Upchurch, in his capacity as master mechanic, "operated the road for two weeks in the interest of the government." In Upchurch's view, the train engineers were essentially dupes of the unions, which he regarded as powerful institutions acting unjustly "not only to capital, but to laboring men, whom they profess to befriend." Union antagonism, in Upchurch's opinion, was counterproductive; what was needed instead was some attempt "to try to harmonize the two great interests of our country, capital and labor."[51]

[50] Upchurch and Dewey, *Life of Father Upchurch*, passim.
[51] Ibid., pp. 22–23.

Upchurch did not act on his convictions until 1869, when he was employed in the lathe shop of the Atlantic Great Western Railroad at Meadville, Pennsylvania. His actions were precipitated by his experience in the League of Friendship, Supreme Mechanical Order of the Sun, the large fraternal labor reform organization. The Meadville Lodge was under pressure from the Grand Council of the League of Friendship to assume an additional degree, the "Knight of the Iron Ring," at a cost of five dollars. Upchurch "came to the conclusion that the whole thing was rotten to the core, gotten up for the purpose of fraud, and therefore unworthy of confidence and support of workingmen." Once again, seeing workers as dupes of a corrupt and dictatorial organization, Upchurch determined to found his own, which was "calculated to benefit the working people more than anything I know of" and which had as a goal "To use all legitimate means in their power to adjust all differences which may arise between employers and employees, and to labor for the development of a plan of action that may be beneficial to both parties, based on the eternal truth that the interests of labor and capital are equal and should receive equal protection."[52]

With his dislike of labor organizations, his desire to unite labor and capital, and his belief that this could be done, Upchurch's founding of the Ancient Order of United Workmen must be seen as a specifically conservative intervention into the working-class movement of the time. Yet it emerged from within and spoke the vocabulary of 1860s labor reform. This explains the rather contradictory character that the early organization assumed. Upchurch had originally wanted "to unite employer and employee into an organization and obligate them to the same great principles of 'the greatest good to the greatest number.'" Yet the organization's first constitution, as written by Upchurch, provided that membership be limited to "mechanics, artisans, engi-

---

[52] Ibid., p. 28; Article II, Section 5, "First Constitution of the Ancient Order of United Workmen," in ibid., p. 57.

141

neers, firemen, train conductors, blacksmith helpers . . . and their assistants of all the various branches." Moreover, the language spoken was that of (opposing) interest: the purpose of the order was "to unite all mechanics and mechanics' helpers . . . so that they may form a united body for the defense and protection of their interests against all encroachments, by elevating labor to the standard it is justly entitled to."[53]

Indeed, the AOUW showed remarkable similarities to the Knights of Labor, established in 1869, one year later. Both organizations shared a commitment to education and self-improvement via the creation of reading rooms, lectures, and discussions; both articulated a disapproval of strikes except, in the words of the AOUW constitution, "when they become absolutely necessary for their [the mechanics and mechanics' helpers] protection, and then only after all efforts at adjustment have failed."[54] With its membership limited to mechanics, the AOUW was initially more of a self-defined workingmen's organization than the Knights, who barred lawyers and bankers, but admitted other proprietors. In 1870 the AOUW relaxed its membership restrictions, but in terms once again reminiscent of the Knights, continuing to exclude not only lawyers and saloon-keepers but also "the man of wealth who will not invest his capital in some manufacture, so as to give employment to the laboring classes."[55]

What separated them was the overall perspective within which they operated. Here the Knights' critique of the wage system contrasted with the Workmen's desire, following Upchurch, for "a plan of action that may be beneficial to both parties, based on the eternal truth that the interest of

[53] Ibid., p. 23; AOUW constitution in ibid., pp. 56–58.

[54] AOUW constitution in ibid., p. 57.

[55] Sackett, *Early History*, pp. 47–48. The grouping of manufacturers with wage laborers rather than with bankers and landlords is part of the nineteenth-century conception of the "producing classes." "Producerist" conceptions of class relations were an important part of late nineteenth-century politics. See, for example, Montgomery, *Beyond Equality*, p. 14.

labor and capital are equal and should receive equal protection." In calling for such a plan, Upchurch apparently had in mind an attempt to use the fraternal bond to create some sort of institutionalized system of resolving differences between workers and employers in order to circumvent the strike. Again, this was not dissimilar to the Knights' goal of "persuading employers to agree to arbitrate all differences which may arise between them and their employees, in order that the bonds of sympathy between them may be strengthened and that strikes may be rendered unnecessary."[56]

Both organizations found this to be an unworkable goal, but the Knights turned toward a more militant activism while interest in the AOUW began to gravitate, to Upchurch's disappointment, toward the insurance provision as the organization's distinctive characteristic.

Upchurch's original constitution had provided that when the order reached a membership of one thousand an insurance program should be created that would pay a minimum of $500 to each member's family upon his death. The systematic payment of death benefits would become an important trend in the fraternal movement, but within the AOUW it assumed a special significance by seeming to represent in altered form the fulfillment of Upchurch's dream. Making available to workers a degree of security for their families was to minimize the dislocations and costs of the wage system and thus reduce class antagonism. At the same time, Upchurch's original vision of the order as a means of *institutional* reconciliation of labor and capital was supplanted by a vision of *personal* reconciliation, as the membership diversified. "Today," wrote Upchurch in his last speech, "we have members from the highest professions and the lowest grades of mechanical labor. We come into this organization on the same great level. It is not money, but it is purity of

---

[56] AOUW constitution in Upchurch and Dewey, *Life of Father Upchurch*, p. 57; Sackett, *Early History*, pp. 27–28; *Knights of Labor Illustrated*, p. 49.

character and uprightness that bring us here, and we can take each brother by the hand as an equal. Brothers, in this organization we have done more to harmonize the human family, high and low, than all the other organizations that ever existed."[57]

Both the AOUW and the Knights of Labor were grounded in the affinity between fraternalism and workers' organization. Given the many similarities between the two organizations, it may seem strange that they developed in such different directions: the Knights emerging, for a brief but crucial period, as the leading organization of American working-class radicalism, the AOUW growing into an important agency of class reconciliation (or collaboration, depending on one's perspective). But in neither case was fraternalism an incidental part of their identities. The seemingly contradictory visions of labor militancy and class cooperation were equally a part of the fraternal model that the Knights of Labor and the United Workmen drew upon. From different yet related perspectives each reflected not only fraternalism's institutional preoccupation with class identity, but also its special character as a cultural form growing out of the artisanal workshop.

[57] Upchurch and Dewey, *Life of Father Upchurch*, p. 214.

FIVE

Social Fraternalism and the
Artisanal Ideal

CHAPTER Two described the process by which Freemasonry emerged from the culture of the artisanal workshop to become a vehicle for a developing bourgeois sociability. This chapter argues that it was Masonic fraternalism's origins in craft production and its continuing idealization of artisanal values and modes of interaction that were at the heart of its appeal in nineteenth-century America.

Throughout the nineteenth century, the processes of capitalist development combined to undermine the craft organization of production. Yet this attack was rarely swift, abrupt, or uniform; rather, it was a process of erosion and gradual reorganization that varied greatly from industry to industry in its pace and its detail. In some industries, like metal working and machine production, a variant of the craft system remained the modal form of organization right up to the end of the century, while in many others, mass production emerged not via the factory system but through the more subtle transformation of the artisanal workshop, a process that changed the "social context of production" while leaving "the shell of the old artisan system" largely intact.[1] With some justification, the craftsman could con-

---

[1] David M. Gordon, Richard Edwards, and Michael Reich, *Segmented Work, Divided Workers: The Historical Transformation of Labor in the U.S.* (Cambridge: Cambridge University Press, 1982), p. 92; Sean Wilentz, "Artisan Republican Festivals and the Rise of Class Conflict in New York City, 1788–1837," in Michael H. Frisch and Daniel J. Walkowitz, eds., *Working Class America: Essays in Labor, Community, and American Society* (Urbana, Ill.: University of Illinois Press, 1983), pp. 42–43.

tinue to be seen as the typical male worker, and the artisanal identity a realistic if precarious one for a significant proportion of the white male population.

This identity was founded in the social relations of the craft workshop, relations that may be understood as fraternal in character. The elements of this fraternal mode—the mutuality inherent in corporatist conceptions of social life, the rituals of sociability and camaraderie, the intertwining of proprietorship and masculinity—provided the raw materials from which social fraternalism was constructed. During the nineteenth century the fraternalism of the workshop was under persistent attack; craft ideals were increasingly less possible to realize within the workplace. The rise of social fraternalism closely parallels this decline of traditional craft relations in the work world. If these ideals could no longer be realized at work, they could instead be transferred to a purely social setting, the fraternal order. If the temperance movement ended the use of drink as the cement for such relations, fraternalism provided a ritual to create the togetherness formerly engendered by alcohol. Through its re-creation of such modes of sociability, social fraternalism both denied and affirmed class distinctions; it simultaneously offered a critique of capitalist development and an accommodation to it. In doing so, it provided nineteenth-century American men with an enormously appealing source of mutual support and camaraderie.

THE ARTISAN AS A SOCIAL FIGURE

Looking at the occupational structure of late eighteenth-century Philadelphia, Eric Foner defined the artisan as "a property-owning producer of commodities (but artisanal "property" includes skill and tools) or a skilled craftsman owning his own tools but working for a contractor."[2] The

[2] Eric Foner, *Tom Paine and Revolutionary America* (New York: Oxford University Press, 1976), p. 279, n. 19.

bifurcated character of this definition is indicative of the difficulties inherent in defining the artisan, for it reflects what Wilentz has called the "duality in the social relations of the [artisanal] workshop," a duality that capitalist development increasingly renders a contradiction.[3]

The artisan is a figure defined not by his relation to property but by his relation to skill and to the social institutions through which skill is acquired and put to use: apprenticeship, the workshop, the trade association. The concept has its roots in the handicraft production of pre-capitalist Europe, where the property-based distinction between master and apprentice or journeyman is but a temporal one. Handicraft production, as regulated by the trade associations described in Chapter One, does not envision a permanent class of wage laborers. Because it assumes that every apprentice and journeyman will become a master, just as every master was once an apprentice and journeyman, it posits an ultimate unity of interest among them. The propertyless figures of apprentice and journeyman and the propertied figure of the master represent three developmental stages of the same socioeconomic role, rather than permanently fixed and opposing social categories. In such a system, the possibilities for individual entrepreneurship or self-aggrandizement much beyond the norm were limited by the more static, nonexpansionary character of the market and by the collective regulation of the trade, which specified not only the standards to be met but the production methods to be used and the number of apprentices who could be trained at any given time. The master was as much the temporary trustee of a collective body of knowledge as he was an individual entrepreneur.[4]

[3] Sean Wilentz, *Chants Democratic: New York City and the Rise of the American Working Class, 1788–1850* (New York: Oxford University Press, 1984), p. 4.

[4] See William H. Sewell, Jr., *Work and Revolution in France: The Language of Labor from the Old Regime to 1848* (Cambridge: Cambridge University

CHAPTER FIVE

If pre-capitalist handicraft production synthesizes these dualities, capitalism breaks down the synthesis. The growth of the market allows more competitive masters to expand at the expense of other less competitive ones, while the enlarged scale of production demands an increase in the number of apprentices and journeymen to provide the needed labor power. They tend to become permanent wage laborers as opportunities to become independent masters constrict.

But early capitalism brought about changes in the dynamic of production more than in the methods and organization of production. Traditional conceptions of economic history have tended to equate capitalist development with the coming of the factory system, the textile industry standing as the model for a system characterized by the use of power-driven machinery, an advanced division of labor, and a high degree of supervision by foremen and managers. More recent scholarship treats the factory system as one variant of early capitalist development, a type of production that arose primarily in those industries that lacked strong craft traditions. In many other cases manufacture continued to be organized by the social institutions of handicraft production. In their analysis of American labor history, Gordon, Edwards, and Reich conclude that for most of the nineteenth century the work force is best characterized as "proletarianized but largely untransformed labor."

> Capitalists hired labor but relied on traditional techniques of production. They organized the production process in the social sense, gathering together labor, materials, tools, and other essential ingredients of production and disposing of the output. Yet, except where there was no preexisting organization of production to draw upon, they did not organize or transform the labor process in detail. Instead they adopted existing methods, including major reliance on the workers' own

Press, 1980), Chapter 2, "Mechanical arts and the corporate idiom," for the most powerful recent description of this system.

knowledge of production. Although producers lost their tools and independence when they became wage workers, large numbers of them retained their skills and control over their work process.[5]

Thus despite the effects of early capitalist development, the social system of artisanal production tended to remain in place. In the early part of the nineteenth century, a precarious equilibrium continued to be achieved, the individualizing tendencies of the market checked for a time by the social institutions of trade solidarity. What I want to do here is to depict the system in its equilibrium, then to show the reactions of both journeymen and masters to that loss of equilibrium as both were drawn into a process in which corporatism and proprietorship, mutuality and individualism, began to appear as alternative directions rather than as elements of a coherent whole. Ultimately I will argue that the fraternal order was a social form which, having grown out of the culture of the artisanal workshop, represented an attempt to reconstruct the fraternal character of handicraft production in a sphere separated from the labor market and the capitalist enterprise.

THE CORPORATE AND REPUBLICAN CHARACTER OF ANTEBELLUM ARTISANS

As Marx points out, the master is indeed a capitalist. He owns "the conditions of production—tools, materials, etc. . . . and he owns the product." But, Marx goes on to emphasize, his identity at this point remains a dual one, for "it is not as a capitalist that he is a master. He is an artisan in the first instance and is supposed to be a master of his craft. Within the process of production he appears as an artisan, like his journeymen, and it is he who initiates his apprentices into the mysteries of the craft. He has precisely the same relationship to his apprentices as a professor to his stu-

[5] Gordon et al., *Segmented Work*, p. 79.

dents. Hence his approach is not that of a capitalist but a *master* of his craft."[6] Here the master's authority is grounded in his superior skill and experience rather than in his control over capital. He and his men are all products of the same system of skill acquisition, with its common rituals and customs. As long as the master continued to work alongside the men, as a practicing artisan, he remained enmeshed in the social relations of the workshop, subject to the coercive and affective powers of a work group of which he was still a part. In such circumstances, it was still possible to conceive of the trade as a corporate body, a moral and social community of men bound to each other by more than economic motives.

This corporate conception of the craft was expressed through organization and ritual. Trade corporations of the classic European type, with their quasi-governmental status and regulatory powers, were never established in colonial American cities, probably because such bodies were already on the decline in Britain by the time of colonization. Indeed, the small towns of North America, which had few craftsmen to begin with, did not require and could not sustain such elaborate levels of organization. But the basic outlines of handicraft production were consistent with their British analogues. And craftsmen in the larger commercial centers, like New York and Philadelphia, did organize trade associations that attempted to fulfill the mutualistic functions of the trade corporation on a more voluntary basis. Indeed, Wilentz finds that as late as the 1840s and 1850s craft benefit societies composed of both masters and journeymen were one of the two most prevalent kinds of workers' organizations in New York. Both in their opposition to strikes and in their provision of mutual aid benefits to needy members of the trade, such societies expressed the corporate ideal of a unity of interest between masters and journeymen.[7] To the

---

[6] Karl Marx, *Capital*, quoted in Wilentz, *Chants*, pp. 4–5. My analysis of artisanal production and politics in the early nineteenth century is deeply indebted to Wilentz's work.

[7] Ibid., p. 365.

extent that they participated in such organizations, masters continued to express a paternalistic commitment to their employees' welfare. By this time such sentiments had become problematic to some number of workers and employers, but earlier in the century, they commanded a powerful allegiance that expressed itself in public rituals that were strikingly similar to those of the traditional European trade corporations.

In 1788, for example, thousands of New York masters, journeymen, and apprentices marched, by trade, to support the adoption of the Constitution. Wilentz notes that the parade "resembled an old Lord Mayor's Show in almost every detail," as the craftsmen marched bedecked with banners, flags, and insignias that "would have been familiar to any Elizabethan Londoner."

> The tailors' banners, like those in English parades, depicted Adam and Eve and bore the legend 'And They Sewed Fig Leaves Together.' The cordwainers' flag included a view of the good ship Crispin arriving in New York harbor, as if the kindly saint himself had made the voyage from the Old World. Several trades not only carried banners but performed the rolling platform displays that had been the theatrical high points of the English festivities. Whether as a continuation of trade traditions or, more likely as a retrieval of those traditions, the artisans' displays suggested that they continued to respect and cherish long-established images of the crafts.[8]

The power of these images may be discerned from the fact that, in the United States as in France and Britain, when journeymen began to meet and organize on their own, they continued to make use of the rhetoric and paraphernalia of the unified trade association. Although they now marched separately, they marched behind the same banners. The

[8] Wilentz, "Festivals," p. 47.

early journeymen's societies were, in Wilentz's words, "as much fraternal associations as trade unions: all mirrored, to some degree, the masters' dedication to mutual aid and to the harmony of 'the Trade.' "[9] Even when societies shifted their focus from the planning of celebrations and the payment of sick benefits to more militant actions, their actions reflected a conception of the trade as a mutualistic, collectively regulated body, rather than an aggregation of competing enterprises.

In the early nineteenth-century United States, as in seventeenth- and eighteenth-century France, journeymen's strikes most often revolved around issues such as the enforcement of apprenticeship regulations and other attempts to prevent the erosion of the regulatory capabilities of artisanal production. Journeymen in New York in the 1830s even made attempts to reinstitute regularized, craft-wide rate schedules similar to the tariff imposed by the seventeenth-century compagnonnage, as discussed in Chapter One. If these schedules had been observed, they would have prevented employers from putting out work to sweatshops, a practice that clearly threatened the viability of artisanal production. "By striking for an equalized rate, one group of unionists proclaimed, the journeymen would benefit the trade as a whole by 'setting an efficient standard,' by ending 'the necessity of giving work out of the shop,' and by halting 'the formation of a system which will ultimately, if not promptly met, lead us to the annihilation of our rights and finally cause us to become mere vassals of the wealthy employer.' "[10] Such sentiments tell us much about the response of at least some American journeymen to a process that was, if not destroying artisanal production, at least transforming its context and its imperatives. It was a response shaped by a fundamental continuity with earlier craft traditions.

The willingness of journeymen to organize separately

[9] Wilentz, *Chants*, p. 56.
[10] Ibid., pp. 231–32.

from masters and to act militantly suggests that they accepted, at least in practice, the permanence of their status as journeymen and wage laborers. Nonetheless they fought primarily to preserve the institutions of artisanal production. Although they were themselves propertyless wage workers, they sought to protect their collective control over the skills that were themselves a form of property, the crucial resource separating them from the ranks of the unskilled, whom they did not see as part of their moral and social universe.

Their unwillingness to become the "vassals of the wealthy employer" displays the particular political connotations that were attached to artisanal identity in the American context, where the critique of economic subjugation could be assimilated to the defense of political freedom and the ideal of republican citizenship. The artisan was frequently held to be the model citizen of the republic, his political independence based upon his economic self-sufficiency. Artisans were seen as "peculiarly virtuous men, imbued with the spirit of independence, fellowship, and commonwealth and free from the economic dependence that bred corruption . . . On the other hand, a republic was the ideal polity for craftsmen, for it allowed them to practice their arts untrammeled by the arbitrary economic and political power of any privileged class."[11] Thus the threat to artisanal skill was interpreted as a threat to the American concept of an egalitarian republic. Yet the notion of the artisan-citizen was a direct descendent of the earlier European specification of proprietorship as the basis of adult manhood and the necessary qualification for participation in craft and civic affairs.

Like this earlier concept, the notion of the artisan as virtuous republican proposed a concept of citizenship that excluded both the unskilled and women. Indeed the two categories were often merged symbolically as well as in practice. Artisanal identity continued to be a masculine identity despite the entrance of increasing numbers of

[11] Wilentz, "Festivals," p. 50.

153

women into the paid labor force. Apprenticeship was not only an institution for the inculcation and acquisition of craft knowledge; it was a vehicle of masculine socialization.

Except in the textile industry, women entered the industrial labor force primarily as outworkers, and thus most often worked alone. Even when such women worked with others, their "workplace associations were family- rather than gender- or trade-based, as men's were." Even, Christine Stansell has noted, when a man was relegated to performing outwork, "he sustained the bonds of his trade, bonds which were exclusively masculine . . . He fraternized with other men on the basis of their shared trade, and carried with him a history of work associations with men dating back to his apprenticeship . . . A journeyman brought a sense of himself as a man bound to other men to whatever other work relations he had in a sweater's garret or his own home . . ."[12] So powerful was what Wilentz calls "the gender-system of 'the Trade,' " that any work performed by outworkers or sweatshop workers had the aura of women's work about it. Bruce Laurie describes the "aristocratic" members of Philadelphia's Journeymen Tailors Association, who "considered 'costly broad cloth' and other fine garments made to order worthy of their skillful hands, but not 'a light summer coatee' or slop work, which they demeaned as the work of women, and . . . not . . . so dignified a subject of employment as the former, which men alone have the honor to make.' "[13] The distinctions drawn by the Philadelphia tailors were typical ones, which display the inseparability of masculine honor and craft pride and make it clear that the feelings attached to the defense of artisanal production were intensified by the fact that it was simultaneously

[12] Christine Stansell, "The Origins of the Sweatshop: Women and Early Industrialization in New York City," in Frisch and Walkowitz, *Working Class America*, pp. 94–95.

[13] Bruce Laurie, *Working People of Philadelphia, 1800–1850* (Philadelphia: Temple University Press, 1980), p. 86.

a defense of a particular kind of institutionalized male solidarity.

DRINK AND THE ANTEBELLUM WORKPLACE

Customs and rituals surrounding alcohol consumption provide especially revealing insights into the fraternal character of artisanal production. In the traditional workshop, the normative practice of workplace drinking had served to unite masters and journeymen in their mutually confirming identities as skilled workers and as men. In the 1820s and 1830s, growing differences between employers and workers about drinking expressed tensions emanating from more fundamental changes in the organization of production.

In the early nineteenth-century United States, drinking was an intrinsic part of the routine of work for most men. In this regard, the workplace was not distinguished from other social settings, for liquor was, in Paul Johnson's words, "an absolutely normal accompaniment to whatever men did in groups," a part of the fabric of everyday life. W. J. Rorabaugh estimates that only about 20 per cent of alcohol consumption in the early century took place at taverns, that is at places specifically intended for drinking; the remaining 80 per cent occurred in the course of commercial transactions, manufacture, elections, and other communal gatherings.[14]

Within this general context, two factors made drinking especially significant to the constitution of artisanal identity and fraternal relationships within the workshop. First, drinking was largely a male prerogative. Liquor consumption demanded access to discretionary income that most women did not have, and its anti-inhibiting properties led drinkers to engage in types of expressive behavior consid-

[14] Paul E. Johnson, *A Shopkeeper's Millennium: Society and Revivals in Rochester, New York, 1815–1837* (New York: Hill and Wang, 1978), p. 56; W. J. Rorabaugh, *The Alcoholic Republic: An American Tradition* (New York: Oxford University Press, 1979), p. 10.

CHAPTER FIVE

ered inappropriate and dangerous for women. The right to
drink was a badge of male privilege and the camaraderie fostered by men's public drinking was a significant part of masculine group identity.[15] The practice of drinking on the job
reaffirmed the association between craft labor and manhood.

Second, drinking was conceived as positively helpful to
manual laborers, and thus particularly appropriate for them.
Until the late eighteenth century, informed medical opinion
as well as social custom held that "drink was an aid to physical labor" and should be consumed by workers "to relieve
fatigue and to bolster their reserves of energy."[16] Liquor
consumption was both legitimate and normal, "embedded
in the pattern of irregular work and easy sociability sustained by the household economy"; it was, moreover, ritually central, "a sort of secular sacrament, to seal the journeymen's social bonds within the customary artisanal regime,"
"a bond between men who lived, worked, and played together."[17]

Drinking customs formed part of the initiation rites associated with the admission of apprentices into their crafts;
similarly, the practice of 'footing'—the payment of whiskey
to the shop by every newly hired journeyman on his first day
of work—established a ritualized means for new workers to
be incorporated into the workplace. In both cases, the right
to drink was linked to the acquisition or display of skill
while the provision of alcohol for the entire shop made the
point that becoming an apprentice or a journeyman was not
simply an individual achievement but represented admis-

[15] Ruth Bordin, *Woman and Temperance: The Quest for Power and Liberty,
1873–1900* (Philadelphia: Temple University Press, 1981), p. 7; Joseph Gusfield, *Symbolic Crusade: Status Politics and the American Temperance Movement*
(Urbana, Ill.: University of Illinois Press, 1963), pp. 26–29.

[16] Rorabaugh, *Alcoholic Republic*, p. 25; Ian R. Tyrell, *Sobering Up: From
Temperance to Prohibition in Antebellum America, 1800–1860* (Westport,
Conn.: Greenwood Press, 1979), p. 107.

[17] Johnson, *Shopkeeper's Millennium*, p. 56; Wilentz, *Chants*, pp. 53–54;
Johnson, *Shopkeeper's Millennium*, p. 56.

sion into a social system and commitment to a set of mutual obligations.

As in the trade associations of early modern Europe, the mutuality of the workshop did not imply an equality. As Paul Johnson notes, "workmen drank with their employers, in situations that employers controlled"; drinking thus "remained within the bounds of what the master considered appropriate." The master's right to set the limits of acceptable behavior was derived from his overall dominance of the shop, yet it was a "unique kind of domination" in which "the informal mixing of work and leisure and of master and wage earner softened and helped legitimate inequality."[18] The workers were indeed subject to the master, but as long as he worked alongside them, sharing in their tasks and their pleasures, he could not isolate himself from the persuasive and coercive powers of the workshop's interpersonal networks. Drinking helped to make the workshop a place where achievement was inseparable from, at times subordinate to, camaraderie.

By the 1820s, however, employers were beginning to attack the custom. The larger context for this initiative was a growing concern about the exceedingly high rate of liquor consumption, which had reached five gallons of distilled spirits per capita per year in the 1820s, nearly triple today's rate.[19] The widespread belief in the healthful properties of distilled spirits had begun to be challenged in the late eighteenth and early nineteenth centuries. At this time, fears about public drunkenness and disorder, as well as concerns about health, led to calls for a more temperate use of alcohol, but it was evangelical revivalism that both established temperance as the basis for an actual social movement and directed the temperance cause toward the goal of total abstinence.

Evangelicalism's emphasis on the evils of drink was part

18 Ibid., p. 57.
19 Rorabaugh, *Alcoholic Republic*, p. 8.

of a larger societal preoccupation with forces outside the individual that would seem to deprive him or her of rationality and free will. Anti-Catholicism and anti-Masonry as well as temperance may be interpreted in terms of this concern to protect the individual from controlling influences. Temperance advocates envisioned a society made up of autonomous actors, self-disciplined and self motivated, unconstrained by social or institutional pressures. The appropriateness of such a vision to the development of a market economy makes it clear that temperance held economic as well as moral and cultural implications.

Thus the liquor question, Paul Johnson has argued, was tied to disturbances in traditional class relations and especially to emerging patterns of class separation in work, family life, and neighborhood composition: "nowhere was the making of distinct classes and the collapse of old social controls dramatized more neatly, more angrily, and in so many aspects of life" as it was in the debate over drinking. The intensification of production made employers more concerned about the efficiency of their workers and led many of them to try to impose stricter standards of work discipline, including the prohibition of drinking on the job. But the fact that masters were willing even to attempt such a violation of traditional workshop custom symbolized the growing divisions between workers and employers. As they enlarged the scale and intensified the pace of production, employers disengaged themselves from their roles as master artisans, and thus became increasingly detached from the social relations of the workplace. They were thus much less subject to the kinds of persuasion that journeymen previously had at their disposal. Their new distance from the workshop culture also gave employers a greater incentive to end on-the-job drinking because their absence gave drinking by workers a new meaning. Previously the presence and participation of the master had helped unite master and men; now drinking became part of a workers-only sociability that "forged sensibilities that were specific to the class of wage-earning crafts-men."[20]

But employers did not just confine themselves to banning on-the-job drinking; many became involved in the temperance movement, which had tended, as a movement, to gravitate towards a total abstinence position. For many, this included active efforts to foster abstinence not just among their own employees but among the working classes more generally. Evidence from several sources indicates that those businessmen who were most drawn to such efforts were precisely those most committed to the new economic order. Ian Tyrell found that opponents to a prohibition measure in Worcester, Massachusetts, were largely retail merchants and lawyers, while the supporters of prohibition were disproportionately manufacturers. Tyrell concludes that the conflict, stemming from the "changing attitudes toward work and leisure which employers were promoting," was between "people who looked to the emerging industrial society and those who found their allegiance in the mercantile economy." Similarly, Johnson's study of Rochester finds that converts to evangelicalism were disproportionately masters in industries where changes in work organization had been greatest: that is, "entrepreneurs who bore direct responsibility for disordered relations between classes."[21]

It is important to realize that the relationship between masters and their espousal of the temperance cause was a complex one. As both Johnson and Wilentz have argued, getting their workers to stop drinking was not simply a self-interested effort, a calculation of material benefit, on the part of employers (though it certainly was that). It also fulfilled employers' needs to see their own actions as legitimate. Their withdrawal from traditional and mutualistic modes of interaction as they intensified labor discipline and changed the character of workshop relations must have represented a

[20] Johnson, *Shopkeeper's Millennium*, pp. 56, 42.
[21] Tyrell, *Sobering Up*, p. 98; Johnson, *Shopkeeper's Millennium*, p. 106.

psychic loss to many masters, a denial of some significant part of their own identity. Many clung to the ideal, continuing to assert their right and "responsibility to govern wage earners" even as they "severed the relationships through which they had always dominated those men."[22]

Temperance was one answer to this dilemma. In promoting temperance, employers could see themselves as continuing to take responsibility for the welfare of their men and thus as still implicated in the relations of a paternalistic mutuality. It was a way of reasserting their "moral stewardship of the trades," which they were in the process of abdicating. Moreover, workers' abuse of alcohol offered an explanation for the failure of some and the success of others; it located the growing distance between the classes in the character of individuals rather than in terms of systemic change. At a time when journeymen were increasingly calling the justice of the system into question, "master craftsmen found in temperance both an explanation for conditions in the crafts and an invigorated social purpose, to set things right for everyone. Once more, the employers were good republican masters, whose efforts to perfect the abilities of all artisans to accumulate their competence (and, not coincidentally, to increase their own profits) would expand national prosperity and increase the store of virtue."[23]

Within this context the attack on conviviality within the Odd Fellows makes greater sense. Drinking now seemed undesirable to middle-class men in two ways. It was a practical hindrance to mobility because it made people less efficient, less diligent workers and caused them to squander money that might be better spent. But drinking was never just an individual mode of consumption. As masters had withdrawn from the workplace, drinking had become part of a more autonomous working-class sociability, a sign of workers' increasing independence from ties with their em-

---

[22] Ibid., p. 140.
[23] Wilentz, *Chants*, pp. 248, 284.

ployers. The struggle to banish drinking from the lodge room was thus part of a struggle to change the class character of the organization, to transform it from an institution of working-class mutuality to one emphasizing individual advancement and cross-class unity.

TEMPERANCE AS AN ATTACK ON MASCULINE CULTURE

The temperance campaigns of the 1820s, 1830s, and 1840s exerted an enormous effect upon the role of alcohol consumption in American culture. Drinking lost respectability and it declined. The consumption of distilled spirits fell precipitously from a high of nearly five gallons per capita in 1830 to less than two by 1850 (remaining around two ever since).[24]

Obviously men were the most affected by this decline in liquor consumption, since they were the primary consumers. Rorabaugh estimates that adult males, who made up one quarter of the total population in 1830, drank sixty million gallons or 83 percent of the distilled spirits consumed in that year.[25] Moreover this decrease in drinking was felt throughout the male population. The emergence of indigenous working-class temperance organizations such as the Washingtonians meant that by the 1840s temperance was no longer simply a middle-class movement.[26]

After reaching an all-time low in 1850, the production and use of alcohol rose somewhat during and after the Civil War, causing renewed concern among temperance advocates. But this increase is of little significance here. First, it never came close to the levels of the early part of the century. Second, most of the increase occurred in the consumption of beer and wine, which suggests that it reflected the habits of

[24] Rorabaugh, *Alcoholic Republic*, p. 8.
[25] Ibid., p. 10.
[26] Tyrell, *Sobering Up*, pp. 165–67; Wilentz, *Chants*, pp. 308–9.

the growing immigrant population and did not signify a massive return to drinking among native-born men.

It is reasonable to assume that alcohol consumption remained low among the population of white Protestant men from which the fraternal movement drew most of its members. Indeed the resurgence of the temperance movement in the 1870s and 1880s, spearheaded this time by the Women's Christian Temperance Union, probably increased the pressures for them to abstain from alcohol. But it also presented such men with a significant problem. In both practice and symbol, the call for temperance, especially when defined as total abstinence, represented an attack upon masculine identity as it was constituted during the first half of the nineteenth century. This was the case in three distinct ways.

First, in practical terms, the prohibition on drinking deprived men of the tavern, which was not just a source of liquor but a masculine social space from which women were barred. The loss of the tavern left teetotaling men with two options: either a turn toward the home and a more sexually integrated social and emotional life or the creation of new masculine social spaces.

Second, it deprived men of the solidarity-promoting aspects of liquor consumption itself. In physiological terms, alcohol acts to reduce "the reserve and distance with which conventional social norms and personality structure often prevent a sense of group affiliation and a mood of intimacy." At the same time, the act of drinking with other people serves as a ritualistic symbol of group affiliation.[27]

Third, drinking as a social rite can indicate not just masculine separateness but masculine superiority. As Gusfield points out, societies always develop rules about who can and cannot drink. The fact that the right to drink is so often defined in terms of age and sex suggests that drinking is typically used to connote maturity and social adulthood. More-

---

[27] Gusfield, *Symbolic Crusade*, pp. 26–27.

over, since drinking is both costly and unnecessary to sustain life, its use is honorific. It thus points to the higher status of men, since in order to drink they must make use of their right to control disposable family income.[28]

The temperance movement of the 1830s and 1840s, a movement led by men as well as directed toward them, posed significant problems for the constitution of a male social world in that abstention from liquor deprived men of a traditional social space and source of solidarity. In the 1840s working-class temperance advocates created their own organizations, such as the Washingtonians, organizations that through their provision of alternative leisure activities both recognized and attempted to deal with drinking's role as the "centerpiece" of the working-man's culture.[29] But the Washingtonians' appeal was limited both by its class base and by the fact that it was an organization specifically for the rehabilitation of drunkards and had little to offer men who did not define themselves in these terms. In general, organizations designed specifically to promote abstinence were probably too ideological and monolithic to meet the social needs of the much larger numbers of men who practiced temperance or total abstinence simply because it had become normative in their social realm.

The late nineteenth-century temperance movement posed an even greater challenge. Led by women and directed specifically against the evil of male drinking, the movement was infused with the rhetoric of domesticity and feminine moral superiority. Working-class immigrant men were obviously those most practically threatened by the possibility that prohibition might actually be enacted, but until such time, the efforts of women temperance advocates did not really penetrate ethnic subcultures. Native-born Protestant men, on the other hand, could not help but experience the moral suasion and social pressures of the temperance crusade. Work-

[28] Ibid., pp. 27–29.
[29] Wilentz, *Chants*, p. 53.

ing to divest men of their rituals of masculine difference and superiority, it constituted a threat to the integrity of their masculine culture and identity.

Such men could, of course, comply with the implicit agenda of the women's temperance movement, with its enshrinement of domesticity. Alternatively, they could seek or construct institutions and practices that would meet some of the same needs as had social drinking. The fraternal order, once cleansed of its convivial past, provided a uniquely appropriate alternative. The ritual of the lodge was, like the act of drinking, a ritual of male solidarity and superiority. And the lodge itself could serve as an equivalent of the tavern, a sex-segregated, male-only social space suitable for casual socializing as well as more solemn endeavors. The fraternal order provided a way for men to comply with the norm of temperance without acceding to the attack on the male social world that it could imply. By providing a masculine sphere, defined ritually, organizationally, and spatially, the fraternal order represented a refusal on the part of numerous men to endorse in toto domesticity's identification of the home as the primary source of emotional life for men as well as women.

THE PERSISTENCE OF ARTISANAL IDEALS: THE MANLY CRAFT WORKER

At the same time that the temperance movement was attacking one of the foundations of working-class male culture and identity, capitalism was attacking another. The growth of large-scale capitalist enterprise and the de-skilling of labor first eroded and then destroyed the social relations of mutuality at the workplace that formed the basis of the ideal of the manly craft worker.

Two sets of changes were brought about by nineteenth-century capitalist development: changes in property relations and changes in the actual organization of production. In the first instance, the growth of larger firms and the simultaneous eclipsing of small and medium-size proprietors as the primary manufacturers meant changes in the typical life chances of artisanal workers as opportunities to advance to proprietorship contracted and owners withdrew from active involvement in the labor process. By the 1860s, an American industrial economy had emerged as a self-generating system in which, "despite all fluctuations of trade and employment, the increase of industrial power consistently surpassed that of population."[30]

Changes in the scale of production and in the role of the entrepreneur would seem to suggest significant changes in the organization of production itself and thus in the character of the work force and the work experience. But to a surprising extent this was not the case. During the mid-century, American industrialization, as David Montgomery has pointed out, was fueled primarily by external economies: "reductions in unit production costs related to transportation, the urban environment, and governmental encouragement to suppliers of new materials clearly played a larger role in fostering growth and in the thinking of most entrepreneurs than did economies of scale or organization within the plant."[31]

Even after the Civil War the industrial economy was characterized by a considerable diversity. Manufacturing was carried on in large factories that might or might not use power-driven equipment, in sweatshops, in traditional artisanal shops, and by outworkers in their homes. Similarly, the organization of production ranged from what Gordon, Edwards, and Reich call "simple control," in which the capitalist himself organized the details of the production process, to varieties of craft production in which responsibility continued to depend primarily upon the expertise of skilled workers.

[30] David Montgomery, *Beyond Equality: Labor and the Radical Republicans, 1862–1872* (New York: Vintage, 1967), p. 3.
[31] Ibid., p. 6.

What this meant was that although the economic and social context of manufacture had been transformed into a highly competitive, expansionary system operating in a truly national market, the actual social organization of production had remained remarkably unchanged. Until the late nineteenth century, "simple" control was concentrated primarily in those industries, such as textiles, that had lacked strong craft organization prior to industrialization. In most other industries, production, or at least that core of production not amenable to simplification, continued to be organized by craft workers whose expertise allowed them to monopolize control over the labor process, a control that did not begin to be challenged seriously by capitalists until the 1870s. Because the production process evaded any fundamental reorganization in so many cases, the actual scale of production tended to remain small even in quite large enterprises, which were often composed of "the agglomerated operations of small shops rather than integrated production using subdivided tasks."[32]

This first change intensified the pace of production and subjected relations between owners and workers to the increased pressures of the market, but did not generally challenge the place of the skilled craftsman as the critical figure in production. Proprietorship was no longer a realistic aspiration for most skilled workers. But the ideal of independence that had been expressed in the impetus to proprietorship was replaced by a new understanding. The independent, fully adult artisan was now defined not by his control over property and his status as a self-employed person, but rather in his possession of skill. The power and thus the manly independence of skilled workers now resided in the considerable autonomy they retained over their work and in their awareness of the essential role they played in organizing production and controlling the details of the labor process.

[32] Gordon et al., *Segmented Work*, p. 86.

In contrast, the second type of change typically involved a shift from some version of craft production toward a system characterized by management control, an advanced division of labor, and the de-skilling of craft workers. Although different sectors of manufacture underwent these changes at different times, not all at once, it seems to be the case that in most industries, with the major exception of textiles, the second kind of change, the actual reorganization of production, was not successfully instituted or even attempted until the last third of the century.

It was not a simple or an easy task for employers to assert their control over the production process. The power of skilled workers was based on both a monopoly over technical knowledge and well-entrenched social institutions of mutuality and self-defense. As David Montgomery has pointed out, the bourgeois initiative of the late nineteenth century necessarily involved new ways of dealing with workers' organization as well as "profound structural changes in the society itself." The former, involving "a more systematic resistance to strikes, through employers' associations, court orders, private detective agencies, state militia, expanded use of lock-outs, and massive discharge of defeated strikers," coupled with the equally massive and militant resistance of workers to them, was responsible for an unprecedented period of labor unrest, beginning in the late 1870s and culminating, most authorities agree, in a decisive defeat for labor by the late 1890s.[33]

This setback was accompanied by structural changes that included a centralization of ownership under the sponsorship of finance capital, more sophisticated attempts by business to make use of the regulatory powers of government, and changes in the composition of the working-class through the incorporation of Southern and Eastern European immigrants into the labor force. These changes helped

[33] David Montgomery, "Labor and the Republic in Industrial America: 1860–1920," *Le Mouvement Social*, no. 111 (April–June, 1980): pp. 208–9.

to alter the balance of power between capitalists and workers and facilitated the more fundamental and successful attack on the social organization of craft labor that was occurring in many industries in the 1890s and early 1900s. This attack produced a fundamental change in the role of the artisan. Skilled workers continued to maintain significant material advantages over the unskilled but their monopoly of knowledge and thus their power was diminished. The artisan lost his practical and symbolic centrality in the productive process.

The nineteenth century can be seen, then, as one of uneven but unrelenting erosion of the economic and social bases of craft production, culminating in the large-scale offensive of the final decades. For those embedded within the changing institutions of craft production, a range of responses were possible, responses that drew directly upon common artisanal traditions even as they expressed highly divergent appraisals of what was happening. This was the case, as Sean Wilentz has emphasized, because of craft production's dual character—its tenuous reconciliation of values and practices that were always potentially at odds with one another. The artisanal workshop of the pre-capitalist and early capitalist era combined egalitarianism with deference and hierarchy; it rested on a practical and moral collectivism while it simultaneously idealized the individual advancement of the successful master-proprietor. As the institutional structure of craft production was dismantled, the synthesis broke down. Both masters and journeymen, employers and wage earners continued to interpret these changes in terms of the fraternal values of the artisanal workshop. Both continued especially to assert the mutuality of interest between workers and owners and the corporate identity of the trade. But this involved increasingly divergent interpretations of what this common interest meant in practice.

Wilentz argues that the first fifty years of the nineteenth century was the period that saw "the transformation of the rituals of mutuality into declarations of class."[34] Positions which emerged in the struggles of the 1820s would be central to American political discourse in the post–Civil War period. In their collective actions, antebellum wage workers struggled to achieve a "just" wage and to maintain the integrity of the institutions of craft production, especially apprenticeship. In the post-Civil War period, workers' continued opposition took two forms: the militancy of the shop floor, and the more politicized opposition to the "wages system" that found its most significant expression in the Knights of Labor. In each period workers emphasized mutuality, the corporatist aspects of the fraternal culture of the workshop, and rejected the idea that the market should be the sole arbiter of industrial production and individual well-being.

Masters, on the other hand, emphasized those elements in the artisanal synthesis that had stressed proprietorship and individual advancement. By the 1830s, masters in New York had articulated a defense of capitalist growth and wage labor which asserted that in the republican American society, there was a fundamental harmony of interest between employers and workers. Their claim was founded on a view of the United States as a classless society, by which they meant a society in which individual mobility was unhindered by the existence of a legally established aristocracy. In such a society all industrious men could better themselves, and economic development was to the advantage of all. Often referred to as the "free-labor" ideology, this mutuality of interest between employers and wage earners was based on the "reciprocity and essential fairness of the wage, the promise of social mobility and independent competence for all industrious men, a model of private charity and benevolence, a nearly religious devotion to the market as an economic arbiter." In this view, "industrialization, seen as an accretion of piecemeal improvements by independent men,

[34] Wilentz, "Festivals," p. 56.

CHAPTER FIVE

augured no social dislocations, no disruption of the fraternal links between masters and men."³⁵

Two points should be made about this republican free-labor ideology. First, some version of it was espoused by many workers as well as by employers.³⁶ Many of them adhered to it in the sphere of electoral politics even as their militant actions on the shop floor seemed at times to deny its logic.³⁷ Free-labor politics was just as much a product of the fractured synthesis of artisanal production as was the more class-based critique of capitalist development that emerged parallel to it. This continuity was probably the source of much of its appeal to workers whose experience was still framed by the traditions and institutions of craft labor.

Second, true to their craft origins, both free-labor republicanism and working-class solidarity implied and were partially organized around conceptions of manhood and brotherhood. In the first instance, what we might call an individualistic fraternalism drew selectively upon artisanal traditions to emphasize self-advancement and social mobility. In this view, the cultivation of the " 'manly virtues' counted for more than financial differences between men"; thus, it "applauded the common bond held to exist between employer and worker." This was the version of fraternalism that drew the young Eugene V. Debs to the Brotherhood of Locomotive Firemen, a fraternalism that encouraged benevolence, sobriety, and industry as the key to individual success and the basis of "the high moral position of manliness."³⁸

In contrast to this was the more collective concept of manliness found in the shop-floor practice of the most organized craft workers. It was not just that skilled craft labor, with its

³⁵ Wilentz, *Chants*, pp. 285, 284.
³⁶ Laurie, *Working People*, pp. 132–33, 142; Nick Salvatore, *Eugene V. Debs: Citizen and Socialist* (Urbana, Ill: University of Illinois Press, 1982).
³⁷ Montgomery, *Beyond Equality*; see especially chapters 5, 7, and 8 for an account of tensions between workplace and electoral activism.
³⁸ Salvatore, *Debs*, pp. 23–24.

170

special prerogatives and freedoms, was a kind of work re-served for men and uniquely their own. Beyond this, the qualities of manliness, "with all its connotations of dignity, respectability, defiant egalitarianism, and patriarchal male supremacy," were seen as essential to the defense of craft prerogatives.

As David Montgomery has argued, the technological control over the labor process possessed by skilled workers had to be collectively maintained and defended. "Technical knowledge was embedded in a mutualistic ethical code, also acquired on the job, and together these attributes provided skilled workers with considerable autonomy at their work and power of resistance to the wishes of their employers."[39] This ethical code relied, in large part, upon a concept of manly conduct toward one's employer and fellow workers. It involved the bold refusal to accept demeaning treatment at the hands of the boss or foreman and the equivalently ve-hement refusal to get ahead at the expense of fellow workers. Collective restriction of output was the regularized expres-sion of this ethic. "A quiver full of epithets awaited" those who violated it: " 'hog,' 'hogger in,' 'leader,' 'rooter,' 'chaser,' 'rucker,' 'runner,' 'swift,' 'boss's pet' to mention some politer versions." "On the other hand, those who held fast to the carefully measured stint, despite the curses of their employers and the lure of higher earnings, depicted themselves as sober and trustworthy masters of their trades ... Rationally restricted output ... reflected 'unselfish brotherhood,' personal dignity, and 'cultivation of the mind.' "[40] Once again it is important to recognize that both conceptions of manliness and brotherhood, the individual-istic and the collective, were grounded in the experience of an earlier form of craft production, in which fraternal bonds between masters and men were not at odds with the collec-

---

[39] David Montgomery, "Workers' Control of Machine Production in the Nineteenth Century," in Montgomery, *Workers' Control in America* (Cambridge: Cambridge University Press, 1979), pp. 13, 14.

[40] Ibid., p. 13.

tive preservation of craft institutions. Differences in the meaning of manhood were thus part of a larger struggle over the meaning of the artisanal heritage.

SOCIAL FRATERNALISM:
PSEUDO-RECONSTITUTION OF THE
ARTISANAL WORLD

The ritual and relations of mutuality between employers and workers could not easily be maintained within the capitalist workplace of the postwar period, despite the wishes of either masters or men. But this did not necessarily lead to "declarations of class." Instead, the traditional mutuality of the workplace could be recreated outside the sphere of production, in a social organization such as the fraternal order. Social fraternalism reproduced many of the features of the artisanal culture from which it had emerged, but it abstracted them from their origins in the relations of production and in the community of artisanal workers, presenting them as the basis for a larger social solidarity.

As Ann Swidler has argued, "cultural products . . . derive their power not from their ability to express one consistent sensibility or set of meanings, but from their ability to fuse together apparently irreconcilable elements of social life."[41] In the nineteenth century, the Masonic model of fraternalism was such a product. With its origins in the social and cultural practices of the artisanal workplace, Freemasonry was symbolically organized around the figure of the craftsman. Because craft production retained its economic centrality for so much of the century, the skilled craftsman remained a credible and resonant figure, both as an economic actor and as a symbol of republican manhood.

But if the world of the craftsman was politically and cul-

<hr>

[41] Ann Swidler, "Interpretive Versus Explanatory Approaches to the Sociology of Culture," paper presented at the 74th Annual Meeting of the American Sociological Association, Boston, Mass., August, 1979, p. 16.

turally legitimated, even sanctified, it was increasingly subject to attack from two different sources. First, the process of capitalist industrial development destroyed craft skills, practices, and social relations of production. Second, the fraternal relations of the male social world were not only eroded by this process, but explicitly assaulted by the attack on drinking. As the social system of craft production became increasingly less able to reconcile the tensions precipitated by these challenges to its integrity, social fraternalism, with its affirmation of the artisanal values of corporatism, ritual, masculinity, and proprietorship, became ever more popular as an alternative. It attempted to reestablish in a social organization the precarious equilibrium of mutuality and proprietorship, corporatism and individuality, that had been banished from the workplace. It allowed both workers and employers to recreate mutualistic relationships between subordinates and superiors in an environment removed from the practical conflicts of everyday work life.

In denying the significance of class difference and rejecting a collective identity based upon workplace solidarity, social fraternalism inevitably emphasized other grounds of unity, especially masculinity. In its emphasis on male identity, social fraternalism was analogous to the cult of domesticity as an ideology of femininity. Each represented a response to economic change; each implied a model of social relations organized around gender. But fraternalism was an alternative to domesticity, one that worked to preserve rather than deny the primacy of masculine social organization.

Domesticity was an ideology of femininity that emphasized woman's role as nurturer and as moral exemplar. As a cultural product of the nineteenth century, it has been convincingly interpreted by Nancy Cott as a response to the transformation of economic life. To the competitive, impersonal, and amoral world of the market economy, domesticity opposed the alternative of the home, with woman as its spiritual and emotional center. In this view, the world of business appeared as a sphere of life in which "every principle of justice and honor, and even the dictates of common honesty [are] disregarded," a place where "the general good [is] sacrificed to the advancement of personal interest." Men, in their role as provider, had to exist and function in that world, but in their hours of leisure they could retreat to the home, that "oasis in the desert" where man "seeks a refuge from the vexations and embarrassments of business, an enchanting repose from exertion, a relaxation from care by the interchange of affection: where some of his finest sympathies, tastes, and moral and religious feelings are formed and nourished; —where is the treasury of pure disinterested love, such as is seldom found in the busy walks of a selfish and calculating world."[42] In "constituting the home as a redemptive counterpart to the market economy," and asserting the necessity of such a refuge, domesticity presented a powerful, if implicit, critique of capitalist development. But in the end, Cott has argued, it acted as a force for/and of accommodation; it "undercut opposition to exploitative pecuniary standards in the work world, by upholding a 'separate sphere' of comfort and compensation."[43]

In defining a new feminine role, domesticity offered both costs and benefits to women and men. It assumed that men would compensate themselves for the loss of a more humane work experience by making the home the emotional center of their lives. This solution implied the demise of a sex-segregated social life that many men were loath to give up.

Fraternalism provided an answer to this dilemma: a type of relationship that sought social collective and moral ends within the context of traditional masculine organization. Fraternalism recognized that capitalist development involved an attack upon a historically specific version of masculine identity as well as an alteration in class relations and

[42] Nancy Cott, *The Bonds of Womanhood: "Woman's Sphere" in New England, 1780–1835* (New Haven, Conn.: Yale University Press, 1977), pp. 64–65.
[43] Ibid., p. 70.

a more competitive, depersonalized work life. Much of the fraternal order's appeal was located in its defense of this identity.

Like domesticity, fraternalism implied both critique and accommodation. It too accepted the necessity for a sphere of life in which responsibility for others would supersede the pursuit of individual self-interest. It too recognized that "the impersonal world of money-making lacked institutions to effect moral restraint" and generate moral character.[44] And it identified some form of kin relation, in this case the creation of fictive fraternal bonds, as the most likely source of such mutually responsible relations.

In a capitalist society, the family is conceived as the one institution where market values do not reign. Thus, family becomes the central metaphor for a corporatist, anti-individualist ethos and the use of familial imagery invariably indicates a desire to constitute a community.[45] The ideology of domesticity located this community in the nuclear family itself and organized it around woman's supposedly unique capacities as wife and mother. Fraternalism took the same overarching metaphor of the family but specified a different content, based on the brotherhood of men. At the same time it drew upon the imagery of other corporate bodies, such as the guild and the chivalric order.

This in fact helps to explain the curious juxtaposition of craft and chivalric images within the fraternal movement, sometimes within the same order. William Sewell, Jr., has noted that the symbolism of French journeymen's associations was based on a variety of sources, including, but not limited to, that of the traditional masters' corporations. "But it is striking," he observes, " that they borrowed almost exclusively from other types of corporate bodies—the church,

[44] Ibid., p. 97
[45] Sewell, *Work and Revolution*, p. 256; see Mary Lowenthal Felstiner, "Family Metaphors: The Language of an Independence Revolution," *Comparative Studies in Society and History*, for a discussion of the use of kinship metaphors.

175

the Freemasons, or religious and chivalric orders—and not from such other domains as scientific discourse, legal contracts, administrative practice, or Enlightenment doctrines."[46] Similarly, the identities of nineteenth-century fraternal orders referred exclusively to corporate bodies—the kin group, the trade corporation, the order of knighthood—that is, from the pre-capitalist, noncontractual forms of association. Like domesticity, fraternalism's presentation of a compensatory and specifically nonmarket institution implied a critique of capitalist relations.

But at the same time fraternalism, like domesticity, provided a means of accommodation to the demands of capitalist development; indeed, it emerged as a perfect complement to the free-labor ideology. Its emphasis on mutual obligation and benevolence provided an essential, if ultimately inadequate, compensation for the dislocations of capitalist development. Its structure of degrees, ascended by all members, upheld the vision of a social mobility available to all industrious men who would care to take advantage of it. And its definition of the lodge as a cross-class institution that bound men together, regardless of who they were, enabled the fraternal order to legitimate the operation of the market in the workplace by denying its consequences for social life. The fraternal order claimed to define brotherhood as the liberal state defined citizenship: without regard to economic position. "There is no favored or privileged class in the Modern Woodmen Society. Every good citizen, be he laborer in the streets, or a judge, a farmer, mechanic, or capitalist, stands on a footing of exact equality in the Modern Woodmen of America."[47]

Domesticity had ratified the split between the competitive individualism of the economy and the supposed moral accountability of noneconomic life by assimilating it to a con-

[46] Sewell, *Work and Revolution*, p. 60.
[47] C.H.T. Riepen, *History of the Modern Woodmen of America, 1883–1911* (Omaha, Neb., 1911), p. 41.

cept of gender difference; men worked in the competitive world of paid labor, women acted as nurturers within the home, each doing what they were by nature best fitted for. In contrast, fraternalism assumed that men could continue to create their own sphere of mutuality in the lodge room, even if this were no longer feasible in the workplace.

In part this could be accomplished through the ritual, and the "characteristic friendship [it] imposed" as it "call[ed] all to a common level, the rich from his mansion, the poor from his cottage . . ." In part it was grounded in the commonality of a masculine identity that was as much an achievement as an inherent quality: "our society [the Ancient Order of United Workmen] considers not rank nor pedigree, but recognizes the development of manliness, which it is ever ready to commend and reward."[48]

[48] J. J. Upchurch and A. T. Dewey, *Life and Times of Father Upchurch, Written by Himself* (San Francisco, 1887), pp. 179–80.

SIX

The Rise of the Women's Auxiliary

Brethren of our mystic union—
Sisters of our social band—
Here in peaceful, pure communion,
We at FRIENDSHIP's altar stand.

Opening Ode, Lodge of the
Daughters of Rebekah

THE fraternal order, as an institution, was one component of a wider array of masculine associations in the nineteenth-century United States. Participation in games and sporting events, many of the activities surrounding party politics and electioneering, and, most centrally, public drinking—all these were activities that were collective, public, extra-familial, and restricted to men (though women might in some cases be present as onlookers).[1] Their effect was to promote solidarity among men, to make them aware of their separation from women, and thus to enforce and facilitate the exercise of masculine power. While the fraternal order was an integral part of this world of masculine institutions, it played a special role because of the fact that explicit organization around the concept of the male bond is a defining character-

[1] John Mack Faragher, *Women and Men on the Overland Trail* (New Haven, Conn.: Yale University Press, 1979); W. J. Rorabaugh, *The Alcoholic Republic* (Oxford: Oxford University Press, 1979); pp. 11–13, 19–20; Jon M. Kingsdale, "The 'Poor Man's Club': Social Functions of the Urban Working-Class Saloon," in *The American Man*, ed. Elizabeth H. Pleck and Joseph H. Pleck, (Englewood Cliffs, N.J.: Prentice-Hall, 1980), pp. 255–84; Roy Rosenzweig, *Eight Hours for What We Will: Work and Leisure in an Industrial City 1870–1920* (Cambridge: Cambridge University Press, 1983), pp. 58–63.

istic of fraternal organization. With their emphasis on ritual testing, their hierarchical structures, and their frank identification of themselves as all-male organizations, nineteenth-century fraternal orders rendered explicit many of the assumptions and values of the wider masculine world.

As the nineteenth century progressed, the inviolability of this world seemed increasingly under attack. Within the home, the cult of domesticity seemed to sanction a degree of feminine authority. In the public sphere, suffragists openly challenged the masculine monopoly of political power, while larger numbers of women entered public life in less challenging ways, via higher education and participation in social reform movements.

For the most part, nineteenth-century women justified their activities by portraying them as an expansion, rather than a rejection, of woman's role as wife and mother. But despite their theoretical restriction to an expanded women's sphere, such institutions often did impinge upon either male prerogatives or the integrity of male power bases. The case of the temperance movement illustrates this point. When the Women's Christian Temperance Union attacked men's right to drink, they were attacking an activity that was an important symbol of male privilege and difference and a social institution, the tavern, that was one of the central sites of male camaraderie.[2] The tremendous popularity of fraternal orders in the late nineteenth century was one consequence of such attacks upon a traditional masculine culture. Fraternal orders not only offered an alternative social space for the expression of male solidarity, but dignified and idealized it by means of rituals that excluded women and celebrated the creation of specifically male social bonds.

If their emphasis on masculine identity made fraternalism appealing to many men, it also put the movement at odds

[2] Ruth Bordin, *Woman and Temperance: The Quest for Power and Liberty, 1873–1900* (Philadelphia: Temple University Press, 1981), pp. 7–9; Kingsdale, "Poor Man's Club"; Rosenzweig, *Eight Hours*.

with some of the century's strongest social currents. In particular, the assumptions implicit in the Masonic model placed fraternalism in conflict with changing notions of womanly capacities and manly prerogatives and provoked challenges to the legitimacy of secret societies. At first, the fraternal response consisted of attempts to incorporate women symbolically into the fraternal system while leaving its masculine organizational character intact. But in the late nineteenth century, as the participation of women in organized public activities became common, fraternal orders were forced to accommodate to demands by women for active participation. The male orders had to consider whether these demands could be recognized without jeopardizing their masculine character, while the women's auxiliaries strove to reconcile their conflicting desires for autonomy and masculine recognition.

FREEMASONRY AND MASCULINE ENLIGHTENMENT

American fraternal orders were distinguished from other voluntary associations by their character as quasi-Masonic brotherhoods. Organizations like the Odd Fellows, the Knights of Pythias, the Modern Woodmen of America, and the Ancient Order of United Workmen frankly recognized a kinship to one another that rested in their common use of forms and imagery derived from Freemasonry. Chief among these was the initiation ritual.

Following the Masons, all of the orders working within this tradition had as their central ritual theme the rite of initiation, in which the candidate, by means of a symbolic ordeal of terror or humiliation, proved himself worthy of admission to membership. In the paradigmatic "Making of a Master Mason," for example, the initiate assumes the role of Hiram Abif, in Masonic legend the heroic architect and grand master mason of King Solomon's Temple who was slain by jealous apprentices for refusing to reveal the secrets of the craft. The initiation is a reenactment of this drama:

the candidate is blindfolded, the secrets are demanded from him, and when he resists answering, his opponents pretend to attack and then to murder him. Only by standing up to this trial could he be reborn to his new status of Master Mason.[3]

Initiation was not, however, a one-time event in the life-history of a fraternal brother. Orders typically organized their membership into ranks or degrees, which were ascended one by one. All Masons were expected to be initiated into the three degrees of Entered Apprentice, Fellowcraft, and Master Mason, titles whose antecedents in the hierarchies of European craft organizations are clear, just as all Odd Fellows were expected to receive the four degrees of White, Pink, Blue, and Scarlet. But Odd Fellows who wished to could receive three optional higher ranks, the Patriarchal, Golden Rule, and Royal Purple, known collectively as the patriarchal degrees, while ambitious Master Masons could aspire to a total of ten additional degrees within the American Rite or thirty within the elaborate Scottish Rite.[4]

Thus a key feature of Masonic and quasi-Masonic fraternalism was its interposition of numerous layers of hierarchy into relations among members. Fraternal ritual articulated themes that are closely identified with the constitution of masculine social order: brotherhood/manhood as an achieved identity, society as a hierarchically organized structure of subordination and deference. To these more general characteristics were added the historically specific gender conceptions of Freemasonry as it emerged in the eighteenth century.

Freemasonry originated in Britain in the seventeenth century and spread throughout Europe and the British Empire

---

[3] James Dewar, *The Unlocked Secret: Freemasonry Examined* (London: William Kimber and Company, 1966), pp. 98–100.

[4] Albert C. Stevens, *The Cyclopaedia of Fraternities* (New York: E. B. Treat and Company, 1907; Detroit: Gale Research Company, 1966), pp. 254–55; 40–45.

during the eighteenth. Its deistic imagery, its religious tolerance and secularism, and its rhetorical emphasis on reason and equality all mark it as a product of the Enlightenment. So, too, does its treatment of gender.

The male-only character of the Masonic lodge is clearly related to its descent from earlier craft institutions. But the exclusion of women from guilds admitted of practical exceptions, while in Masonry it did not. Here it may be relevant that the Grand Lodge of England, the body that played the central role in defining the character of official Masonry, was a social and political project of the mechanical philosophers.[5]

This is significant because, as Evelyn Fox Keller has argued, the mechanists, in contrast to their rivals the alchemists, sought what they self-consciously termed a masculine science, one that would render nature subservient to human, or more accurately, to masculine purpose. Whereas the alchemists had proposed science as an enterprise involving the intermingling of masculine and feminine principles—of rationality and intuition, of spirit and matter—on terms of metaphorical equality, the mechanical philosophers, in their concern to dominate nature, enjoined a strict separation between the two principles and tried to ensure that the masculine activity of science not be contaminated with the feminine qualities of emotionalism, disorder, and irrationality.[6] The mechanical philosophers' view of science as a masculine enterprise and their concern for a more rigid demarcation between masculine and feminine may explain the zeal with which Masonic ritual and practice enforced its exclusion of

[5] More than one-fourth of the Masons affiliated with the early Grand Lodge were also members of the Royal Society, the institutional center of mechanical philosophy. Jean-Theosphile Desaguliers, the Grand Lodge's influential early leader, was also a leader of the Royal Society and a prominent spokesman for popular Newtonianism. Margaret C. Jacob, *The Radical Enlightenment: Pantheists, Freemasons, and Republicans* (London: Allen and Unwin, 1981), pp. 110–12.

[6] Evelyn Fox Keller, *Reflections on Gender and Science* (New Haven, Conn.: Yale University Press, 1985), pp. 53–54, 60–61.

women. Indeed, the 1738 *Constitution of the Free-Masons* barred not only women but eunuchs, which clearly indicates a concern about the blurring of gender distinctions and may even imply a reference to the alchemists' use of the hermaphrodite as the symbol for a good science.

The Masonic exclusion of women was consistent with the more general approach of the Enlightenment, which did not in most cases extend its critique of authority to arrangements between the sexes. Indeed, as Nancy Cott points out, Enlightenment thought had the effect of intensifying sex-role stereotypes in its attempt to systematize and rationalize them. "The placement of new authority in Nature and Reason engendered a new kind of pseudo-scientific cataloguing of differences between the sexes. Rather than alter their beliefs in the subordination of women, 'enlightened' thinkers altered, refined (even amplified) their reasons for it, discovering 'natural' and 'rational' explanations in place of solely God-given ones." Thus, much of the Enlightenment's evaluation of women revealed clear continuities with earlier traditions, but clothed them in the guise of natural and immutable law, at a time when other hierarchical arrangements were beginning to be understood as social in origin.[7]

Such views are revealed in the rites of the Lodge of Adoption, the eighteenth-century version of a Masonic initiation for women, and in *The Magic Flute*, Mozart's classic opera of Freemasonry. In both cases women appear as impulsive, irrational, excessively emotional, and given to idle and uncontrollable chatter. The Lodge of Adoption based its ritual on the need to overcome so-called feminine vices; in the sec-

[7] Maurice Block and Jean H. Block, "Women and the Dialectics of Nature in Eighteenth Century French Thought," in Carol P. MacCormack and Marilyn Strathern, eds., *Nature, Culture and Gender* (Cambridge: Cambridge University Press, 1980); Abby R. Kleinbaum, "Women in the Age of Light," in Renate Bridenthal and Claudia Koonz, eds., *Becoming Visible: Women in European History* (Boston: Houghton Mifflin, 1977); Nancy Cott, *The Bonds of Womanhood: 'Women's Sphere' in New England, 1780–1835* (New Haven, Conn.: Yale University Press, 1977), p. 161.

ond degree, for example, the candidate is warned against the perils of garrulity by having her mouth symbolically padlocked and then plastered shut with the Masonic trowel. (The traditional Masonic justification for the exclusion of women was their supposed inability to keep a secret.) The adoption ritual also made frequent reference to the Biblical theme of the temptation in the Garden of Eden and so emphasized both the covetousness and the weakness of woman as personified in Eve.[8] *The Magic Flute* presents the figure of the Queen of Night, who represents the impulsiveness, the hostility, the arrogant wish to rule that characterize the woman "who does not have a man to hold her within limits." The opera also emphasizes the garrulity of women, "the repeated tittle-tattle of women, made up of lies," to which is contrasted "the resolute spirit" of "a man who thinks before he speaks."[9]

But Freemasonry went beyond a mere cataloging of sex-linked traits and the articulation of a particular view of masculine and feminine capacities. For it not only expressed the importance of rationality and enlightenment, it offered the means by which they could be realized, through participation in the Masonic brotherhood and initiation into its secrets, a participation and a revelation from which women were excluded. Thus, it was implied, the cultivation of these key Enlightenment virtues through social means was not a possibility even available to women, in the way that the Christian virtues of piety, spirituality, and good works have traditionally been, through the institutional medium of the Church.

Eighteenth-century Freemasonry was occasionally criticized for its exclusion of women, and Masonic literature tried to deal with such objections by writing approvingly of

[8] Jacques Chailley, *The Magic Flute, Masonic Opera: An Interpretation of the Libretto and the Music*, trans. Herbert Weinstock (New York: Alfred A. Knopf, 1971), p. 111.

[9] Rose Coser, "The Principle of Patriarchy: The Case of the Magic Flute," *Signs* 4 (Winter, 1978): pp. 337–48.

free choice in marriage and pointing to the superiority of Masons as husbands.[10] In France, the Lodges of Adoption provided for a few women the experience of a quasi-Masonic initiation, while accepting the basic definitions of masculinity and femininity that Freemasonry upheld. It was these definitions, and their implications for the attainment of morality and enlightenment, that placed Freemasonry in clear opposition to the alternative set of ideals that it encountered in nineteenth-century American society.

NINETEENTH-CENTURY FREEMASONRY AND THE CULT OF DOMESTICITY

The new conception of womanhood that emerged in the late eighteenth- and early nineteenth-century United States portrayed woman as uniquely virtuous and compassionate. It was an ideology that assigned to women a special responsibility for moral education and spiritual influence through the agency of the family and woman's role within the family as wife and mother. In its identification of women as the moral custodians of society, the doctrine of the separate spheres gave a new content to the sexual division of labor and valorized women's contributions to the social enterprise.

In opposition to this, Freemasonry negated the role of the family and claimed that men could attain morality through participation in an all-male brotherhood. Its simultaneous exclusion of women and portrayal of men as morally self-sufficient could not help being called into question at a time when so many Americans, both men and women, believed that virtue could be secured only by the agency of woman.[11]

This conflict between the view of women as "custodians of social morality" and the Masonic lodges' claim to be "pur-

[10] Jacob, *Radical Enlightenment*, p. 207.
[11] David Brion Davis, "Some Themes of Counter-Subversion: An Analysis of Anti-Masonic, Anti-Catholic, and Anti-Mormon Literature," *Mississippi Valley Historical Review* 27 (September, 1960): p. 219.

CHAPTER SIX

veyors of moral education" most certainly represents one of
the major sources of the anti-Masonic movement that swept
the Northeast during the 1820s, 1830s, and 1840s. Anti-
Masonic propaganda often argued

> that any deviation from the romantic ideal of marriage
> and respect for women's sensibility, modesty and sanc-
> tity, which were seen as balancing forces to the hard
> necessities of the business world, undermined the very
> foundations of society. Thus the Masons were repeat-
> edly condemned for being cut off from the ennobling
> influence of women; it was said that their rites were de-
> vised to harden the heart, stultify the conscience, and to
> eradicate every degree of moral sensibility.[12]

Moreover, it is likely that much of this opposition came
from women themselves. The doctrine of woman's sphere
was not simply a masculine ideology imposed on passive
women to their complete detriment. American women used
it to build not only their own private networks of sisterhood
but also the beginnings of a sphere of public competence,
through the creation of religious societies and moral reform
organizations.[13] The doctrine of separate spheres may have
implied a high degree of separation between men and
women, which frequently rendered their personal relations
with each other distant and problematic, but it was nonetheless a theory of complementarity and taken seriously as such.
Women's antipathy to Freemasonry was therefore rooted
not simply in resentment against their exclusion, but in the
Masonic claim to inculcate morality without feminine intervention. It challenged them in the central area reserved for

[12] Dorothy Ann Lipson, *Freemasonry in Federal Connecticut* (Princeton,
N.J.: Princeton University Press, 1977), p. 188; Davis, "Counter-Subver-
sion," p. 219.
[13] Mary Ryan, "The Power of Women's Networks: A Case Study of Female
Moral Reform in Antebellum America," *Feminist Studies* 5:1 (1979): pp. 66–85;
Cott, *Bonds of Womanhood*; Barbara Leslie Epstein, *The Politics of Domesticity:
Women, Evangelism, and Temperance in Nineteenth-Century America* (Middle-
town, Conn.: Wesleyan University Press, 1981).

them by the canons of domesticity, an area that they occupied in ever more assertive ways as the century progressed. In opposition to the claims of an evangelical religion increasingly associated with women, Freemasonry offered men an institution that provided not only solidarity but an explicit defense of male secularism and moral autonomy. Because of the tensions that inhered in the claims of such conflicting ideologies, a generalized social anti-Masonry continued to exist well after anti-Masonry as a political movement had collapsed; it seems likely that women's antagonism was especially important in fueling this social reaction.[14]

Masons had of course tried to deflect this opposition and to elicit tolerance, if not approval, from women. Masonic writings emphasized the order's respect for the family, its protection of defenseless women, and its aid to widows and orphans of Masons. Masons also tried to combine a defense of their exclusionary position with an acknowledgment of women's moral claims by arguing that Masonic ritual was in fact unnecessary for them "because of their superior virtue."[15] This marked an alteration of earlier Masonic views that women, because of their infirm nature, required masculine guidance to help them attain morality. Yet it missed the mark because while it paid homage to the virtue inherent in women as individuals, it failed to acknowledge men's spiritual dependence on them. The boldest attempts to deal with this issue, to defuse feminine opposition to secret fraternalism and to accommodate secret fraternalism to the claims of domesticity, were the proposals, emerging in both the Masons and the Odd Fellows, to establish honorary degrees for women.

HONORARY DEGREES FOR WOMEN:
THE FIRST COMPROMISE

The first fraternal rituals for American women were the Odd Fellows' Rebekah degree and the Masonic degrees of

[14] Lipson, *Freemasonry*, pp. 187–200, 329–38.
[15] Ibid., p. 193.

the Eastern Star, both devised in the early 1850s. This was the period when fraternalism was beginning to recover from the destructive effects of the anti-Masonic movement, which had prompted the dissolution of most Masonic lodges and had tended to discredit other orders as well. That experience necessarily provoked reflection about what could be done to avoid future attacks and to deal with remaining antagonisms. It is clear from the fraternal literature that antipathy among women was a major issue. A concern to defuse feminine antagonism is revealed in the sentimental Masonic fiction of Robert Morris, creator of the Eastern Star, and in the arguments of Schuyler Colfax, the chief supporter of the Rebekah degree within the Odd Fellows.[16]

The first line of attack was an attempt to demonstrate that fraternalism was beneficial to women, despite their exclusion from it. Some of Morris's stories deal with women, especially widows, who receive Masonic aid when their personal connection to Masonry is recognized. In the story of "The Tongue Too Silent," a widow dies for want of the help she would have received "had she exhibited any little token of a Masonic character that would barely have caught the eye without shocking the mind with a brazen effrontery."[17] Morris was concerned that the Masons lacked a way for their female relatives to identify themselves and even more concerned that women, in their indifference to, or distaste for, Masonry, did not realize the support that could be theirs in time of need. Similar concerns were voiced in the Independent Order of Odd Fellows, which in 1846 granted its local lodges the right to issue official identification cards to

[16] In addition to participating in the Odd Fellows, Schuylor Colfax of Indiana was a nationally prominent Republican who served as speaker of the House of Representatives, 1863–1869, and vice-president of the United States 1869–1873, under Ulysses S. Grant. Allen Johnson and Dumas Malone, eds., *Dictionary of American Biography* (New York: Charles Scribner's Sons, 1958), p. 297.

[17] Robert Morris, *Lights and Shadows of Freemasonry* (Louisville, Ky.: J. F. Brennan, 1852), p. 226. See also "The Mason's Widow" in the same volume.

the wives and widows of members.[18] This was surely an attempt to make good on the order's rhetoric of family devotion and to demonstrate to women its commitment to their well-being. It was apparently not sufficient, for by 1850 there were calls for something "more pleasant and more honorary."[19]

For the claim that fraternalism was beneficial to women to be convincing, it had to be inserted into a portrayal of the masculine and feminine that was more acceptable to nineteenth-century sensibilities. Accordingly, Robert Morris, in his fictionalized Masonic propaganda, portrays the exclusion of women as a logical outgrowth of the doctrine of the separate spheres. He acknowledges the images of Victorian true womanhood, alluding to the joys of woman's "light footsteps," "soft voice," and "the sunshine of her presence," but it is a presence that must remain "outside the door." "Her sphere is in the heavens, ours within the lodge, and though her light and warmth may reach us, her form cannot enter."

This exclusion was justified through an appeal to domesticity and to a sexual division of labor that called for men, as providers, to confront life's sordid realities while women remained at home protected from them. Masonry was an institution that had "originated among *men*—was designed to protect laboring *men* in their rights,—to add the lightness of superior knowledge to the inherent hardships of their profession,—to enable *men* to overcome the peculiar temptations to which in their exposed position they were peculiarly liable.

[18] Theodore A. Ross, *Odd Fellowship: Its History and Manual* (New York: The M. W. Hazen Company, 1888), p. 64. Theodore Ross was a longtime Grand Secretary of the national organization. It should be noted that manuals like this were official or semi-official publications, intended for the use of members rather than for a general readership.

[19] Independent Order of Odd Fellows, Sovereign Grand Lodge, *Journal of Proceedings of the Right Worthy Grand Lodge of the United States from Its Formation in February, 1821*, vol. 2 (Baltimore, Md.: 1884), p. 1618.

"Thus the answer must be this, Why is not Masonry open to the female sex? because females are not *men*." Thus the practice of Masonry was assimilated to the nineteenth-century view of man as sole provider and woman as the beneficiary, whose contribution was spiritual rather than material. "For you shall the golden harvest of Masonry be gathered, although we may not demand your presence in the tiresome sowing or in the hot reaping."[20]

The fate that might befall women who dared to question this arrangement is suggested in Morris's story, "Catherine Williams: or, Husband and Wife." The haughty and beautiful heiress Catherine refuses to marry her fiancé Herbert Crosswell when she learns he is a Mason. "Never," she declared, "will I marry a man whose secrets I cannot share. When God pronounced concerning man and wife, these twain shall be one flesh, he meant that their knowledge and aims, as well as their enjoyments and sorrows, should be mutual . . . there can be no permanent affection where there is concealment." Her gentler and more womanly cousin Martha disagrees: "do you expect that your husband will share with you all his secrets? all that is connected with his business affairs, with his worldly plans, his combinations, his dealings with men, often running into altercations, harsh and perhaps unfeminine?"[21] A woman exposed to these masculine secrets risks the loss of her innocence, her purity, her femininity. But Catherine persists in her rejection of the noble Herbert, with the end result that Martha gets Herbert while Catherine marries a fortune-hunter who turns out to have a few non-Masonic secrets—he is a spendthrift, a thief, and a bigamist. A woman who attempts to penetrate the wall that separates the sexes risks ruination, as she forfeits the protection it had assured her.

Morris maintains that the doctrine of separate spheres necessitates secrecy between the sexes, a secrecy of which Ma-

---

[20] Morris, *Lights and Shadows*, pp. 95, 122–23, 124.
[21] Ibid., p. 104

sonry is only one instance: "in the very constitution of the sexes, in their different spheres of action, in their different tastes, capacities, and temptations, there must be, and there is, a history for each, which the other is forbidden to know, and which nothing but an unclean curiosity ever induces the desire to know." As a result, he argues, attempts by women to be admitted to or to learn the secrets of the craft constitute an attack upon the intrinsic differences that properly divide the sexes, and "it is only those viragos who yearn for a beard, and who unsex themselves in their conventions for Woman's Rights," who attempt to violate its sanctity.[22]

Despite the vehemence of this attack, Morris apparently suspected that some greater concession would have to be made, because in the same volume in which this tirade appears, he presents his Eastern Star degrees for women. The Odd Fellows had come to similar conclusions two years earlier, when they instituted the Rebekah degree, suggesting that feminine antipathy to fraternalism extended beyond the presumably limited ranks of "viragos" yearning for beards. It was to address this opposition more effectively that Morris proposed for the Masons and the Odd Fellows actually established honorary degrees for women.

The subject of a Ladies' Degree, the Odd Fellow Schuyler Colfax stated in 1851, "may be calculated to excite a smile," but its institution would benefit the order greatly. First, it would provide an incentive for men to ascend to higher degrees, since the Ladies' Degree would be restricted to Scarlet Degree holders and their wives. Second, female degree holders could be requisitioned by the order to help in the visiting of sick members, which was one of the Odd Fellow's duties. Here Colfax's acceptance of the tenets of domesticity becomes evident, as he argues that this would be especially advantageous because of the greater abilities of women as nurses, their "kindly nursing" being much more effective than "the assiduous and constant attendance of man." This

[22] Ibid., pp. 123, 124.

was because "she was formed to minister at the couch of affliction . . . we only strive to compel the observance by laws and penalties of what in her is Instinct, the promptings of Nature, the impulse of the Heart." This argument represents not only a typically nineteenth-century portrayal of woman's special gifts but some backing off from the idea of full fraternal self-sufficiency in the performance of moral obligations. Most importantly, Colfax argues that the initiation into a Ladies' Degree will "lessen and ultimately destroy the prejudice felt against the Order, by many of the fairer sex." The past exclusion of women suggests to them that the order "exhibits no confidence, reposes no trust in them"; and this discourages men from joining the order. As a result, their symbolic admission can only increase the interest felt in the order among "that sex who wield an influence that few deny and all obey."[23]

The tenets of domesticity are similarly acknowledged in the symbolism of the ladies' degrees, a symbolism that is in distinct contrast to that of the eighteenth-century Masonic Lodges of Adoption, with their serpents, apples, and trowels making clear reference to feminine sexuality and moral infirmity. The symbols for the Degree of Rebekah were the beehive, symbolizing associated industry (to which we might add industry occurring within the enclosed domestic space of the hive, that is, the home), the moon and seven stars, representing order and the laws of nature, and the dove, implying, of course, innocence, gentleness, and purity. The five points of the Eastern Star referred to five Biblical heroines who achieved virtue in the five roles of woman's life: daughter, sister, wife, mother, and widow.[24] The point is obvious: women achieve virtue only through family roles and by means of their relationships to men. Indeed this

---

[23] Odd Fellows, *Journal of Proceedings*, pp. 1618–19.

[24] Ross, *Odd-Fellowship*, p. 476; *Order of the Eastern Star, An Instructive Manual on the Organization of Chapters of the Order with Ritual and Ceremonies* (Chicago: Ezra A. Cook, 1923).

recognition of women in terms of their family roles is a central theme of both these honorary degrees.

It should not be supposed that these degrees were intended to establish separate women's organizations. Rather, they were proposals to initiate women into honorary membership. By symbolically incorporating women into the male order, the honorary degrees were to reconcile the claims of domesticity and brotherhood. Even such a limited incorporation could only be extended to those women related to Masons or Odd Fellows. In the case of the Degree of Rebekah, in fact, it was conferred on women with their husbands. The institution of a special ritual for married couples solved a number of problems. It not only honored women, but it publicly acknowledged the central and sanctifying role of the marital bond, a bond that was now given ritual representation within Odd Fellowship. At the same time, by restricting the degree to the wives of Odd Fellows, it preserved the primacy of the order, since a connection to a male member was the necessary basis for female participation and since female participation took the form of a special ritual for women rather than initiation into masculine secrets. The Rebekah degree united women to their husbands and husbands to their wives, but at the same time it affirmed the male bond while creating no parallel bond for women. Finally it was a way of arguing, via the ritual, that Odd Fellowship was an autonomous moral institution. The Rebekah degree was an opportunity for women to "comprehend the Institution." Through it they were afforded a glimpse into its mysteries in order that they might recognize its moral character and so accept its claim upon their husbands.

Women's Auxiliaries after the Civil War

If the problem of male fraternalism in the early to mid-nineteenth century was to recognize the claims of feminine spirituality, its problem after the Civil War was to accommodate the demands for actual women's *organizations* to the requirement of continued masculine separation and primacy. These demands had their roots in two trends that characterize the period. First, male secret fraternalism achieved tremendous popularity during the last third of the century. Not only did the already-existing associations of Masons and Odd Fellows grow to massive proportions, but literally hundreds of new orders were formed, some of which, such as the Knights of Pythias, the Ancient Order of United Workmen, and the Modern Woodmen of America, became large national organizations with members numbering in the hundreds of thousands by 1900.[25]

Second, the same period saw the development of women's organizations on a national and secular basis. The years prior to the Civil War had witnessed the beginnings of women's participation in activities of a more public, formal, and collective nature. With the exception of the relatively small number of women who participated in the abolitionist and early suffrage movements, this occurred primarily through the formation of women's religious and moral reform societies, organizations that grew directly out of female religiosity and retained a sectarian and local character. Only after the Civil War do we see the emergence of national organizations that were either restricted to or dominated by a female membership and leadership. Among these were the suffrage organizations, the Women's Christian Temperance Union, and the women's club movement.[26]

The creation of fraternal women's organizations is clearly a recognizable part of this impulse toward feminine participation in public membership organizations, but one central

[25] Stevens found that more than 600 fraternal associations were established in the nineteenth-century United States, of which about 350 survived for some period. *Cyclopaedia*, p. xvi.

[26] See Bordin, *Woman and Temperance*, for an account of the Woman's Christian Temperance Union, and Karen J. Blair, *The Clubwoman as Feminist: True Womanhood Redefined, 1868–1914* (New York: Holmes and Meier, 1980), for the women's club movement.

difference must be emphasized. Almost all the other organizations being established at this time were independent associations that either barred or discouraged male participation. In distinct contrast to this, the women's orders such as the Order of the Eastern Star, the Daughters of Rebekah, and the Pythian Sisters were defined by their connection to already-existing male organizations. In what seems an almost demeaning act of subjugation, they constructed their organizational identities on their relationship to the orders that for so many years had vociferously excluded them. Looked at in this way, it is tempting to see them as representing a reactionary countertendency to the impulse toward autonomy expressed by the other women's organizations emerging at this time (and perhaps representing something similar to women's participation in the New Right today).

A look at the conditions for membership seems to confirm the male-dominated character of these organizations. To join the Order of the Eastern Star, for example, a woman had to be the wife, mother, sister, or daughter of a Master Mason.[27] Eligibility was thus determined not by her individual qualities, but by her relationship to a man. In addition, men could themselves become members of these supposed women's orders. Indeed, the Eastern Star and the Daughters of Rebekah *required* male participation, since certain offices were reserved for men. Thus an organization like the Eastern Star offered the female relatives of Masons the option of participation in a public organization, but it was a participation consistent with the structures of a male-dominated society in which women are defined and recognized only in terms of their relationships to the family. They participate in public life, if at all, as wards or dependents of men.

[27] The Daughters of Rebekah and Pythian Sisters also determined eligibility on this basis. I have selected the Eastern Star, Daughters of Rebekah, and Pythian Sisters for analysis because they were auxiliaries for the three largest male orders of the late nineteenth century.

Given this, a number of questions arise. Why did women enter into organizations conceived in these terms? Was their desire for participation a challenge to existing gender relations, which was then co-opted, or did their participation represent a self-conscious ratification of masculine authority? Did the male orders actively devise and promote the formation of such associations? What was the character of women's participation, once in them? Was the fraternal auxiliary a device for the reproduction of male dominance or a vehicle for women's advance?

Such questions are best answered by looking at the major features of the women's auxiliaries—especially the rituals and the legal structures—and at the social context surrounding their establishment and operation. What emerges from such an analysis is a process beginning with women's initiative, followed by accommodation and negotiation rather than a one-sided imposition of male power.

WOMEN'S AUXILIARIES: RITUAL

The starting point for such an analysis is the ritual, the activity that most distinguishes fraternal orders from other types of association. The performance of the rituals of opening and closing the lodge and initiating new members provided the central activity of each meeting and comprised the secret knowledge that united members in bonds of sisterhood or brotherhood. The repeated enactment of these minidramas portrayed, in vivid terms, the values deemed most worthy of emulation. Their content allows us to contrast the models of masculine and feminine conduct that the orders propounded.

The men's rituals display (although in attenuated form) the features of a classic rite of passage.[28] They begin with

---

[28] The three stages of separation, marginality, and incorporation or reincorporation were first outlined in Arnold van Gennep's *The Rites of Passage*, trans. Monika B. Vizedom and Gabrielle L. Coffee (London: Routledge and Kegan Paul, 1960).

the blindfolding of the candidate and some kind of alteration in his dress to make it more uniform and anonymous. The change in dress works to divest him of his identity and status in the outside world, while the blindfold disorients him, isolates him from social contact or cues and infuses him with a sense of vulnerability. He must overcome his fears and pass a ritual test in order to be transformed and incorporated into the fraternal union.[29]

The women's rituals lack the features of detachment, testing, and incorporation into a new and higher social category.[30] In the Eastern Star and Rebekah rituals, the candidate is neither blindfolded nor dressed differently. She is not placed in a situation of physical vulnerability or social disequilibrium; she remains who and what she is. Nor is she challenged, frightened, or threatened in any way; thus there is no need or opportunity for her to display courage in the face of danger. She is simply admitted into the organization, given the oath, and taught the lessons, signs, and passwords.

The Pythian Sisters' ritual seems initially to be an exception to this, for here the candidate is dressed in a white robe and given a visor to act as a blindfold. In addition there is an attempt to frighten her through the use of sound effects simulating thunder and lightning. Most significantly, she is subjected to a kind of challenge, as her escort deserts her, leaving her to the hostile inquiries of the lodge members, who pretend to be angered that a stranger has made her way into the lodge. The Pythian Sisters ritual is most closely

---

[29] The analysis of men's rituals is based on "The Making of a Master Mason," reprinted in Dewar *Unlocked Secret; Revised Odd-Fellowship Illustrated: The Complete Revised Ritual of the Lodge, Encampment, Patriarchs Militant and the Rebekah Degrees* (Chicago: Ezra A. Cook, 1897), p. 236; and Douglas Roberts, ed., *Ritual for Subordinate Lodges of Knights of Pythias* (New York: Dick S. Fitzgerald, 1894).

[30] Analysis of women's initiation rituals is based on "Initiation Ritual, Order of the Eastern Star," in *Order of the Eastern Star, An Instructive Manual,* cited above, pp. 60–109; "Initiation Ritual, Daughters of Rebekah," in *Revised Odd-Fellowship Illustrated,* pp. 238–55; and J. A. Hill, *Ritual of the Order of Pythian Sisters* (Green Castle, Ind.: 1889), pp. 15–28.

modeled on a masculine fraternal initiation, yet a reworking of these similar elements affords a significantly different resolution. For instead of standing up to the test on her own, the candidate is quickly rescued by the Mistress of the Temple, who volunteers to give the passwords and signs for her and in general act as her sponsor and guide. Note the difference here: the male initiate is expected to prove himself on the basis of his own courage; this is what makes him worthy to be incorporated into the brotherhood. The woman, on the other hand, is rescued and adopted into the sisterhood, dependent for her well-being on the goodwill and pity of others. As the most Excellent Chief of the Temple explains: "A stranger, alone, blind and friendless. How sad the sight! Fit representation of woman's condition when unorganized, unaided, dependent!"[31] While the man is transformed and raised up by the test, the woman remains unchanged. She is taken into the organization by virtue of her helpless state, a state that is natural to her sex. The man, moreover, proves himself several times over as he ascends the degrees of his order. For women in all three auxiliaries there is only one initiation ceremony, making the point that women do not function in the hierarchical world of the male social order. Their destiny as women is relatively fixed, and remains remote from the striving in which men must engage.

Indeed, the Rebekah ritual specifically cautions women to avoid this striving after worldly achievement. Citing the examples of biblical heroines such as Esther, Ruth, Sarah, and of course Rebecca, the ritual points to the links between their histories and "our own realization of domestic life" (which is thus accorded a trans-historical status). The lives of these women, the ritual claims, constitute

> a nobler testimony to woman, a worthier eulogy of her rank and honor than she can find in the histories of thousands of Earth's mightiest—of Elizabeth, of Cleopatra, of Catharine or Isabella. *Such* we do not cite for

[31] Hill, *Pythian Sisters*, p. 16.

your emulation and imitation. But rather the record of those whom the Bible commends—who signalized their lives, not by bloody victories on fields of carnage and of death—not by despotic sway over a nation of millions—not by the meretricious charms of beauty—but by their zeal in doing good—in vindicating the true modesty and worth of woman's natural character—in pouring the oil of consolation into the wounds of the afflicted—in whispering words of sympathy in the ears of the heart-stricken.[32]

Virtue for women is domestic virtue and the enactment of feminine roles, a statement made equally clearly, albeit with less brutal explicitness, by the Eastern Star, its five points symbolizing the five stations of woman's life—daughter, widow, wife, sister, and mother—and by the Pythian Sisters, with their principles of love, fidelity, and purity.

Accounts from late nineteenth-century sources indicate that many lodges had begun to conduct their rituals in the so-called "beatified" or "exemplified" form, which meant the elaborate acting out of each passage, each historical or biblical reference, often with appropriate costumes. This meant that women played a stronger and more efficacious role as ritual actors, instead of being the passive recipients of lectures conducted most frequently by men. Yet despite changes in their presentation the content of the rituals remained impervious to changing conceptions of womanhood. The Opening Ode of the Rebekah degree aptly summed up the typical interpretation of the differences between the men's and women's associations when it sang of "Brethren of our mystic union— / Sisters of our social band." The male ritual created a higher bond between men that then permitted women to enter into social relationship with one another, a relationship that was worthy, but ultimately secondary and dependent.

[32] *Revised Odd-Fellowship Illustrated*, pp. 250–51.

199

CHAPTER SIX

WOMEN'S STRUGGLE FOR POWER WITHIN THE AUXILIARIES

If we were to base our understanding of these organizations solely on their rituals, we would have to conclude that they were initiated by men to placate or co-opt their women relatives, to provide them with a "suitable" outlet for public participation. But that would totally miss what is most striking about the auxiliaries, their contradictory character. It would above all fail to recognize two significant factors: the depth of male opposition and the commitment to feminine advance that characterized their proponents.

Masculine opposition to the creation of women's auxiliaries was widespread, persistent, and often effective. It is important to realize that not one of the three largest orders actually initiated the creation of an auxiliary. Instead, the issue was whether such auxiliaries should be opposed, tolerated, or recognized. The opposition that arose, in almost all orders, to women's participation, even in the form of auxiliary organization, indicates real concern about the violation of these organizations' masculine character and precludes a view of auxiliaries as a recognized strategy for cooptation. The Knights of Pythias, for example, did not recognize their women's auxiliary, the Order of Pythian Sisters, as an official Pythian organization, until 1904, twenty-seven years after it was initially proposed. The Masons have never officially acknowledged the Order of the Eastern Star as Masonic in character, despite the fact that it has existed for more than one hundred years as an organization for the female relatives of Masons.[33] Even the Odd Fellows, who were the first to recognize both an honorary woman's degree and then an auxiliary, encountered significant resistance among their ranks. The early history of the Daughters of

[33] Ida M. Jayne-Weaver and Emma D. Wood, *History of the Order of Pythian Sisters* (Seattle, Wash.: Peters Publishing Company, 1925), pp. 94–95; Alvin J. Schmidt, *Fraternal Organizations* (Westport, Conn.: Greenwood Press, 1980), p. 97.

Rebekah exemplifies the kinds of issues that were typically raised in the transition from honorary degree to organization for women.

In establishing the Rebekah degree, the Odd Fellows had no idea of creating a women's organization; they simply wanted to devise an honorary title with which to defuse feminine antipathy. But by the mid-1860s, women holders of the degree had apparently concluded that it created a bond among themselves, as well as a relationship to the male order. Consequently they began to form their own lodges.[34]

When the legality of women's lodges was put to a vote, in 1864, it was defeated, and for several years the order attempted to suppress them, ruling them "irregular, unauthorized, and in contravention with the legislation of the Grand Lodge." But the meetings continued to be held, in defiance of the order, so that in 1867 the newly elected Grand Sire conceded defeat and suggested that Rebekah-degree lodges be incorporated into the order. As Theodore Ross, a later Grand Secretary comments, "The ladies were at all times in advance of the Grand Lodge, in their views of the needs and wants of the Degree, and it was owing to their persistent efforts, and not always legal ones . . . that the Grand Lodge made wider the pathway of progress."[35]

The Rebekah lodges were recognized by the Odd Fellows primarily because in practice they could not be contained. But this did not mean the creation of anything resembling an autonomous woman's organization. Permission had been granted to form local lodges, but they were headed by male officers and supervised by the all-male state Grand Lodges.

The years from 1868 to 1888 witnessed many disputes through which the powers of the Rebekah lodges and their female members were incrementally expanded in response to constant pressure. The changes enacted gave Rebekah lodges the power to select their own members and to hold

[34] Ross, *Odd-Fellowship*, p. 464.
[35] Ibid., pp. 465–66.

meetings without men present (a quorum had originally been defined as five men and five women). In 1878 women became eligible to head local lodges and preside over meetings and in 1884 were granted representation at the state, but not the national, level.[36]

Similar pressures led to changes in the authority structure of the Order of the Eastern Star. On the state level, the Grand Patron, who was necessarily a man and a Master Mason, was originally designated as executive officer, with the right to preside at meetings and appoint all committees. The role of the Grand Matron, the highest woman officer, was to assist him in his duties. But by the mid 1870s, there were demands throughout the nation for the Grand Matron to be recognized as head of the order in each state, a demand that was quickly adopted on a state-by-state basis, despite the objections of the original male leaders, Robert Morris, author of the ritual, and Robert Maccoy, its publisher and promoter.[37]

The issues that women fraternalists were struggling over, the rights they were trying to acquire, have a clear feminist significance. This is best appreciated by placing them in the context of the norms governing women's public behavior in the 1860s and 1870s. The right of women to associate with each other in secular public settings was not yet totally accepted. More controversial was the propriety of a woman presiding over meetings, at a time when it was still relatively unusual for women to speak in public.[38] The acceptability of a woman chairing meetings may, in fact, have been more difficult in the mixed-sex fraternal auxiliaries than it was in the single-sex reform and religious organizations in which

[36] Ibid., pp. 467–71.

[37] Order of the Eastern Star, State of Connecticut, *Proceedings of the Grand Chapter*, 1874 and 1875 (Bridgeport, Conn.: Farmer Office Steam Presses, 1876), pp. 13–15.

[38] Blair, *Clubwoman as Feminist*, provides a good account of the women's clubs as social settings in which women could develop the confidence to speak in public and chair meetings, pp. 66–71.

most women's participation was concentrated. Thus the seemingly trivial changes in the rules governing these organizations indicate significant reevaluations of women's capacities for self-government and public competence.

It is equally important to realize that the early leaders of the auxiliaries were themselves fully cognizant of these implications. Their participation was not motivated by a general conservatism about woman's place. Addie Barrio, for example, the outspoken Grand Matron of the Connecticut Order of the Eastern Star, justified the existence of the Eastern Star in terms of the "spirit of the age," which "had demanded an extension of woman's influence and usefulness. It had called her to stations of the greatest responsibility as author, teacher, preacher, and physician, and made her a prominent factor in all the moral, intellectual, and social activities of society." In such a period, she asked, "Shall the spirit that is moving all other institutions in woman's behalf leave Masonry untouched?"[39]

The Reverend Frank W. Evans saw the Daughters of Rebekah in similar terms, pointing to the successes of women as lawyers, physicians, professors, clergy, and proprietors and managers of "large mercantile and manufacturing establishments."

> These facts show that woman is as intellectual as man, as capable of participating in the management of benevolent institutions, like Odd Fellowship and kindred associations, as men are. The entire modern history of woman shows that she is as capable of self-government, as well qualified for business, ballots, and office as are most men . . . This is not designed to be an article on woman's suffrage, yet that topic is somewhat incidentally connected with a discussion introductory to the history of the Rebekah degree in Odd Fellowship.[40]

[39] Order of the Eastern Star, *Proceedings*, 1880, p. 29.
[40] Henry Stillson, *The History and Literature of Odd Fellowship, the Three-Link Fraternity* (Boston: Fraternity Publishing Co., 1897), p. 710.

Ida Jayne-Weaver, the first Supreme Chief and a powerful figure in the Pythian Sisters for some thirty years, was an active, committed suffragist. Under her leadership the Pythian Sisters even joined the National Council of Women, a federation of women's organizations instituted by Elizabeth Cady Stanton and Susan B. Anthony in an effort to broaden support for suffrage.[41]

It should be clear that auxiliary leaders and supporters not only conceived of their organizations as part of the century's feminine advance. They connected them quite specifically to women's growing public competence rather than to the retiring domestic virtues emphasized by the rituals. At the same time, however, they sought to strengthen their ties to the male orders, and to maintain the recognition and participation of male representatives, on whatever terms of subordination that might require.

They revealed their determination in a number of ways. First, through continued acceptance of the idea that eligibility for membership would be determined in the first instance by a familial relationship to a Mason, Odd Fellow, or Pythian. Second, in the varying strategies that were used to allay male fears of feminine encroachment.

In the Order of the Eastern Star, the Masonic connection was maintained through the continued importance of the Worthy Patron. While the Worthy Matron was the executive officer of the lodge, the Patron remained the central ritual figure, the king to her prime minister. Only he, a Master Mason, could confer the degree admitting someone to membership; the Eastern Star lodge thus derived its authority from Masonic approval and involvement. At the same time, membership was predicated upon a woman's willingness to acknowledge that the Eastern Star was not "a part of the Masonic institution" and that Masonic exclusion was legitimate. "To us are given all the advantages of the society, its

---

[41] Jayne-Weaver and Wood, *Pythian Sisters*, pp. 82–83. For more information on the National Council of Women, see Blair, *Clubwoman as Feminist*, pp. 93–94, 104.

shield of protection, its hand of relief, and its voice of sympathy. The only Masonic privilege denied to us is that of visiting the lodge. Women cannot be Masons."[42]

The Pythian Sisters, on the other hand, did not have any male officers; men were considered honorary members who could not hold office, offer resolutions, or vote. As one Sister explained in 1910, "they are allowed the same position in the Temple that they accord to us in politics: 'They may mold public sentiment, but cannot express their own opinions in the form of a vote.' "[43] Yet the Pythian Sisters so valued the participation of the Knights and the Pythian recognition it seemed to imply, that when the Supreme Lodge of the Knights prohibited its members from belonging to any other organization with the word Pythian in its title, the women's order reluctantly but immediately changed its name, to Rathbone Sisters, in order to retain their male members.[44] Obviously their commitment to the male order and to an identity based upon it was a strong one. Their actions, like those of their Eastern Star and Rebekah counterparts, were consistently directed at the double goals of greater autonomy for women and greater recognition by men, goals that did not seem to *them* to be in necessary conflict. We can only speculate about the sources of their motivation and the character of the organization that such compromises produced.

CONCLUSION

Despite the profound differences of opinion that exist as to the universality of male dominance, anthropologists gener-

[42] Order of the Eastern Star, *Ritual*, p. 95.

[43] Mattie H. Woodruff, "The Order of Pythian Sisters," in Hugh C. Webb, *A History of the Knights of Pythias and Its Branches and Auxiliaries* (Uniform Rank Co-Operative Association, 1910), p. 92.

[44] Jayne-Weaver and Wood, *Pythian Sisters*, pp. 75–77. Justus H. Rathbone was the founder of the Knights of Pythias. In 1904, when the Sisters were officially recognized as a Pythian organization, they regained their original title.

ally agree that the degree and character of same-sex association is a key variable determining the relative position of men and women. In contrast to women, men typically have access to a culturally valued set of roles and activities based upon their associations outside the family. This organized, extra-familial existence provides them with the resources of symbolic authority, access to material goods, and the empowerment that is afforded by institutionalized relations of solidarity.[45]

For women, as for men, organization is a source of power. Women are most vulnerable when they are socially isolated, lacking significant ties to other women. Involvement in well-developed domestic networks strengthens women's position, but the societies that most closely approach sexual egalitarianism seem to be those in which women possess forms of public organization that parallel those of men. Traditional Western African societies, for example, were characterized by the maintenance of a separate women's world that included not only domestic activities and relationships but also publicly sanctioned religious, political, and economic functions that women performed (and were understood to perform) for the society as a whole. In such societies, the resource of culturally validated extra-familial organization is available to women as well as to men and the negotiation of gender-based prerogatives is conducted upon

[45] For example, Michelle Zimbalist Rosaldo, "Woman, Culture and Society: A Theoretical Overview," in Michelle Zimbalist Rosaldo and Louise Lamphere, eds., *Woman, Culture and Society* (Stanford, Ca.: Stanford University Press, 1974), and Peggy Sanday, *Female Power and Male Dominance: On the Origins of Sexual Inequality* (Cambridge: Cambridge University Press, 1981), differ on the universality of male dominance, yet both emphasize the importance of extra-familial social networks. For a more general statement of the importance of social networks to collective action and the exercise of power, see Charles Tilly, *From Mobilization to Revolution* (Reading, Mass.: Addison-Wesley, 1978), and for an application to the genesis of the contemporary women's movement, Jo Freeman, *The Politics of Women's Liberation* (New York: Longman, 1975).

a more nearly equal basis.[46] Same-sex social organization should be seen, then, as a constituting element in any gender-based system of institutionally structured power relations. Within such a context, the ambiguous character of nineteenth-century fraternal auxiliaries becomes apparent.

Orders like the Eastern Star and the Daughters of Rebekah represented an advance over the honorary degrees of the earlier period in that they allowed the creation of active social bonds among women, bonds that had been created by a largely feminine initiative. But the legitimacy of those bonds was derived from an already-existing relation among men. Membership thus represented an extension of a familial role rather than a form of independent and coequal participation. The men retained their autonomous associations in which they could be free of feminine scrutiny or influence, while their women relations participated in organizations that were practically as well as symbolically subject to masculine authority. In this sense the auxiliaries were little different from the honorary degrees they replaced. If the creation of separate women's networks, activities, and institutions is a potential source of power, then the presence of men within supposed women's organizations presumably acts to inhibit such possibilities. What motivated the continued advocacy of such ties by leaders who seemed generally committed to women's empowerment?

THROUGHOUT the century, women had made known their disapproval of male-only fraternalism, disliking especially the practice of secrecy. From Morris's fictional Catherine Williams to the Eastern Star's quite genuine Addie Barrio of a generation later, opposition to fraternal secrecy remained a consistent theme. Catherine denounced Masonic secrecy as an impediment to the complete confidence that should exist between husband and wife, while Barrio ar-

---

[46] Rosaldo, "Woman, Culture and Society," pp. 36–39; Sanday, *Female Power*, chapters 6 and 7.

gued that since women were already forced to be complicit in masculine secrets, their exclusion from fraternal secrecy was simply an exercise in hypocrisy. How, she asked, could Freemasonry exclude women on the grounds that women cannot be entrusted with secrets, when "the very man who thus libels our sex is one whose guilty secret of depraved life, or deeds, a devoted wife is hiding, with almost superhuman care, from even friendly eyes."[47]

The difference between the two generations of women represented here was that, in the post–Civil War era, individual doubts about fraternalism were supported by the articulation of a more explicitly political critique, which identified fraternal secrecy as one of the bulwarks of an undesirable system of sex segregation that was especially detrimental to women. Against this system, many feminists and other reformers emphasized the need to bring the sexes together in a common social life based upon frank communication.[48]

Those who opposed the fraternal order as an institutional embodiment of masculine secrecy and sex segregation had two choices. They could voice their disapproval and call on men to reject all fraternal involvement. This was the course taken by important public critics like the sex educator Burt Wilder Green, the reformer Theodore Tilton, and by Elizabeth Cady Stanton, who called on women to raise their voices against secret societies. Alternatively, they could demand that men share their secrets with women by incorporating them into the orders.[49] In the face of fraternalism's phenomenal growth in this period, this second alternative might seem a more pragmatic one, and to some early proponents, the women's organizations seemed a step in this direction. One model for such a course already existed, in the Patrons of Husbandry, or Grange, an agricultural frater-

[47] Order of the Eastern Star, *Proceedings*, 1878, p. 9.

[48] William Leach, *True Love and Perfect Union: The Feminist Reform of Sex and Society* (New York: Basic Books, 1980), p. 10.

[49] Ibid., pp. 49–50, 60–61.

nal order that had successfully admitted both men and women to all degrees of membership and levels of office. Thus the Reverend Frank W. Evans, an Odd Fellows Past Grand Master, was not being unduly optimistic when he asserted his belief that "all distinctions in eligibility and rank between the sexes will be obliterated, and woman be invested with all the rights enjoyed by men within our noble Order, and that her voice will be heard, her vote cast, and her power and influence be felt in all our lodges, subordinate and grand."[50]

Probably many others were skeptical of such a possibility: Addie Barrio, for example, rejected the Masonic justification for women's exclusion, but believed it was not susceptible to change. "That woman would have keenly appreciated all that is beautiful or worthy in Freemasonry we do not deny; but there is no dignity in clamoring at the fast closed door, and every true woman has *long* since recognized this fact."[51] Still other women must have preferred the idea of separate but closely linked organizations, which, in the Pythian Sisters' formulation, would allow "both Knights and ladies to understand the advantages of organized, cooperative effort, by which means they become mutually auxiliary, while retaining their individuality and independence."[52]

What unites these alternative versions of women's fraternal participation is the vision of close and respectful ties between men and women. Within this context, the insistence upon a mixed-sex membership implied a critique of the segregated and secretive social life idealized by the male orders. Women's fraternal auxiliaries can thus be seen as part of a larger attack upon the inviolability of male social institu-

---

[50] Stillson, *History and Literature*, p. 713. See also Order of the Eastern Star, *Proceedings*, 1876, p. 7, for the similar comments of Grand Patron W. H. Ford: "I believe the day is not far distant when the Masonic fraternity as a body will concede to woman her rights . . ."

[51] Order of the Eastern Star, *Proceedings*, 1878, p. 8.

[52] Jayne-Weaver and Wood, *Pythian Sisters*, p. 27.

tions, an attack that was implicit in the temperance movement as well. In this sense the fraternal auxiliaries anticipated the development of a more couple-oriented sociability that was to emerge in full force during the 1920s.[53]

The costs of that change, the loss to women of a feminine culture, of women's institutions, and of the value they could place on their own friendships, has been convincingly documented.[54] But the history of fraternalism and the feminine response to it suggests another side of the story. Women were concerned and often angered by their absence from an all-male social world that claimed the right to exclude them from its powers and privileges. Their attempts to assert their influence over that world involved a variety of strategies, some of which appear in retrospect to have been dead ends. The basis on which fraternal auxiliaries were constructed was limited, and ultimately limiting, to be sure. Yet it seems equally important to acknowledge the complicated process of challenge, negotiation, and accommodation on both sides that attended the development of these organizations.

[53] Paula Fass, *The Damned and the Beautiful: American Youth in the 1920's* (Oxford: Oxford University Press, 1977), especially chapter 2; Robert S. Lynd and Helen Merrill Lynd, *Middletown: A Study in Modern American Culture* (New York: Harcourt, Brace and World, 1929).

[54] Estelle Freedman, "Separatism as Strategy: Female Institution Building and American Feminism, 1870–1930," *Feminist Studies* 5:3 (1979): pp. 512–29; Carroll Smith-Rosenberg, "The Female World of Love and Ritual: Relations between Women in Nineteenth Century America," *Signs* 1:1 (1975), pp. 1–29; and Linda Gordon, "The Struggle for Reproductive Freedom: Three Stages of Feminism," in Zillah R. Eisenstein, ed., *Capitalist Patriarchy and the Case for Socialist Feminism* (New York: Monthly Review Press, 1979), p. 118, contain interesting discussions of this point.

SEVEN

The Business of Brotherhood

LATE nineteenth-century American society, with its many clubs and societies, represents a case of what Anthony Oberschall has termed the associational mode of solidarity, a society in which collective action is organized through secondary ties of instrumentally motivated voluntary association rather than through bonds that seem either "natural" or "spontaneous." This stands in contrast to communal forms of solidarity, forms of organization based upon kinship, village, or tribal identity, which seem more to emanate from or to be part of the organization of traditional communities than to represent a conscious and separate type of organization.[1]

Seen in these terms, nineteenth-century fraternal orders were without doubt associational: voluntary, dues-paying membership organizations that represented one of many vehicles for participation in social and political life. Yet the fraternal order differed from other voluntary associations of the time in one important way. Its identity was a contradictory one, for it defined its existence, its raison d'être, in terms of a communal and corporatist ideal. Its solidarity was grounded in the notion of brotherhood rather than in the achievement of an instrumental goal, and it staked its appeal on the claim that in a society of secondary institutions, the fraternal order could recreate the ethos of kin-based associations.

The fraternal relationship, E. J. Hobsbawm has written, implies a concept of mutual assistance "given both voluntar-

[1] Anthony Oberschall, *Social Conflict and Social Movements* (Englewood Cliffs, N.J.: Prentice-Hall, 1973) p. 119.

ily and as of right, *but not measured in terms of money or mechanical equality or reciprocal exchange.*" In its use of kin-based imagery, fraternalism invoked the moral community of the family. It proposed a model of social life that was non-contractual, noncompetitive, and anti-individualist, "which did not organize human relations through the mechanism of a market."[2] Like the cult of domesticity, fraternalism represented an implicit critique of capitalism even as it attempted to provide an ameliorative accommodation to it.

The principles of domesticity located the alternative moral dimension within the nuclear family and designated women as the guardians of moral values. Fraternalism stood as an alternative to domesticity because it identified men as the principal moral actors and proposed to extend the moral economy of kinship beyond the nuclear family to a larger sphere of social relations. The bonds of mutual obligation, the image of a self-regulating, caring community, were central to the concept of nineteenth-century fraternalism.

In practice, however, this image stood in an increasingly problematic relationship to the practical realities of fraternal life in the latter part of the nineteenth century. The fraternal vision was a morally and socially limited one, excluding as it did the participation of women, blacks, and members of many immigrant groups. But the late nineteenth-century lodges were subject to additional pressures, from within and without, that called into question their corporatist claims even in regard to their chosen constituency of white men.

Like most other voluntary association leaders, lodge officials sought expansion, solvency, and a measure of operational efficiency. But the fraternal order was not simply another voluntary association like the Women's Christian Temperance Union or the local singing society. Participants at every level found that the fraternal order could become a source of financial gain. By the late nineteenth century, fra-

[2] E. J. Hobsbawm, "Fraternity," *New Society*, November 27, 1975, pp. 471, 472.

ternal membership can be usefully understood as a commodity that was systematically marketed and from which numerous individuals stood to profit. Fraternal orders could offer to their prospective members a ready-made sociability, the promise of financial protection, and, through standardized rituals, a form of entertainment that anticipated aspects of twentieth-century mass culture. The appeal of all of these was predicated upon their supposedly noncommercial, familial character, a character that was compromised by the acquisitive goals and expansionary tactics of fraternal leaders.

WHO STOOD TO GAIN?

In the late nineteenth century, fraternal expansion was increasingly based on the incentives to personal gain that were offered throughout the movement. Regalia manufacturers and merchants, job printers, physicians, and above all fraternal agents and leaders found in the fraternal order a source of material benefit and personal advance.

Several kinds of business enterprises profited through the provision of ancillary services and goods to the orders. The fraternal press, for example, constituted a valued source of business for some small printers and publishers. In addition to incidental job printing for local lodges and regular publication of state and national proceedings, there was a flourishing periodical press in the fraternal world, including at least sixty Masonic periodicals and some forty-five Pythian magazines and newspapers in the late nineteenth and early twentieth centuries.[3]

Even more closely tied to the fraternal movement were the sellers and makers of lodge regalia. In some cases, regalia was sold over the counter by retail merchants; even in

[3] Lynn Dumenil, *Freemasonry and American Culture 1880–1930* (Princeton, N.J.: Princeton University Press, 1984), pp. 283–84; Richardon Riles, *The Official Pythian Lodge Directory* (Jacksonville, Fla.: 1900), n.p.

Poughkeepsie, New York, a town of 20,000, a man like William R. Maloney, beginning with a few hundred dollars worth of merchandise in 1867, was able to create a business worth thirty to forty thousand dollars in 1887, simply by specializing in fraternal regalia.[4] Retail merchants like Maloney could make a good living, but manufacturers, like the seventeen listed in the 1900 Pythian Directory, must have made more sizable sums. A typical manufacturer produced costumes, banners, ritual objects, and stage accessories for most of the important orders, publishing an illustrated catalog for each one. Fraternal leaders at the national level possessed the power to specify the precise nature of the costumes and accessories that their members were to use; it seems likely that leaders and manufacturers enjoyed mutually profitable ties. In at least one case, fraternal founder and regalia manufacturer were one and the same person. The Boston firm of D. Wilson and Company, "Manufacturers and Dealers in Odd Fellows, Masonic, Knights of Pythias, Knights of Honor, Royal Arcanum and All Other Society Regalia, Jewels, Badges, Chapeaux, Swords, Belts, Banners and Flags," was undoubtedly the Darius Wilson who had himself founded the American Legion of Honor and the Royal Arcanum. Either Wilson was creating new organizations in order to expand the market for the regalia he produced, or else he had gone into the regalia business in order to capitalize on his position in the orders. In either case, his fraternal involvement was inseparable from his financial advantage.[5]

Fraternal expansionism could also be advantageous for physicians, especially those starting out in practice. The beneficiary societies required a physical examination prior to admission, and the sick benefits paid by local lodges in or-

[4] Clyde and Sally Griffen, *Natives and Newcomers: The Ordering of Opportunity in Mid-Nineteenth Century Poughkeepsie* (Cambridge, Mass.: Harvard University Press, 1978), p. 126.

[5] Riles, *Pythian Lodge Directory*, n.p.; Albert C. Stevens, *The Cyclopaedia of Fraternities* (New York: E. P. Treat and Company 1907), pp. 123, 186.

ders like the Pythians were increasingly subject to verification by a physician as well.[6] The lodge could be an important way for doctors to recruit patients; the usual quid pro quo was that the doctor had to lend his prestige and standing to the lodge by becoming a member. The ultimate step in the lodge-physician relationship was the institution of the contract practice. This was "an arrangement where a physician agreed to provide medical service to groups of patients such as members of benevolent organizations, fraternal lodges, or employees of industrial companies for a fixed fee per annum."

As a form of prepaid health care, the contract practice violated the ethic of fee for service held by the medical profession. From 1869 through the early twentieth century, the American Medical Association and local medical societies persistently condemned contract practice but lacked the power to prevent it because of the advantages it offered to both patients and doctors with marginal status. A position as a lodge doctor could serve to build up a practice as well as guarantee a secure, if modest, income. "The lodge doctor found that at the bedside he came in contact with a large group of patients who otherwise would not have called upon his services. After establishing a reputation as a busy practitioner, in part due to the recommendations of numerous families whom he had attended as a lodge doctor, and in part as a result of the normal growth of practice, the physician tended to disengage himself from lodge practice." Though the extent of lodge practice is not known, it was considerable in at least some cities and towns. In North Adams, Massachusetts, for example, 8,000 of the town's 22,000 citizens were found to use lodge physicians.[7] Like businessmen, physicians represented an occupational group for

[6] Jno. Van Valkenberg, *The Knights of Pythias Complete Manual and Textbook* (Canton, Ohio: Memento Publishing Company, 1887), p. 113.

[7] George Rosen, "Contract or Lodge Practice and Its Influences on Medical Attitudes to Health Insurance," *American Journal of Public Health* 67:4 (1977): pp. 374, 375.

whom the fraternal order was not simply a voluntary association but a potential source of monetary gain.

The core of fraternal entrepreneurship, however, was composed of agents or lodge organizers, men who in effect *sold* lodge membership. Lodges could be organized by enthusiasts, those who were intrigued by the order and wished to establish it in their locale, but people whose scope of action was geographically confined were of limited use, since they could form only one or at most two or three lodges. As a result, orders relied primarily on travelling agents or organizers who could devote all their energies to the systematic recruitment of members.

A fraternal agent was an individual who organized lodges as an occupation, much as a travelling salesman would sell any other product. Like travelling salesmen they were paid on commission, receiving a set amount for every lodge established or member recruited.[8] The case of the Ancient Order of United Workmen demonstrates the evolution of this system.

The order did not use agents during its first few years, preferring instead to rely on the efforts of its members. The founder and most of the early members were railroad workers who enjoyed a high degree of geographical mobility, which should have facilitated expansion. Nonetheless they found recruitment by volunteers to be slow and ineffective; by 1872, four years after its founding, the order had only 550 members, divided among two factions. In 1872 they accepted the services of a lodge organizer.

Dr. James M. Bunn, who had volunteered for the position, was perhaps typical of the breed, described as "pleasing in person . . . a good conversationalist, energetic, persistent and convincing." He had no interest in the labor reform goals that motivated many of the members. Rather, "he saw

[8] M. W. Sackett, *Early History of Fraternal Beneficiary Societies in America* (Meadville, Pa.: Tribune Publishing Company, 1914), pp. 70–78; Este Erwood Buffum, *Modern Woodmen of America: A History* (Rock Island, Ill.: Modern Woodmen Press, 1927), p. 8; Stevens, *Cyclopaedia* p. 246.

the possibility of interesting men in all vocations, in the matter of insuring their lives for the benefit of all their families," and he was "not averse to reaping the financial gain that might result." For his services, Dr. Bunn was to receive a commission of $150 for each lodge he organized. From this he was to pay the cost of "paraphernalia, consisting of collars and aprons for the officers and members and a set of mechanical tools used by the lodge in conferring degrees, and such record books as were needed."[9] In the last six months of 1872, Bunn made nine visits to Pittsburgh, where fifteen lodges were organized, two to Philadelphia, with no success, and visits to at least twenty smaller towns, resulting in eight lodges. Assuming that the deduction for equipment accounted for no more than $75 of the $150 commission, a generous estimate, Bunn took in at least $1,725 for the twenty-three lodges he established in six months of admittedly arduous travel.

Although Bunn himself was eventually ousted from the order, after an embarrassing attempt to pass off the Masonic ritual as that of the AOUW, the order continued to use agents in its now successful drive toward expansion, for it was widely agreed that agents were essential to increase membership. When the Red Men suffered a series of financial reverses in the early 1870s, the most serious consequence was said to be that it "left practically no funds for expenses of organizers of new tribes." And surely the Modern Woodmen of America could never have attained their astonishing fivefold increase, from 39,000 to 210,000, in *seven* years (1889 to 1896), had it not been for a systematic and aggressive use of salesmanship and promotion.[10]

---

[9] Sackett, *Fraternal Beneficiary Societies*, pp. 71–72.

[10] Stevens, *Cyclopaedia*, pp. 245, 158. By 1911, the Modern Woodmen, now numbering 1,129,805, employed thirty-six Supervising Deputies and 250 District Deputies or field organizers. "The Deputies were not paid out of the General Fund, but only received such compensation as they earned in the field." C.H.T. Riepen, *History of the Modern Woodmen of America, 1883–1911*, (Omaha, Neb., 1911), p. 45.

The case of the rejuvenated Ku Klux Klan provides a good picture of how this pecuniary system typically worked. Although it is best known as a racist and nativist social movement, the twentieth-century version of the Klan began as a conventional fraternal order. Its founder, William J. Simmons, was a seasoned fraternal agent, who claimed to have earned $15,000 a year as a district manager for the Woodmen of the World. "In addition, he belonged to several varieties of Masons and to the Knights Templar . . . 'I am a fraternalist,' he was to explain whenever anyone asked his profession."[11]

In 1915, the massive popularity of D. W. Griffith's film, "The Birth of a Nation," with its glorification of the Klan's role in the Reconstruction South, inspired Simmons to found a new and potentially lucrative order, but despite his prior experience as a fraternal organizer, the organization failed to prosper in its first four years. Simmon's idea remained an appealing one, attracting the interest of professional fund raisers Elizabeth Tyler and Edward Young Clarke, the latter also a former fraternal agent who was now to be in charge of recruitment. The economic arrangement they reached with Simmons is revealing: "Of every ten-dollar initiation fee (Klectoken), four dollars went to the Kleagle (fraternal agent) responsible. The King Kleagle of the state realm got one dollar. The Grand Goblin got fifty cents and the rest went back to Atlanta: two dollars and fifty cents for Clarke and Mrs. Tyler, and two dollars for Simmons."[12] Designation of one official publisher and one company as the sole manufacturer of approved regalia provided an additional source of profit. Under the new regime the Klan met with swift success, recruiting eighty-five thousand members and earning more than $300,000 for Clarke, Tyler, and Simmons in its first fifteen months of operation.[13]

[11] David M. Chalmers, *Hooded Americanism: The History of the Ku Klux Klan* (Chicago: Quadrangle Books, 1968), p. 29.

[12] Ibid., pp. 33–34.

[13] Ibid., p. 35. Also note that the Klan, legally recognized as a benevolent and charitable organization, was not subject to taxation.

It may be objected that the Klan was not a typical fraternal organization, but there is every reason to believe that its leaders drew upon established fraternal procedure in setting up their financial procedures. Joseph Cullen Root, founder of the eminently respectable Modern Woodmen of America a generation earlier, was a figure not very different from Simmons in his use of fraternalism to pursue personal advantage. A compulsive fraternalist, Root was a member of the Knights of Pythias and the Ancient Order of United Workmen, an Odd Fellow, a Thirty-Third Degree Mason, and a founder of the Iowa Legion of Honor. Root began his career in earnest as Chief Rector of the Iowa-based V.A.S. Society. When the V.A.S. resisted his efforts to expand beyond Iowa, Root established the Modern Woodmen, leaving the V.A.S. in a state of financial disarray. Later, ousted from the MWA in a dispute, he immediately created still another organization, the Woodmen of the World, which also became large and well known.

Root treated fraternal orders as businesses; failure at one simply prompted him to start another. As the history of the Klan suggests, such efforts could be profitable. In a similar case, success in building up the Loyal Order of the Moose allowed James J. Davis, its Supreme Dictator, to obtain a seat in the United States Senate and then to *sell* his interest in the Moose for $600,000, no small sum in the 1920s.[14]

To be sure, some orders resisted the trend. The Masons could afford to; their greater fame and prestige allowed them to enforce a ban against solicitation of members and thus to retain their voluntary character. But in general, an order that renounced the use of agents and solicitation had to recognize that it would remain small. As the Most Eminent Recorder of the Artisans Order of Mutual Protection wrote in 1914: "We are very proud of our little old-fashioned organization, we work on the original plan, no organizers, no commissions, our members are our agents, and we think we

[14] Buffum, *Modern Woodmen*, pp. 1, 5; Charles W. Ferguson, *Fifty Million Brothers* (New York: Farrar and Rinehart, 1937), p. 291.

favor a good man by admitting him."[15] The alternatives seemed to be small, minimal growth organizations with recruiting based on the activation of already-existing friendship networks and large, expansionary organizations created through an aggressive sales effort. The result was that by the end of the century, the fraternal experience of many, if not most, members occurred within lodges governed by agents and national leaders pursuing their own financial goals.

If fraternal orders were to prosper, and fraternal agents to operate successfully as salesmen, they needed a product to sell. Most basically, lodges offered a kind of ready-made sociability, an organizationally constructed friendship, at a designated time and space and with a group of people assembled for that purpose. Here the orders' national character was significant to their appeal because of the high rates of geographic mobility that characterized the late nineteenth-century United States. Unlike most other organizations, the largest of the fraternal orders could offer their members social entrée to groups of men in communities all over the country, a feat made possible by the lodge's claim to create brotherhood among strangers. In addition, fraternal orders offered two other incentives to membership: the provision of death and sickness benefits and the entertainment that was afforded by the enactment of rituals and parades. These too were dependent for their power on the lodge's supposed ability to create a personalistic tie with moral and emotional dimensions. It was this tie that gave fraternal benefit societies their advantage over commercial life insurance companies and rendered fraternal ritual an emotionally compelling experience. But in each case the moral and emotional component that gave fraternal mem-

[15] Quoted in Sackett, *Fraternal Beneficiary Societies*, p. 218. Although the Masons certainly never used agents, Dumenil reports that competition between lodges led to erosion of the ban on solicitation of new members in the early twentieth century. *Freemasonry and American Culture*, pp. 153–54.

bership its appeal was contradicted by the acquisitive uses
to which it was put.

FRATERNAL INSURANCE AND THE
IDEAL OF MUTUALITY

Fraternal benefit societies, which provided life insurance for
their members, became an important part of the fraternal
movement in the 1870s and 1880s. Lodges had always dispensed benefits in times of sickness and death as part of their
practice of mutual aid, but these were usually modest sums
distributed by the local lodge. In contrast, benefit societies
like the Ancient Order of United Workmen, the Legion of
Honor, and the Modern Woodmen of America paid out
larger, predetermined sums, derived from assessments lev-
ied on the entire state or national membership. For example,
the AOUW, the earliest insurance fraternity, specified a death
benefit of $2,000 in 1869.[16]

The emergence of fraternal life insurance was at one and
the same time part of a larger trend toward the adoption of
life insurance and the expression of a deeper cultural ambiv-
alence regarding the trend. Life insurance achieved popular
acceptance much later than fire or marine insurance, and
long after the development of adequate actuarial tables made
it a rational economic proposition. The obstacles to the practice of insuring human life, Viviana A. Zelizer has argued,
were primarily cultural, located in "a value system that condemned a strictly financial evaluation of human life." "Putting death on the market offended a system of values that
upheld the sanctity of human life and its incommensurability. It defied a powerful normative pattern: the division between the marketable and the nonmarketable, or the sacred
and the profane . . . Sacred things are distinguished by the
fact that men will not treat them in a calculating, utilitarian
manner."[17]

[16] Stevens, *Cyclopaedia*, p. 122.
[17] Viviana A. Rotman Zelizer, *Morals and Markets: The Development of Life*

In addition to altering the valuation of human life, life insurance implied a change in the social organization of provision to the needy, from a gift relationship to a contractual one. The eighteenth-century ideal stipulated that a needy widow and orphans were to be aided by their kin and community; life insurance violated this vision by making the protection of families a "purchasable commodity." "In a gift-exchange system, men are bound by trust and community solidarity, but in the impersonal economic market they come together as buyers and sellers of commodities . . . although life insurance provided an efficient financial alternative to co-operative means of support, it did not qualify as their moral substitute. Systems of voluntary mutual aid were deemed morally and socially superior to paid protection, which obliterated 'spontaneous love and duty.' "[18]

Fraternal insurance offered a way to deal with this moral dilemma, because it denied the commodified character of insurance provision by defining it as a system of mutual aid based in quasi kin relations. As a result, it was immensely popular, outselling commercial life insurance in the 1890s despite the greater security offered by the regular insurance companies.[19] But the success of the fraternal benefit societies was always tenuous. The practical need to administer an actuarially and fiscally sound enterprise conflicted with the claims of fraternal mutuality and led to tensions between different concepts of what a fraternal benefit society should be. The contrasting cases of the Ancient Order of United Workmen and the Modern Woodmen of America suggest alternative responses to this dilemma.

The Ancient Order of United Workmen was the first American order of any importance to offer a substantial death benefit, initially set at $500, roughly a year's income

Insurance in the United States (New York: Columbia University Press, 1979) pp. xi, 43–44.

[18] Ibid., pp. 91–92.

[19] Ibid., p. 93.

for a moderately skilled worker, and later raised to $2,000.[20] Because it was a pioneer, its procedures had to be improvised or else copied from existing commercial life insurance companies. Myron W. Sackett was the person most responsible for the implementation of the AOUW's insurance scheme. Sackett was well placed for this task, since he served simultaneously as Grand Recorder of the Pennsylvania Grand Lodge, by *far* the largest state body at this time, and as Supreme Receiver of the national organization. Because he operated from a firm power base in Pennsylvania but a less secure position in the Supreme Lodge, Sackett worked by instituting changes at the state level, then attempting to persuade the Supreme Lodge that they should be extended to the entire order. As a salaried official with a paid office staff, Sackett was able to institute standardized record-keeping and, most important, regular procedures for determining membership eligibility and eligibility for death benefits.[21]

To this end, Sackett introduced a battery of standardized forms, borrowed from life insurance companies, including a death report form, a medical examiner's report, and what was essentially an insurance policy, five pages long, stating the exact requirements for payment. He also compiled an assessment book, which was a register of benefit certificates currently in force; before this the Grand Lodge had no record of how many members held potential claims on the organization. In addition, officers of subordinate lodges were now required to keep monthly financial records that were forwarded to the Grand Lodge.

Most controversial were Sackett's attempts to introduce rudimentary actuarial principles. These included a more stringent medical examination prior to admission, an attempt to limit the age of eligibility by restricting new mem-

---

[20] J. J. Upchurch and A. T. Dewey, *Life and Times of Father Upchurch, Written by Himself* (San Francisco, 1887), p. 68; Stevens, *Cyclopaedia*, p. 128.
[21] Sackett, *Fraternal Beneficiary Societies*, pp. 132, 148.

bers to the ages from 21 to 60, and an attempt to introduce age-graded fees so that older members would have to pay more because of the greater losses incurred in insuring them.

The AOUW had originated, it must be remembered, as a type of labor reform fraternity, to which the insurance benefit was incidental. A substantial proportion of the membership still thought of the order in those terms and resisted Sackett's initiatives. Opposition was especially strong in the Supreme Lodge, which initially allowed Sackett's innovations within Pennsylvania but refused their extension to the rest of the order. To some extent the resistance stemmed from an antipathy to the detailed and exacting record-keeping that Sackett was proposing in an era when many businesses used only the most minimal bookkeeping procedures. As the Supreme Lodge commented in 1874, "the system of 'red tape' is growing entirely too much for the comfort of subordinate lodges." But the greater part of the opposition came from the fear that the order was being transformed from a fraternity into a business. The adoption of the more stringent medical examiner's report, which implied a much stricter eligibility requirement, was barely adopted even in Pennsylvania. It was "vigorously opposed upon the ground that we were drifting away from the broad humanitarian ideas of the founders and were endeavoring to turn the Order into an insurance company."[22]

By the end of the 1870s the Supreme Lodge had acquiesced in the requirements of record-keeping and the use of medical examiners' reports, but resisted further changes. Retention of a decentralized system meant that the Grand Lodges rather than the national order were responsible for payment of benefits within the individual states. When a state or region experienced an unusually high death rate, as for example in the yellow fever epidemic of 1878, an additional assessment could be made by the Supreme Lodge on

[22] Ibid., pp. 57–58, 143.

the order as a whole, but the assessments were voluntary and compliance was not always good. Most significantly, the order continued to refuse the use of assessments adjusted by age at admission. Opposition to age grading was *not*, as Sackett notes, because the membership failed to understand the financial risks uniform assessment implied. Rather, "They looked upon a graded assessment as a violation of the principle of that perfect mutuality to be accorded one brother to another and while recognizing the added risk of advancing age, were willing to pay the added cost in order to maintain the simplicity of like contribution and like benefit to all."[23]

By 1895 the AOUW was the only fraternal beneficiary society to retain what were now regarded as dangerous practices. The *Cyclopaedia of Fraternities* warned that "while the A.O.U.W. is perhaps the oldest and among the more successful of its class in the United States, while its affairs are managed capably . . . sooner or later there may develop a necessity for a revision of its assessment insurance system in the direction at least of a grading of payments according to age, and the placing of death benefit funds in the hands of the supreme governing body."[24] But the AOUW retained in large measure its loyalty to the concept of mutuality and brotherhood that had informed its early years.

As a fraternal benefit society organized on business principles from its inception, the Modern Woodmen of America provides a striking contrast to the AOUW. Joseph Cullen Root's provisions for the order reveal his intent to establish it on a solid financial footing by avoiding the unbusinesslike "mistakes" made by orders such as the AOUW. First, the administration of the organization was completely centralized; not only did the Supreme Camp control the benefit funds, but there were no state jurisdictions at all. This eliminated the expense of an entire middle level of officials and pre-

[23] Ibid., p. 148.
[24] Stevens, *Cyclopaedia*, p. 129.

vented the states from emerging as a source of possible op-position to the central administration. Second, the MWA was restricted by its charter to the midwestern states of Illinois, Minnesota, Iowa, Nebraska, Michigan, Kansas, North Da-kota, South Dakota, Missouri, Indiana, and Ohio "from which the cities of Chicago, Detroit, Milwaukee, St. Louis, and Cincinnati are excluded. This, it is claimed, makes its territory the healthiest in the country."[25] Root excluded not only large cities in the Midwest, but all of the industrial northeastern United States, as well as the South, considered a high risk area since the yellow fever epidemic of 1878 had strained the finances of so many fraternal orders. In this way, he intended to use geographical restrictions to build in a principle of lesser risk. Second, the Modern Woodmen ex-cluded members from what were considered high-risk oc-cupations, such as railway brakemen, employees in gun-powder factories, balloonists and sailors, miners, railway engineers, firemen and switchmen, plow grinders, brass workers, firemen, and professional baseball players. The is-sue is not whether the restrictions placed on membership were actuarially correct, but rather that the attempt was being made to reduce risk and to make the MWA a more sta-ble financial institution. Finally, the MWA prevented men over 45 years of age from joining and instituted an age-graded assessment system, "the grading being in proportion to the average expectancy of life by the standard of American tables."[26] The MWA had, in other words, incorporated the operating principles of the commercial life insurance indus-try. It continued to maintain, and indeed to emphasize, a fraternal identity, but in practice, the concept of the MWA as a business enterprise, answerable to strict principles of man-agement, overrode the ideal of fraternalism as unconditional mutuality.

On the basis of these procedures, the Modern Woodmen of America became a highly successful benefit society. In

[25] Ibid., pp. 159, 158.
[26] Buffum, *Modern Woodmen*, p. 103; Stevens, *Cyclopaedia*, p. 158.

1897, fourteen years after its founding, it had 259,584 members, as opposed to the Ancient Order of United Workmen's 347,990. Ten years later the figures had more than reversed themselves, with 234,952 for the Workmen versus 801,254 for the Woodmen. The AOUW's decline could be linked in part to the weakness of the organization at the national level and its consequent inability to engage in extensive promotion, but a series of bankruptcies of Grand Lodges in the early 1900s was probably even more influential. Some Grand Lodges went into receivership; others were merged into surviving Grand Lodges. The Illinois AOUW, for example, reduced to 1,200 members by 1917, was reinsured by the Iowa Grand Lodge, which was itself absorbed by the North Dakota jurisdiction in 1932. Of the forty-three Grand Lodges operating in 1883, only ten remained by 1929 when the national organization disbanded. The MWA continues to exist to this day, with more than 500,000 members in 1979.[27]

The contrasting histories of the Ancient Order of United Workmen and the Modern Woodmen of America suggest that fraternal benefit societies could not survive without abandoning in practice their principle of mutuality. Ultimately the insurance fraternities adopted commercial methods or failed and disbanded. But the image of fraternal insurance as different from and morally superior to commercial insurance continued to attract members well into the twentieth century.

RITUAL AS COMMODITY

Ritual, which formally created a state of brotherhood, was what gave fraternal life insurance its aura of moral superi-

[27] Ibid., p. 114; P. E. Thomas, "A Brief History of the Supreme Lodge Ancient Order of United Workmen and of the Various Grand Lodges Including Those Out of Existence and Also Those Still Operating," (Fargo, N.D.: unpublished manuscript, 1943), pp. 13, 16, 5; Alvin J. Schmidt, *Fraternal Organizations* (Westport, Conn.: Greenwood Press, 1980), p. 219.

ority, what constituted it as a system of mutual obligation rather than a commercial venture. But ritual was valued in and of itself as well.

To men raised in a culture that abhorred idleness, the ritual offered legitimation; its grandiloquent rhetoric ennobled time spent in otherwise aimless socializing. But the ritual went beyond that: it functioned as a form of entertainment that enlivened and gave purpose to the sociability it justified. Indeed, I would argue that the phenomenon of late nineteenth-century fraternalism cannot be understood without seeing it as an entertainment product that was systematically produced and marketed by the national orders as an incentive to membership.

Fraternalism had always been characterized by its theatricality. As we saw in Chapter One, the processions of the confraternities and guilds, the floats and tableaux of the urban charivaris, the traditions of masking, costuming, and symbolic adornment provided an important source of public entertainment in the cities of late medieval and early modern Europe. Ritual is, as Clifford Geertz has argued, an interpretive activity that is appropriately understood as artistic production.[28] Especially, it is a kind of theater, a symbolic activity that is collectively and publicly enacted.

The Masonic version of the European fraternal tradition drew upon the initiation rites of guilds and journeymen's societies, rituals that were secret, but collective and theatrical. The initiation rite is in essence a drama, a miniplay in which the initiate takes on a role, such as that of Hiram Abif, undergoes a test of courage, and demonstrates his bravery and loyalty to the craft. The multiplication of Masonic degrees in the late eighteenth century suggests a steady demand for new dramatic material; for many Masons the high point of their participation was the opportunity to play out these roles. British Masonry also drew upon the public

[28] Clifford Geertz, *The Interpretation of Culture* (New York: Basic Books, 1973), p. 443.

processional traditions of early modern fraternalism. Many Masonic lodges marched in public procession on Masonic feast days and attended the theater in groups wearing their regalia until such practices were outlawed in the mid-eighteenth century by the Grand Lodge of England, which wished to avoid popular attention.

In its characteristic forms, nineteenth-century fraternalism displayed remarkable continuity with earlier fraternal practice. Operating within the Masonic model, the activities of orders such as the Odd Fellows and Knights of Pythias were structured around the repetitive reenactment of their orders' own particular initiation rituals. At the same time, the late nineteenth-century organizations reemphasized participation in public spectacle, as orders competed to see who could field the most rigorously drilled and elaborately dressed parade units. But while the forms, initiation, and procession are amazingly similar to earlier fraternal modes, their context had changed as fraternal orders were increasingly governed by their competition for expansion, solvency, and personal enrichment. Within this competition an appealing ritual was deemed an essential element in the battle for members; this produced a major difference between the ritual of the Masons and that of subsequent fraternal orders.

The first three degrees of the Masonic system were derived from the traditions of operative masonry. While they were substantially reworked by the early Accepted Masons, their evolution was essentially complete by about 1740. From that point on, the ritual was treated as something to be preserved and passed on, not unlike a folk tradition. Since the degrees were transmitted primarily by word of mouth in the eighteenth century, their performance varied in minor detail by region and social stratum, but never were they subject to arbitrary change or replacement.

By contrast, the rituals of the nineteenth-century fraternal orders were written by one enterprising individual, such as Justus H. Rathbone of the Knights of Pythias or Joseph

Cullen Root of the Woodmen, or else by committee, as in the case of the Independent Order of Odd Fellows, the Grand Army of the Republic, and the Ancient Order of United Workmen. What is more, these rituals could be changed at will and frequently were, if they proved ineffective or unappealing. The history of the Red Men provides a notable example of this process.

The Improved Order of Red Men was one of the oldest American orders, extending back to the 1830s, and its leaders were clearly disturbed to see it surpassed by one new order after another. Attributing this lack of success to an unappealing ritual, they responded with recurring attempts to improve it, beginning in 1851 when the desperate Great Council of the United States "offered a premium to the brother who would produce one that would prove satisfactory." During the next twenty years there was a succession of major and minor alterations. "Several changes were made in the title of officers in 1853, and in 1854 a ritual was adopted for 'raising up Chiefs' . . . In 1861 a Beneficial Degree Ceremonial for opening and closing was adopted, and in 1863, after many years of effort, there was secured a 'complete symmetrical and attractive ritual' . . . There was another revision of the ritual in 1869, and from 1866 to 1870 inclusive the work of rehabilitation was pushed . . ."[29] The Red Men were unusual in the amount of trouble they had with their ritual, but almost every order went through some changes and revisions: the Odd Fellows in 1835, 1845, and 1880, the Knights of Pythias in 1866, 1882, and 1892, the Ancient Order of United Workmen in 1874 and 1875, and the Elks "several times" from 1866 to 1895.[30]

The leaders of nineteenth-century fraternal orders saw the ritual in quite instrumental terms, as a marketable commod-

[29] Stevens, *Cyclopaedia*, pp. 244, 245.

[30] Ibid., pp. 255, 264; Van Valkenberg, *Pythian Manual*, p. 119; L. H. Prescott, *History of the Criterion Lodge No. 68, Knights of Pythias* (Cleveland, Ohio: Imperial Press, 1899), p. 25; Sackett, *Fraternal Beneficiary Societies*, pp. 108, 161; Stevens, *Cyclopaedia*, p. 230.

ity, to be modified or replaced as changes in public taste or the innovations of rival orders demanded. Just as the television programmers of today attempt to differentiate themselves from their largely indistinguishable competitors by means of minor programming innovations, so lodge officials tried for interesting effects and catchy themes, which were then evaluated by the cognoscenti and tested in the marketplace.

In his prospectus for the Modern Woodmen, Joseph Cullen Root indicated his acute awareness of this process, an awareness drawn from his prior participation in at least six other fraternal orders. "A pleasing Ritual," he wrote "has been devised, that presents less objectionable features, and has the flavor of more originality than any of the more pretentious and so-called 'Ancient' associations now in existence."[31] Realizing the problem, the *Cyclopaedia of Fraternities* recognized his creative effort, the attempt "to be as original as possible in formulating ritual and ceremonies" that had gone into the Modern Woodmen of America, but could not refrain from commenting that "so much had been done in the way of creating secret societies prior to 1880–83 that some well-traveled ground had to be covered." A similar recognition of the problem facing fraternal ritual writers informs the *Cyclopaedia*'s description of the Royal Arcanum's ceremonial, one " 'well calculated to impress' the meaning of the motto of the Order upon the minds of all novitiates, *even though they have passed through the ordeals required by other societies.*"[32]

PRODUCT DIVERSIFICATION

Such comments reveal a growing concern that there were only so many changes that could be devised for fraternal initiation rituals. Two innovations emerged at least partly in

[31] Quoted in Buffum, *Modern Woodmen*, p. 5.
[32] Stevens, *Cyclopaedia*, pp. 159, 186 (my emphasis).

response to this perception: the playground or recreational lodge and the military branch. Each represented an attempt to elaborate and enliven fraternalism's entertainment dimension. The quintessential playground lodge was the Ancient Arabic Order of the Nobles of the Mystic Shrine, better known as the Shriners. Commonly viewed as a part of the Masons, the Shriners were established in 1871 by an American comedian, William J. (Billy) Florence, who claimed to have been initiated into an Arabic secret order while on a tour of the Middle East. Whatever the truth of this claim, by 1879 the order had begun to develop in a hyper-theatrical and somewhat tongue-in-cheek direction, through the efforts of the members of Mecca Temple of New York, "who laid the foundation for the elaborate ceremonial, gorgeous scenic effects, and realistic dramatic renditions of the ritual of the Order, which have since distinguished it."[33]

The Shriners developed into a highly successful organization, famous, indeed notorious, even today for their comically exaggerated titles, their lavish parades, and their red fezzes. But the idea of the playground lodge was not successfully diffused through the fraternal movement and thus failed to serve as a significant incentive to membership for any save the Masons.

As the Shriners became popular, the Odd Fellows and Knights of Pythias created their own equivalents. Pythians established the fez-wearing Dramatic Order of Knights of Khorassan in 1894 and the Odd Fellows made two attempts, the Imperial Order of Muscovites, which met in Kremlins and was ruled by a Supreme Czar, and the Ancient Order of Samaritans, created after the Muscovites fell flat. Both Khorassans and Samaritans remained marginal organizations.[34]

Undoubtedly this was related to the fact that the Shriners

---

[33] Ferguson, *Fifty Million Brothers*, p. 234; Stevens, *Cyclopaedia*, p. 3.

[34] Stevens, *Cyclopaedia*, pp. 232–33; Ferguson, *Fifty Million Brothers*, p. 80, for Khorassan; Stevens, *Cyclopaedia*, p. 261, for Muscovites and Samaritans.

represented not simply an impulse toward dramatic and fun-loving self-parody, but an extension of Masonic elitism and social differentiation. The Shrine is not, strictly speaking, a Masonic organization: "It is not a Masonic Order and forms no part of Freemasonry, is independent in origin and government, and is associated with the Craft only because it was established by eminent Freemasons and because none but Freemasons of high degree may become acquainted with its mysteries."[35] The requirement that a Shriner must be either a thirty-second-degree Scottish Rite Mason or its equivalent in the American Rite Masonic Knights Templar was frankly attributed to the desire "to insure a 'select class of men to compose its membership.' " The degree requirement created a financial screening mechanism that the Shrine's Pythian and Odd Fellow emulators could not duplicate. At a time in the 1930s when roughly 40 percent of families had incomes under $1,000, initiation into the Shriners cost $150 while the Knights of Khorassan charged $15.[36] They could not rival the panache and prestige of the many-degreed Shriners, nor could their more modestly endowed members afford to create the kinds of elaborate displays that gave the Shriners their public identity. Even in the more affluent Masonic world, the Shriners constituted an economic and social elite, one that no other order could easily sustain. For their members, recreational lodges provided an atmosphere of informal fun that the parent organizations seemed to lack, but only within the Masonic movement did the playground lodge achieve real influence.

In contrast, the idea of the military branch was much more successfully disseminated through the fraternal movement. The Masonic Knights Templar provided an important model for a military fraternalism, but they had been in existence for more than half a century when the other military branches emerged in the 1870s and 1880s. The Odd

[35] Stevens, *Cyclopaedia*, p. 1.
[36] Ferguson, *Fifty Million Brothers*, pp. 240, 80.

Fellows, for example, began to consider the idea in 1870, but the Patriarchs Militant, as their drilling organization was called, was not established until the mid-1880s. The Uniform Rank of the Knights of Pythias was organized in the early 1880s through a reorganization of scattered Pythian drill teams that had already been formed through local initiative.[37]

The appeal here lay quite frankly in spectacle. For men who were attracted by elaborate regalia, the military branches provided an opportunity to indulge their fantasies to the limit. Some indication of the ruling priorities may be derived from the fact that the General Laws of the Uniform Rank, Knights of Pythias, a twenty-four-page document, devoted more than six pages to detailed specification for the regalia to be worn by each officer and member. For example, the "Chapeau or Helmet (full dress)" for officers was described as

> black silk folding chapeau trimmed with two black ostrich plumes running over the top from front to rear, a gold chapeau tassel on each peak, on the right side a black silk rosette five inches in diameter, surmounted by a strap with gold embroidery 1/4 inch wide, strap to be five inches long, two inches wide, including the embroidery, with rounded ends; a silver bullion lily to be embroidered in the upper ends, and a gold emblematic button in the lower end; across the front and back peak on each side a black silk ribbon sashing, one inch wide; chapeau to be worn with the front peak turned slightly to the left, showing the gilt ornament on the right side.[38]

Some were openly derisive of the military branches, criticizing "the overwhelming desire among the younger mem-

---

[37] Stevens, *Cyclopaedia*, p. 256; Ferguson, *Fifty Million Brothers*, p. 79; Van Valkenberg, *Pythian Manual*, p. 417.

[38] Van Valkenberg, *Pythian Manual*, p. 143.

bers of the Order to strut before the world,—clad in the ha-
biliments of war when no danger threatened, to dress
themselves in showy uniforms, which ofttimes meant display of pride and nothing more." The Patriarchs Militant,
wrote one Odd Fellow, have been "found, by practical ex-
periment, to meet in full all the demands of the most ardent
lover of military display, except in one who really wants to
fight."[39] But even opponents agreed that a military branch
served an important role in recruiting new members, especially the young. A Modern Woodmen publication of 1912
noted that the Foresters, the Woodmen's drill team, who
marched with axes rather than guns, were a good advertis-
ing feature, especially through their national drill contests.
The Supreme Chancellor of the Knights of Pythias, writing
one year earlier, agreed: "The military Department of our
Order . . . not only attracts young men toward the Order,
but, in my opinion, is a valuable aid in building up the membership of the order in the subordinate lodge."[40]

Drill teams and parade units were seen as an effective ad-
vertising device because they were the most elaborately costumed and most publicly visible parts of the lodge movement. Bedecked with helmets, gauntlets, epaulets,
chevrons, ribbons, and ornaments and carrying swords, ri-
fles, or axes, they displayed themselves en masse at parades
and other public occasions, giving their parent orders a vivid
public presence and means of promotion. Yet they represented something more than pure spectacle: military
branches were quasi-military organizations, with a structure
of regiments, brigades, divisions, and officers paralleling
those of an army. As such, they were engaged in the glori-

[39] Henry Leonard Stillson, *The History and Literature of Odd Fellowship, the Three-Link Fraternity* (Boston: Fraternity Publishing Company, 1897), pp. 158–59.

[40] Riepen, *Modern Woodmen*, p. 82; Knights of Pythias, *Official Record of Proceedings of the Twenty-Sixth Convention of the Supreme Lodge, Knights of Pythias, Milwaukee, August 2–11, 1910* (Nashville, Tenn.: Brandon Printing Company, 1910), p. 36.

fication of hierarchy and the promotion of a spirit of militarism.

The image of the lodge brother as knight or soldier has always been the chief alternative to that of lodge brother as craft worker. When the eighteenth-century French and German Freemasons wanted to reject Freemasonry's symbolic links to the traditions of operative masons, they recast themselves as descendants of crusader knights. Emulating the higher Masonic degrees, many nineteenth-century fraternal orders based themselves in chivalric or military imagery.

Both artisanal and military metaphors make a corporatist appeal, combining unity of interest with hierarchy in a noncontractual relationship. Yet they differ significantly as well. The military model greatly extends the hierarchy, with many more layers and a much greater distance from top to bottom. It rejects the fellowship of the craft workshop for the precise discipline of the regiment. Both call for the obedience of subordinates to superiors, but the artisanal master evokes an authority based upon expertise and paternalism, while the military officer commands a more abstract, less personalized obedience.

With their precisely drilled ranks of officers and men, the military branches provided the fraternal world with a broadened, revivified, and more authoritarian range of hierarchical relations and metaphors. Their content, however, presented more than an idealization of abstracted hierarchy. Fraternal military branches emerged at a particular moment in United States history, a time of renewed nativism and unprecedented labor unrest. The interest in militarism within the fraternal movement is clearly linked to concerns about social instability and perceptions of the need for both a military spirit and a military capacity.

Some of these links may be seen in the career of James R. Carnahan, one of the initiators of the Knights of Pythias's Uniform Rank. After service in the Civil War and a civilian career as a lawyer and judge, Carnahan took the initiative, in 1877, to organize a Knights of Pythias Drill Corps in

Lafayette, Indiana, since there was as yet no uniform rank at the national level. Although a desire to recreate the military glories of the Civil War was one motivating factor, something more than nostalgia was at work: "He saw, in 1876 and 1877," reports the Knights of Pythias *Manual and Textbook*, "the necessity of a distinctive military rank of the Order."[41]

The reference here is undoubtedly to the massive labor conflicts of 1876 and 1877, climaxed by the great nationwide railroad strike of 1877. To many contemporaries, this seemed more an insurrection than a strike, involving as it did the takeover of railroads by strikers and the contagious expansion of the strike to other workers in many cities. It was a violent upheaval, occurring during a severe depression and defeated through the intervention of local and federal troops. Inspired by the memory of the Paris Commune of seven years earlier, many upper- and middle-class Americans viewed it as the beginning of class war and acted accordingly.

State militias were the chief military bodies used by the state to repress strikes; consequently they assumed an increased importance. Within such a political context, fraternal military branches may be seen as a kind of analogue or auxiliary to the state militias. In Carnahan's case, this identity of purpose was made explicit by his simultaneous service as Adjutant General of the Indiana State Militia (1881–1885) and first Major General or national commanding officer of the Uniform Rank, Knights of Pythias. Of his service in the militia, the *Pythian Manual* comments: "His administration of that important office was characterized with a general revival of the military spirit amongst the people, and a more thorough and effective organization of the State militia."[42]

Fraternal leaders were clear in their identification of the

[41] Van Valkenberg, *Pythian Manual*, p. 416.
[42] Ibid., p. 417.

military branches as an aid to military preparedness. As the Supreme Chancellor of the Knights of Pythias wrote in 1910, "the Military Department of an order . . . serves the purpose of promoting a military spirit among the members." A 1911 account of the Modern Woodmen of America explained the existence of the Forester Department in similar terms: the "idea is that the Woodmen shall have a certain number of fairly well drilled men to serve as the second line of defense when the nation is in trouble. And a second line of defense that will be of far greater value than the ordinary, undrilled undisciplined American."[43]

The promotion of militarism is never abstract; it must be based, however implicitly, upon mobilization against an enemy. Military branches were established in an era when the United States was conspicuously uninvolved in international hostilities and the primary threat appeared to be an internal one: the menace of rebellious workers and immigrant hordes. Thus the stylistic content of the uniformed ranks—a content of hierarchy and discipline—was grounded in a subtext of nativism and working-class repression. Through their membership in fraternal orders, middle-class men proclaimed their commitment to a social order that seemed under assault, while working-class men participated in activities that were symbolically directed against them.

The militarism of fraternal drill teams and parade units represented a shift of emphasis in content and imagery toward the theme of the nation at arms, away from the traditions of the craft workshop. Yet the elaborate parades and costumes were strongly reminiscent of an earlier European fraternalism with its use of the procession as a defining event. Both the initiation rite and the parade, the chief forms of symbolic activity in late nineteenth-century fraternalism, find their direct equivalents in the ritual forms of European popular fraternalism, yet their meaning was altered. The

---

[43] Knights of Pythias, *Proceedings*, p. 35; Riepen, *Modern Woodmen*, p. 82.

nineteenth-century rituals were shaped by the drive for competitive advantage. Subjected to a process of standardization and commodification, they represent a transitional stage in the social organization of popular entertainment.

In both the sixteenth and nineteenth centuries, ritual, with its inherent theatricality, served as a source of entertainment. In contrast to the entertainment presented by modern mass media, this was an entertainment based upon face-to-face communication among people already known to each other. Like the early modern confrere or compagnon, the nineteenth-century lodge brother participated as actor rather than spectator in the ritual performance. The late nineteenth-century lodge bears a marked resemblance to more traditional forms of popular culture in that it was an organizational vehicle through which its members *made their own entertainment*, through their active engagement in the dramatic events that were the center of the lodge meeting.

But while nineteenth-century lodge brothers did make their own entertainment, the process by which this happened had changed, as had its social context. Despite important continuities, early modern and nineteenth-century fraternalism operated within vastly different social systems and were shaped by different structural forces. Early modern fraternalism emerged from the corporate life of traditional collectivities. Nineteenth-century orders appropriated these forms, but incorporated them into what is best understood as a precursor to the commercialized and mechanically reproduced mass media entertainment of the twentieth century.

To say that early modern fraternalism was traditional in character means that its forms and activities seemed to emanate from the social usages of traditionally organized collectivities. They represent practices that were handed down, informally reproduced by their users, and thus open to alteration and reinterpretation. Charivari, for example, could move from a concern with domestic morality and appropriate gender behavior to anti-authoritarian critiques of national rulers, church leaders, and local authorities. Even in their more frequent and "traditional" function of domestic regulation, charivaris attacked a variety of targets, from submissive husbands and elderly men marrying young girls to husbands who beat their wives.[44] The receptivity of fraternal ritualism to changes in popular sentiment revealed its character as a readily understood symbolic system that remained in the hands of its users, available to be reworked within the broad framework of certain generally understood rules.

In sharp contrast to this were the carefully prescribed rituals of the nationally organized nineteenth-century orders. Instead of a relatively spontaneous event, lodge brothers were involved in the precise reenactment of a ritual that was specified for them to the last detail of the regalia they were to wear and the words they were to utter. Thus they made their own entertainment, but its content was determined for them. It was a form of entertainment that was standardized; in the absence of an electronic means of reproduction it was instead socially reproduced through the top-down specification of fraternal rituals and spectacles that were acted out by the lodge members themselves. In this regard, the national fraternal organization represented a new social technology that made possible the marketing and consumption of a standardized entertainment product through organizational rather than electronic means.[45]

Like electronic mass media, fraternal ritual in the late nineteenth century was a process of one-way communica-

[44] Natalie Z. Davis, "The Reasons of Misrule: Youth Groups and Charivaris in Sixteenth Century France," *Past and Present* 50 (February, 1971): pp. 41–75; E. P. Thompson, " 'Rough Music': Le Charivari Anglais," *Annales Economies Societés Civilisation* 27:2 (1972): pp. 285–312; Emmanuel LeRoy Ladurie, *Carnival in Romans*, trans. Mary Feeney (New York: G. Braziller, 1979).

[45] See Charles Perrow, "A Framework for the Comparative Analysis of Organizations," *American Sociological Review* 32 (1967): pp. 194–208, for a discussion of the concept of organizational technology.

tion. The rituals were not subject to alteration by members and could not be easily changed to articulate their concerns or mobilize them to action. The lodge was relatively closed to input from below, but its ritual was subject to modification by the central leadership almost at will. Such modifications were frequently arbitrary from the perspective of local members, though they might be entirely rational from the perspective of a leadership committed to expansion and financial solvency. In contrast to film or broadcast programming, nineteenth-century fraternalism was limited in its ability to present entertainment that was standardized yet engaging. Yet it represents a type of entertainment that anticipated in many ways the experience of modern mass media presentation.

Conclusion

The aggressive tactics of the leading orders produced tremendous growth throughout the late nineteenth century and up through the 1920s. Even the Masons, who eschewed the use of agents and banned solicitation of membership, found themselves caught up in the competition for expansion, setting up contests and other incentives for lodges to increase their size. But well before the movement had reached its numerical peak, thoughtful commentators were beginning to express concern over the consequences of the hard sell. Declines in Masonic attendance at meetings were attributed to the anonymity of the increasingly large lodges produced by the membership drives.[46] Related to low attendance was high turnover. In 1911 the Supreme Chancellor of the Knights of Pythias called attention to the large-scale nonpayment of dues that plagued the order and created enormous turnover. The Knights lost 48,043 members for nonpayment in 1909, a year when 51,673 were initiated. "My own opinion," wrote the Supreme Chancellor, "is that

[46] Dumenil, *Freemasonry*, pp. 186–87, 189–91.

one of the prolific causes . . . is the fact that many men are initiated into the order who are actuated in joining the order simply by the hope that some benefits in the way of pecuniary gain may accrue to them." With a similar analysis, the Grand Sire of the Odd Fellows argued that the order should abolish all benefits. Such concerns seemed to point to a dawning perception that fraternalism had been transformed by commercialism and acquisitiveness, and that "lodges are dominated today by 'Knights for revenue only.' "[47]

In many local lodges, fraternal orders undoubtedly continued to function as organs of informal sociability, devoted to the maintenance of pre-existing friendship networks and the incorporation of new members into such networks. Moreover, the tendencies affecting the lodge were not peculiar to it, but rather part of a larger commodification of social life. Nonetheless, within the context of the fraternal ideal, they represented a decided paradox. That orders should engage in the precise calculation of potential members' longevity and worth, that agents should earn healthy commissions and leaders rake in thousands of dollars, all seemed to contravene the relation of brotherhood, the ideal of mutuality, which stood at the core of fraternal identity.

[47] Knights of Pythias, *Proceedings*, p. 17; Ferguson, *Fifty Million Brothers*, p. 228; Knights of Pythias, *Proceedings*, p. 17.

CONCLUSION

WHAT defined fraternalism as a unique social form was its use of four elements—corporatism, ritual, masculinity, and proprietorship—to create a persuasive model of solidarity. But one more characteristic must be recognized: fraternalism's consistent engagement with contradiction. Its tenuous unification of opposites, its symbolic resolution of conflicts—among religious sectarians, between young and old, men and women, wage workers and entrepreneurs—is part of what made fraternalism so appealing to its enthusiasts and what fascinates us today. Consider, for example, the following points:

- Fraternal youth organizations in early modern Europe articulated patriarchal assumptions and values; at the same time they were used by young men to assert their interest against particular assertions of patriarchal power.
- In a later period, Freemasonry developed as a movement that synthesized the values of the emerging market economy with the social relations of an earlier corporatist order to express the social and cultural agenda of a nascent bourgeoisie.
- Following the Masonic tradition, nineteenth-century American fraternalism offered a vision of mutuality and collective responsibility that did not seem to undercut the republican ideal of the self-made man. In simultaneously affirming and denying class distinction, social fraternalism presented both a critique of capitalist development and an accommodation to it.
- In an era when women were enshrined as the culturally sanctified providers of moral values and emotional nurture, fraternalism rejected the notion of sexual complementarity by proclaiming the emotional self-sufficiency of

men. Women's auxiliaries seemed to represent an acceptance of male dominance, yet they were the product of women's struggles and the target of masculine resistance.

• The commodification of fraternalism represented perhaps a final irony: fuelled by acquisitive interests, lodge membership was aggressively and systematically marketed as a form of belonging, a relation of brotherhood established by ritual and free from the demands of the marketplace.

Fraternalism has never, then, been a simple phenomenon; rather, it has been distinguished by the many uses to which it was put, the differing interpretations its adherents placed on their membership, and the various satisfactions that they derived from their participation. Consequently there are many ways to understand it. My own analysis has been guided by three central questions. What was the meaning of the fraternal order as a social institution? In particular, what was its significance for the formation of collective identities, especially class identity? And finally, what accounts for its tremendous popularity followed by its unremitting decline?

THE COMPLEXITY OF CATEGORIES

"The construction of hegemony," Carrigan, Connell, and Lee have written of gender, "is not a matter of pushing and pulling between ready formed groupings, but is partly a matter of the *formation* of those groupings." E. P. Thompson intended a similar point about class when he asserted that the English working class was "present at its own making." My analysis of fraternalism is concerned above all with this problem: "the historical production of social categories," the formation of collective identities.[1]

My approach assumes the interactional bases of social cat-

[1] Tim Carrigan, Bob Connell, and John Lee, "Toward a New Sociology of Masculinity," *Theory and Society* 14:5 (1985): p. 594; E. P. Thompson, *The Making of the English Working Class* (1963; pbk. ed., New York: Vintage, 1966), p. 9; Carrigan et al., "Masculinity," p. 553.

egory formation. Perhaps the best statement of this perspective is that of Gerson and Peiss, whose conceptualization of gender relations could, with minor modification, be applied to class, ethnic, and racial formation as well. Their formulation asserts that gender is defined by socially constructed relationships between women and men, among women, and among men in social groups. Gender is not a rigid analytic category imposed on human experience, but a fluid one whose meaning emerges in specific social contexts as it is created and recreated through human action.[2] Through these actions men and women constitute themselves and each other as distinct social groups.

Three points should be made with regard to this perspective. To say that gender and class are socially constructed is not to say they are randomly devised and infinitely variable. Significant social categories are necessarily grounded in daily life. The economic processes of capitalist development, for example, result in proletarianization, the creation of a class of propertyless wage workers, and this in turn "provides a necessary, indeed the necessary condition for [working] class formation in the more thickly textured senses of ways of life dispositions, or patterns of collective action."[3] Conceptions of gender are similarly grounded in material life—in biology, family, work, and in the structure of resources differentially available to women and men. For both class and gender, people draw upon the differential resources they derive from a given social organization, which sets parameters even though it does not and cannot *determine* the particular responses they will make.

Second, if gender is, like class, a relational, interactive sys-

[2] Judith M. Gerson and Kathy Peiss, "Boundaries, Negotiation, Consciousness: Reconceptualizing Gender Relations," *Social Problems* 32:4 (1985): p. 317.

[3] Ira Katznelson, "Working-Class Formation: Constructing Cases and Comparisons," in Ira Katznelson and Aristide R. Zolberg, eds., *Working-Class Formation: Nineteenth-Century Patterns in Western Europe and the United States* (Princeton, N.J.: Princeton University Press, 1986), p. 15.

tem, then it becomes necessary to study men as well as women within the framework of gender relations. The articulation of hierarchy between and among men, the resources derived from same-sex bonding, and historical variations in the degree and sources of masculine power and in the ideal forms of masculinity suggest the range of topics to be explored if we are to understand the constitution of male dominance as a social system.

Third, gender and class formation should not be seen as two closed and separate systems. Feminist scholars waged a vigorous and necessary campaign to identify gender oppression as a separate and analytically distinct phenomenon with a logic and dynamic of its own. Yet ultimately it is important to recognize that in the specificity of everyday life, people simultaneously act out the dynamics of class and gender. As Joe Interrante remarks, "men's class/race experiences do not exist 'in addition to' their experiences as men; they are interwoven threads of a single masculine identity."[4] Ideals of masculinity and femininity inevitably contain a class component, while class resistance is often expressed and understood as the defense of masculine privilege or the assertion of women's duty to defend their own virtue or the well-being of their children. It is difficult to conceptualize the fluid and interactive character of the two constructs while guarding their integrity. Fraternalism is a valuable subject precisely because it is so difficult to understand it *except* in terms of class, gender, and the complex interaction between them.[5]

[4] Joe Interrante, "Dancing Along the Precipice: The Men's Movement in the Eighties," *Radical America* 15:5 (1981): p. 67.

[5] In United States history, race is an equally important part of the dynamics of domination and collective identity formation. My text indicates but does not fully document fraternal practices of racial exclusion; neither was I able to consider the creative responses made by black people to their exclusion from white orders. For that reason I have restricted my final discussion to the interaction of class and gender. For consideration of black fraternalism, see William A. Muraskin, *Middle-Class Blacks in a White Society: Prince Hall Freemasonry in America* (Berkeley, Ca.: University of California Press, 1975); Betty M. Kuyk,

CONCLUSION

BOUNDARIES

An interactionist perspective asserts that gender is both a complex of relationships and an emergent way of explaining them, a socially constructed representation of their meaning. It is analogous to Katznelson's third level of class, classes as "formed groups," sharing "cognitive constructs" that "map the terrain of lived experience and define the boundaries between the probable and the improbable."[6] Note that both Katznelson and Gerson and Peiss point to "boundaries" as a useful way to think about the constitution of groups. Gerson and Peiss, in fact, identify the notion of boundary as a crucial construct in their attempt to conceptualize the formation of gender identity.

> The concept of boundaries describes the complex structures—physical, social, ideological, and psychological—which establish the differences and commonalities between women and men, among women, and among men, shaping and constraining the behavior and attitudes of each gender group . . . Boundaries mark the social territories of gender relations, signalling who ought to be admitted or excluded.[7]

The concept of boundaries is a useful way to think about the constitution of groups because it emphasizes that their origins are social. Every society generates a number of ways in which boundaries can be drawn and an even greater variety of ways they can be given meaning. Boundaries are lines of demarcation that people draw; they can only be effective if they are socially recognized and acted on. Thus

"The African Derivation of Black Fraternal Orders in the United States," *Comparative Studies in Society and History* 25:4 (1983): pp. 559–92; Charles Edward Dickerson, "The Benevolent and Protective Order of Elks and the Improved Benevolent and Protective Order of Elks of the World: A Comparative Study of Euro-American and Afro-American Secret Societies" (Ph.D. diss., University of Rochester, 1981).

[6] Katznelson, "Working-Class Formation," pp. 17–18.

[7] Gerson and Peiss, "Boundaries," pp. 318, 319.

class boundaries involve the development of shared dispositions, dispositions that are "trans-individual, not merely
opinions or views of individual actors. They constitute cultural configurations within which people act."[8] Because it
rests upon social consensus, whether enforced or freely
given, the preservation or maintenance of a boundary line,
like its destruction or erosion, is an active, ongoing process
of social reproduction, not a one-time event.

Boundaries have both an institutional and a symbolic
character. They are embedded in and emerge from the organization of everyday life—the distribution of resources,
the division of labor by sex, race, and class. But culture helps
to define some boundaries as important and others as incon-
sequential.

Fraternalism is above all about boundaries, in both their
institutional and symbolic aspects—their construction, their
bridging, and occasionally their dismantling. Membership
in an organized group of any kind creates a boundary between members and nonmembers. Simmel recognized that
the ritualized possession and dissemination of secret knowledge substantially strengthens such a boundary. It sets in
motion a process of differentiation; the exclusion of some
people effects the incorporation of others and bestows a common identity upon them.[9] Simmel's fascination with social
forms at their purest and most abstract allowed him to identify the mechanism of secrecy and ritual that fraternalism
employs, but led him to disregard the substantive content
that is also a necessary part of fraternalism's efficacy. Secrecy
was rarely a sufficient basis for the lasting organization of
solidary relations, even in the days of fraternalism's prime;
in the long run a myth of origin and justification is needed.
A powerful myth will build upon already-existing or at least
incipient boundaries. But to select is to focus attention on

[8] Katznelson, "Working-Class Formation," p. 19.
[9] Georg Simmel, "Secret Societies," *American Journal of Sociology* 11:4
(1906): pp. 441–98.

and thus to intensify. In this way, fraternal orders contributed to ongoing processes of boundary maintenance and reproduction.

Fraternalism implies a structured and bounded set of interactions and a mythic structure that valorizes those interactions. As a result, it had the potential to impact upon two processes that are central to class formation: first, the development of organizational capacity, that is, of the social networks and institutional resources that facilitate mobilization; second, the development of a class culture that expresses and interprets class experience in emotionally convincing terms and thus makes it available as a basis for identity, a meaningful boundary, and a stimulus to action. This potential resided in two key aspects of fraternal identity: its character as a form of explicitly masculine organization and the class perspective it presented, especially as that was articulated by the Masonic model that so dominated the movement.

FRATERNALISM AND CLASS ORGANIZATIONAL CAPACITY

The popularity of the fraternal movement affected class organizational capacity through the interrelated elements of personalistic ties and institution building. Its male-only, cross-class character helped to shape the interactional patterns of American working-class life.

Nineteenth-century social life was in general segregated by gender to a much greater degree than it is today. Fraternalism surely cannot be held responsible for the existence of a complex world of sex-segregated sociability from which men and women derived both pleasure and resources. But fraternalism was a significant part of the institutional structure that organized and maintained these divisions in the mushrooming cities and towns of the mid-to-late nineteenth century. Living in towns opened up new opportunities for leisure and socializing, and fraternalism grew in response to this, providing men with a structured use of time and an outlet for disposable income. It did not create patterns of male-only interaction, but it helped to formalize them. It provided the physical and institutional space in which they could flourish.

This was especially consequential for working-class women. As we have seen, many nineteenth-century women resented and sometimes resisted their exclusion from male-only social life. Women were themselves entering the world of voluntary association in great numbers during this period, through the growth of the women's club movement and the campaigns for temperance, suffrage, and other reforms, but these were primarily middle-class activities. Public life in working-class communities, on the other hand, occurred primarily through electoral politics, trade unionism, and fraternal orders, all of which were closed, in practice when not in principal, to women. As a result, working-class women's already-limited leisure time remained much more closely linked to the world of family and kin.[10] They were excluded from the larger communication networks to which the lodge gave access; they were also deprived of opportunities to learn organizational skills like speaking in public and keeping records, skills that transfer easily to other domains. What this meant for class formation was the virtual exclusion of working-class women from the formal means of

[10] Kathy Peiss, *Cheap Amusements: Working Women and Leisure in Turn-of-the-Century New York* (Philadelphia: Temple University Press, 1986), finds that working-class wives rarely went out and relied primarily on kin networks for sociability (pp. 22, 25). Women's auxiliaries could have offered an opportunity for their participation, as they did later in the twentieth century. But their cost, smaller size (the Daughters of Rebekah, probably the best established auxiliary, had 143,000 female members in 1985, compared with nearly 800,000 Odd Fellows), and the fact that participation by the male relative was a prerequisite for membership, all suggest minimal participation by working-class women at the turn of the century. Membership figures are derived from Henry Leonard Stillson, ed., *The History and Literature of Oddfellowship, the Three-Link Fraternity* (Boston: Fraternity Publishing Company, 1897), pp. 886, 888.

CONCLUSION

collective organizational life in their communities. As Cynthia Cockburn writes of women's exclusion from the power base represented by craft unionism: "The cost had been paid by women—and perhaps we may say, it had been paid for by the working class, properly conceived."[11]

At the same time, the class character of the lodge had implications for working-class formation. The widespread participation of blue-collar workers in the cross-class fraternal order involved significant parts of the American working class in relationships of personal acquaintance and fellowship with non-working-class men. This could lead to a variety of consequences, from the demobilization of workers to the radicalization of the business class, to little or no effect on either group. Currently we lack the kind of evidence that would allow us to evaluate the impact of such systematic cross-class bonding in nineteenth-century communities. Social mingling between small businessmen and workers in lodges may help to explain the remarkable support by local business interests for strikes, which Herbert Gutman found in a number of Gilded Age communities. Evidence from the mid-twentieth century, on the other hand, suggests a different outcome. Friedlander's work on the creation of a United Auto Workers local in the 1930s finds evidence of Masonry as a significant bond between management and workers. Not only were foremen overwhelmingly Masons, but antiunion leaders among the rank-and-file tended to be Masons as well, even functioning as company spies in several instances. And Dalton discovered that as late as the 1950s, Masonic membership was an important vehicle for advancement and perquisites at the factory where he conducted his study.[12] Cases like these reveal the role that Freemasonry

---

[11] Cynthia Cockburn, *Brothers: Male Dominance and Technological Change* (London: Pluto Press, 1983), pp. 158–59.

[12] Herbert Gutman, "Class, Status, and Community Power in Nineteenth Century American Industrial Cities—Patterson, New Jersey: A Case Study," in *Work, Culture and Society in Industrializing America* (New York: Vintage, 1976), and "The Workers' Search for Power," in H. Wayne Morgan, ed., *The*

could play in maintaining cross-class networks and providing the social vehicle by which working-class men expressed loyalty to their employers and were rewarded for doing so, even at a time when fraternalism had lost much of its affective power.

Striking as they were, personal ties of this sort were perhaps less important than the institutional consequences of fraternal membership. White working-class men were faced with a choice, even if they did not generally understand it in self-conscious terms: their time, energy, personal loyalties, and financial resources could go into the construction of autonomous institutions such as unions that increased their capacity to mobilize as a class, or the same resources could be incorporated into the operation of the mixed-class, and ostensibly class-neutral, but increasingly entrepreneurial, fraternal order.

Some union activists who were also lodge members understood this and responded by trying to influence the way fraternal orders conducted their financial affairs. The *Typographical Journal* of Pennsylvania complained in 1903 that "almost without exception every fraternal and beneficial organization in the state of Pennsylvania gets its work done in non-union offices. This is rather strange when we know that a very large percentage of their membership is recruited from the ranks of organized labor." Union members within the Pennsylvania Foresters tried to remedy this by passing a resolution at the state convention requiring all printing to be done by union printers. But, noted the *Typographical Journal*, "the executive officers have ignored this decree and are getting all the work done in non-union offices."[13] Working-class men had played an important role in building up

---

Gilded Age: A Reappraisal (Syracuse, N.Y.: University of Syracuse Press, 1963); Peter Friedlander, *The Making of a U.A.W. Local, 1936–1939: A Study in Class and Culture* (Pittsburgh, Pa.: University of Pittsburgh Press, 1979), pp. 47, 60, 129–30; Melville Dalton, *Men Who Manage* (New York: John Wiley, 1959).

[13] *The Typographical Journal*, March, 1903, p. 276.

the financial resources of many fraternal orders, yet they were limited in the extent to which they could use the orders to advance or defend working-class interests.

As this example indicates, many working-class men participated in both unions and fraternal orders, but many others preferred or found it necessary to choose between the two; this could pose an even greater problem for the labor movement. Adolph Strasser of the Cigarmakers' International Union of America identified fraternal membership as one of the three major obstacles to successful organizing in the smaller towns of Pennsylvania, where the benefit features of the fraternal order offered direct competition to those of unions: "that the trades union protects wages and conditions, and pays out of work benefits in addition to other benefits, which the fraternal order does not, is either ignored or not understood."[14]

Unions themselves had a fraternal character, but, as Strasser's comment indicates, they made a different statement in class terms than the social order did. Through the provision of unemployment benefits, unions could attempt to respond to the particular circumstances of working-class life; through the payment of strike benefits they could provide material resources for class mobilization. In contrast, the sickness and death benefits provided by the lodges proclaimed a universality by concentrating on those misfortunes to which men of all classes were subject. The choice between the union and the lodge was sometimes a practical one, but it was always a symbolic one, for the fraternal order, with ritual as its raison d'être, idealized the cross-class relationships that it encompassed. It was the fraternal order's symbolic content, organized around the implicit figure of the artisan, which allowed the lodge to flourish.

[14] "Organizer's Report," *Cigar Makers International Journal*, June 15, 1910, p. 10. I am grateful to Ken Fones-Wolf for this reference and the one preceding it.

RITUAL AND CLASS FORMATION

As dramas of social relationships, rituals are representations of the social world. But the social world is a complicated place, the product of multiple interests, perspectives, and propensities. To evoke recognition and sympathetic identification, rituals must express the contradictions intrinsic to social life, but at the same time they must order and resolve the contradictions they display. Thus it is often the case, as Ann Swidler has written, that "cultural products . . . derive their power not from their ability to express one consistent sensibility or set of meanings, but from their ability to fuse together apparently irreconcilable elements of social life." Often this works through the vivid portrayal of a central symbol. The theme of romantic love, for example, Swidler writes, "achieved its great power from its ability to synthesize in one symbolic image, both individual aspirations for independence, autonomy, and personal integrity, and the very demands of the social world with which these aspirations were in tension. In loving, both hero and heroine could find themselves and simultaneously define their place in the social world."[15] The portrayal of such a synthesis through art or ritual authorizes a particular version of social reality. Ritual thus plays a cognitive role for its participants; it helps to structure "their knowledge of the past and their capacity to imagine the future."[16] Masonic fraternalism was such a ritual complex. At a time when it was an assumed part of American community life, it articulated a vision of the social world that spoke to and attempted to resolve some of the culture's most troubling questions about relations between the sexes and the classes. Through its ritual, it constructed bonds of loyalty across class lines and thus demonstrated the

---

[15] Ann Swidler, "Interpretive Versus Explanatory Approaches to the Sociology of Culture," paper presented at the 74th Annual Meeting of the American Sociological Association, Boston, Mass., August, 1979, p. 16.

[16] Steven Lukes, "Political Ritual and Social Integration," *Sociology* 9:2 (1975): p. 302.

possibility of a social order founded on harmonious class relations. And, as a cultural institution that maintained and idealized solidarity among white men, it offered gender and race as the most logical and legitimate categories for the organization of collective identity.

THE MASONIC VISION OF CLASS SOCIETY

As Chapter Two demonstrated, Freemasonry offered a set of ideas, values, and social relations that were congruent with the needs of an emerging capitalist society. Freemasonry rejected the importance of ascribed characteristics through its creation of brotherhood among men of different ranks, classes, and religions. It celebrated the social worth of productive labor through the use of masons' tools as ritual objects and by the wearing of the leather apron as the central symbol of Masonic identity. When men became Accepted Masons, they became, in a symbolic sense, craft workers, industrious artisans who would contribute to the growth of the emerging market economy. Finally, Freemasonry presented a model of class structure and social mobility in a capitalist society. Like the outside world, the lodge was built around a structure of inequality, in the system of degrees that members were to ascend. Yet the analogy between the lodge and the world was an imperfect one. The lodge differed significantly from the society in which it existed, just as marriage differs from romantic love. Based on an initial rite of leveling, Masonic fraternalism constructed a society in which everyone began symbolically at the bottom, on an equal footing, and rose as a matter of course to the top. It thus presented capitalist society as one without competition, which offered success and well-being to everyone wiling to ascend the ladder.

This was a depiction of the social world that resonated powerfully with some of the central dilemmas created by the juxtaposition of capitalist development and American egalitarianism. On the one hand, fraternalism maintained that class boundaries were irrelevant to the formation of group loyalties, were rendered permeable and thus insignificant by the universal process of mobility and by the unifying effects of the fraternal bond. In so doing, fraternalism articulated a particularly middle-class version of class awareness, in which the "denial of the existence or reality of classes" is founded upon the supposedly near-universal availability of individual achievement.[17] On the other hand, fraternalism claimed to create a bond of brotherhood that transcended rationality or self-interested calculation. Taking their imagery from pre-capitalist, noncontractual forms of association—the kin group, the craft corporation, the order of knighthood—nineteenth-century fraternal orders articulated a vision of social relations based on mutual obligation and collective solidarity. In its insistence that lodge brothers were ritually obligated to aid one another in time of need, fraternalism acknowledged that need was an inevitable by-product of capitalism. In identifying the lodge as a sphere of collective responsibility for others, fraternalism implicitly recognized that the market and the values it encouraged were not sufficient or desirable for the conduct of moral life. And in constituting the lodge as a male-only preserve, fraternalism rejected the claims of domesticity and asserted the moral authority of masculine community. Fraternalism thus defined manhood as an alternative reference point to a collective identity and critique based upon class difference and workplace solidarity.

Fraternalism and the Meaning of Class

It is important to see that the ideal of fraternal manhood could embody resistance as well as accommodation. It could represent a simple alternative to class identity, as when working-class and middle-class men bonded together on the

[17] Anthony Giddens, *The Class Structure of the Advanced Societies* (New York: Harper, 1973).

basis of their common masculine identity. But it could also involve a more subtle shaping of the meaning of working-class identity itself.

Social fraternalism drew upon deep roots in American working-class life; indeed, a fraternal version of masculinity was central to working-class culture at work and at leisure. The defense of craft workers' prerogatives was typically and simultaneously understood as a fraternal defense of manhood. This was a perspective on the meaning of workers' collective action and self-interest that was explicitly articulated and formalized in the trade union movement's conception of itself as a brotherhood.

At the same time, working-class leisure was infused with a spirit of fraternity. Urban public spaces such as the pool room, the street corner, and above all the saloon represented, for workingmen, "a realm of autonomy and choice, a sphere of life separate from the obligations of the workplace." Through their socializing, workers articulated an implicit opposition to the "dominant value system of competitive individualism." The treating of rounds of beer or games of billiards was one of the chief manifestations of this ethos. Treating created a debt of honor; it was a ritual of reciprocity and a proclamation that the needs, interests, and preferences of the group superseded those of the individual.[18]

In large cities with immigrant populations where the consumption of alcohol remained an integral and legitimate part of public life, the lodge was part of the world of the saloon, with saloon halls and back rooms commonly used as fraternal meeting places. In those parts of the United States where drinking had become delegitimized as a public activity, the lodge served as an alternative to the drinking culture. In either case, the fraternal movement, with its more explicit and formalized rituals, served to articulate the assumptions

[18] Peiss, *Cheap Amusements*, pp. 4, 20–21.

of the larger world of male sociability and to place them on a morally higher ground.

For if leisure was a source and a sphere of resistance, it was a highly problematic one. Treating was just as much a ritual of male bonding as it was a statement of working-class solidarity. "The public culture of workingmen was not only a potential bulwark of solidarity against the ravages of capitalism; it was also," as Kathy Peiss has written, "a system of male privilege in which workers' self-determination, solidarity, and mutual assistance were understood as 'manliness.' " This was equally true of workplace resistance, where a "culture of male camaraderie has been a vital part of union 'brotherhood' and a source of flexibility and spontaneity in shop-floor politics."[19]

Within these nineteenth-century class subcultures, fraternal ritual played a special role. First, as we have seen, ritual creates solidarity; at the same time, it tends to elevate, to heighten the significance of, the relationships it enacts. In the case of fraternalism, its ritual drew upon the metaphor of kinship to intensify its potential for creating solidarity. In doing so, it recommended a model of social life that placed the welfare of the group above that of the individual. But any metaphor of kinship implies assumptions about gender relations as well as a more general conception of social life. In this case the metaphor was that of brotherhood. Thus the model of solidarity, the very *image* of solidarity, was an image of men joined and joining together, a social possibility from which women were cognitively excluded even in those cases where their participation was countenanced in practice. What this involved, as Anne Phillips has written, "was a partial redefinition of the working class as male. Instead of class solidarity we have seen a more mongrel variant, in which class and brotherhood are subtly elided. Workers did come to see themselves as brothers, not in the abstract

[19] Ibid., pp. 4–5; Interrante, "Dancing," p. 67.

phrases of the 'brotherhood of man' but as real, live, working men. Class unity became the prerogative of male workers."[20]

Women were not just cognitively absent, overlooked, or missing from the image of class solidarity. Ritual creates solidarity by highlighting solidarity, through contrast with difference. This is nowhere more true than in rituals of gender. There the typical focus of ritual is the insistence that the differences between the sexes are of "essence, substance, and inherent quality" rather than of degree or point along a single continuum. "The pervasive message of ritual with regard to sex," remarks Sydel Silverman, "is the incommensurability of male and female." Such rituals assert that men are essentially different from women, but that all men are basically similar to each other. As a result they can reach common understandings and act together in ways that men and women never can. In ritual, "the symbolic statement of the gender contrast crosscuts class and social categories of all other kinds," acting "to obscure and defuse socio-economic cleavages."[21]

Fraternalism identified masculinity as a focal point for individual identity and collective loyalty. If the differences between men and women were so basic, so essential, then it became all the more difficult for men and women to imagine themselves as partners in collective struggle. Fraternalism surely did not by itself *create* such boundaries, but it was part of the process that did.

THE DECLINE OF AMERICAN FRATERNALISM

Well before fraternalism had entered the absolute and seemingly irrevocable decline of the current era, interested observers had noted a loss of commitment and enthusiasm. In

[20] Anne Phillips, "Images of Fraternity: Socialist Slogan, Feminist Values," *Dissent* 32 (Winter, 1985): p. 73.

[21] Sydel Silverman, "Rituals of Inequality: Stratification and Symbol in Central Italy," in Gerald D. Berreman, ed., *Social Inequality: Comparative and Developmental Approaches* (New York: Academic Press, 1981), pp. 169, 170.

many orders, turnover was exceptionally high. In his annual report of 1910, the Supreme Chancellor of the Knights of Pythias pointed to the fact that while a total of 78,819 men had entered the order in 1909, 68,749 or almost 10 percent of the membership had either withdrawn or been suspended for nonpayment of dues. These losses, combined with 6,544 deaths, meant a net gain of less than 4,000. Fraternal leaders worried about a loss of the old spirit even in the face of the still-expanding membership figures. The Middletown of the 1920s and 1930s was perhaps a typical case: the Lynds found that fraternal membership had grown, but attendance and participation was greatly diminished. "The ritual is said on every hand to mean little today, apparently far less than even a generation ago."[22]

The reasons for this declining engagement with the fraternal ideal are clearly related to the sources of its original appeal: its evocation of artisanal culture, its creation of a world of male fellowship, and its provision of entertainment. By the early twentieth century, the attack on craft production, changes in social relations between men and women, and the development of mass media entertainment had combined to begin the erosion of the lodge's appeal.

The gradual destruction of craft production deprived the fraternal orders of both their social base and their symbolic power. Fraternalism's origins in the institutions of craft workers, its frequent designation of the artisan as a model figure in capitalist society, and its emphasis on mutuality and male camaraderie combined to make social fraternalism a recognizable extension of the social and cultural life of the craft workshop. In the last third of the nineteenth century these artisanal experiences and ideals, though threatened and eroded, remained a concrete and potent memory, if not

[22] Knights of Pythias, *Official Record of Proceedings of the Twenty-Sixth Convention of the Supreme Lodge, Knights of Pythias, Milwaukee, August 2–11, 1910* (Nashville, Tenn.: Brandon Printing Company, 1910), p. 17; Robert S. Lynd and Helen M. Lynd, *Middletown: A Study in American Culture* (New York: Harcourt, Brace and World, 1929), p. 307.

CONCLUSION

a lived reality, for a large proportion of the adult male population. By the early to mid-twentieth century this was much less true. As the experience and the ideal of artisanal culture became more remote, enthusiasm and commitment to social fraternalism declined as well.

As the artisanal ideal eroded, other models replaced it. In mid-nineteenth-century Toulouse, France, cross-class organizations had ended because of the withdrawal of working-class participation, and the formation of exclusively working-class organizations. In the early twentieth-century United States, cross-class social fraternalism was weakened by the rise of organizations with membership restricted to proprietors and professionals: service clubs. The major service club federations—Rotary, Kiwanis, and Lions—along with many minor ones, were founded in the early 1900s and had achieved a widespread popularity by the 1920s. In the popular imagination, service clubs and fraternal orders tend to be perceived as essentially similar types of men's social organizations. In fact, the creation of the first service club, Rotary, in 1910, represented a sharp break with fraternal tradition, for the service club limited its membership to proprietors and professionals.[23] The creation of service clubs did not lead to a wholesale exodus of businessmen from fraternal orders, but it did offer a new and prestigious rival for their energy, commitment, and leadership ambitions. Again, in Middletown, businessmen were now "too busy" to find the time that they formerly reserved for lodge meetings. The man who goes weekly to Rotary will confess that he gets around to the Masons "only two or three times a year."[24]

[23] For the rise of the service club, see Charles F. Marden, *Rotary and Its Brothers: An Analysis and Interpretation of the Men's Service Club* (Princeton, N.J.: Princeton University Press, 1935); Paul P. Harris, *My Road to Rotary* (Chicago: A. Krock and Sons, 1948); and C. R. Hewitt, *Towards My Neighbor: The Social Influence of the Rotary Club Movement in Great Britain and Ireland* (London: Longmans, Green and Co., 1950).
[24] Lynd and Lynd, *Middletown*, p. 306.

CONCLUSION

In its repudiation of the open-class policy of the fraternal order, the service club expressed an increasing tendency for small proprietors to distance themselves symbolically from wage workers. The contrasting ethos of the service club and the fraternal order reflected the differences in the two kinds of association. Instead of the mutuality of the fraternal order, in which brothers were obligated to protect and defend one another, the service club sought to reconcile individual self-interest with a more abstract notion of concern for the community beyond the club, best exemplified in the Rotary slogan, "He profits most who serves best."

Changes in the social relations between men and women also reduced the appeal of the male-only fraternal order. The emergence of the dance hall, the amusement park, and the movies offered young working-class men and women opportunities to meet in pleasurable settings without adult supervision. The lure of these new forms of commercialized recreation greatly reduced the appeal of the lodge to young unmarried working-class men.[25] At the same time, middle-class culture had begun to emphasize new images of masculinity and femininity. The ideal of companionate marriage was accompanied by new expectations of a more sexually integrated social life, beginning with dating and courtship and continuing throughout married life. These expectations posed a challenge to the fraternal order's staunch defense of masculine camaraderie.[26]

The service club was better equipped to deal with this challenge. Although it too was a male-only organization, its meetings were typically held over lunch, unlike the lodges, which met on weekday evenings. By meeting at lunch, that is, within that part of the day when men and women were still expected to be separate, the service club respected the evening as a time for marriage and the family. But this was

[25] See Peiss, *Cheap Amusements*, for a fascinating account of this process.
[26] See Paula Fass, *The Damned and the Beautiful: American Youth in the 1920s* (Oxford: Oxford University Press, 1977), especially chapter 2, and Lynd and Lynd, *Middletown*.

a solution only available to those men working in white collar occupations in which they could take an hour for lunch; thus it was a response open to the service club but not to the mixed-class fraternal order.

Alternatively, fraternal orders could adjust their sex-segregated mode of operation, and some of the orders that experienced the greatest growth in the twentieth century were those, like the Elks and Moose, that de-emphasized ritual and offered a more couple-oriented sociability to their members. The orders that had enjoyed the most popularity in the nineteenth century, like the Odd Fellows and Pythians, were seemingly less able to make alterations in response to the changing norms of social life and suffered accordingly.

The third factor contributing to the decline of fraternal orders was the development of new mass media products. If, following the analysis put forward in Chapter Seven, we see the fraternal order as an entertainment product, then the development of the movies, records, and radio, followed a generation later by television, emerges as perhaps the most crucial factor affecting the fate of the lodge. The orders made some attempts to meet the competition by assimilating these technological innovations into their ritual: a Knights of Pythias manual published in the 1930s suggests the use of recorded music and slide projections to enliven the ritual at appropriate moments. But the new mass media provided not only technological sophistication but a content that was thematically more varied and innovative, a presence more massive, than fraternal ritual and pageantry could possibly offer. The new entertainment media could, moreover, be integrated into the new, more sexually integrated social life.

FRATERNAL orders still exist today, but their greatly diminished size, aging memberships, and public marginality mark them as anachronisms. Their inflated rhetoric and unselfconscious depiction of hierarchy has made them the stuff of comedy for at least a generation. So much is this the case that we take them seriously only through an effort of imagination and scholarship.

Much in fact remains to be done. By providing a conceptual framework, I hope I have laid the groundwork for further study of fraternal institutions. We need to know, for example, exactly how use of the fraternal form affected the workings of trade unions and political groups in nineteenth- and early twentieth-century America. We need systematic comparisons of American and European versions of fraternal organization. And we need more exploration of the role that social fraternalism played in the lives and consciousness of ordinary people.

My own analysis of Masonic fraternalism has tended to emphasize its retrogressive content: its grounding in sexual and racial exclusion, its increasingly commodified character and its idealized depiction of social relations in capitalist society. Indeed, I remain convinced that despite its complexities and contradictions, American fraternalism was primarily a force for social order. Yet it is important to recognize the positive features that it simultaneously offered to American culture and that are too often missing from the politics of today: an insistence on the moral dimension of social relations and a vision of solidaristic bonds among strangers created by ritual, enlivened by theatricality, and motivated by an ethos of mutuality and collective responsibility.

INDEX

alcohol use. *See* drinking
"American exceptionalism," 106, 107n
American Miners Association, 103
Aminzade, Ronald, 92
Anderson, Rev. James, 54, 57
Anthony, Susan B., 204
artisans: capitalist development and, 28, 40–41, 63–64, 145, 147–49, 164–68; fraternalism and, 13–14, 16–17, 145–77, 260–61; Freemasonry and, 81–82; masculinity and, 153–55; social identity of, 146–50, 153–54; workplace drinking, 155–60
Ashmole, Elias, 60

Bacon, Sir Frances, 56, 63–64
Barrio, Addie, 203, 207, 209
Beal, John, 69
Beinicke, Fred, 103
Belleville, Ill., 98–103; fraternal orders, 3, 87, 97–101; miners, 102–3
"Birth of a Nation, The," 218
Bossy, John, 25n.
Boyle, Robert, 58
Bricklayers and Masons International Union, 137
Buffalo, N.Y., 87, 103–5
Bunn, Dr. James M., 128, 216–17

Carnahan, James R., 236–37
Carrigan, Tim, 244
Catholic Church, 34–35, 42–45, 66, 126, 130, 138
Catholic Knights of America, 130

charivari, 32–33, 35–37, 49, 239–40. *See also* processions and parades
Cigar Makers' International Union, 138, 253
Clarke, Edward Young, 218
class formation/identity, 9–10, 88–110, 147–55, 168–77, 245–48, 258–59
clubs: British, 54–55; service, 261–63; women's, 194, 202n.38
Cockburn, Cynthia, 251
coffee houses, 54, 65
Colfax, Schuyler, 188, 191–92
compagnonnages. *See* journeymen's associations
confraternities, religious, 34–35, 41, 42–45
Connell, Bob, 244
corporatism, 150–52, 169–71, 175–77; fraternalism and, 4, 38–42, 211–12, 236; trade associations and, 39, 40–41
Coser, Rose Laub, 31n.19
Cott, Nancy, 173, 174, 183
craft workers. *See* artisans
Cumbler, John, 88–89

Dalton, Melville, 251
Davis, James J., 4, 219
Davis, Natalie Zemon, 33
Davis, Susan G., 13
Dee, John, 58, 60, 61
Dermott, Laurence, 75, 79
Desaguliers, John Theophile, 69–71, 75, 182
Digges, Thomas, 61

domesticity, ideology of, 173–77, 185–87, 212

drinking, 119–20, 155–64, 179, 257–58. *See also* temperance

Dumenil, Lynn, 88, 95

Eastern Star, Order of the, 192–93, 195, 197, 202

Edwards, Richard, 148, 165

Elks, Benevolent and Protective Order of, 123, 128, 263

Elks, Improved Benevolent and Protective Order of, 132

entrepreneurialism, fraternal, 17, 211–42

Evans, Rev. Frank W., 203, 209

family, patriarchal. *See* patriarchalism

Farmers' Alliance, 4, 5, 136

Fink, Leon, 6

Florence, William J., 232

Fludd, Robert, 58

Foner, Eric, 146

Foresters, Pennsylvania Order of, 252

Franklin, Benjamin, 77, 113

fraternal orders: Afro-Americans and, 131–35, 264n.5; agents, 4, 17, 213, 216–20; class composition of, 95–101, 103–5, 107–8, 251; class formation/identity and, 88–89, 106–7, 109–10, 243, 248–49, 251–53, 257–61; decline, 259–63; drinking and, 119–21, 162–64, 179; entrepreneurial activities, 211–42, 244; immigrants and, 130–31; labor organizations and, 3, 102–3, 111, 136–44, 252–53; life insurance and, 139, 143, 221–27, 253; Masonic influence on, 11–12, 125–29, 180–81; military branches, 233–38; playground lodge, 232–33;

press, 213; physicians, 214–16; regalia manufacture, 213–14; ritual, 122–23, 125, 131, 180–81, 196–97, 229–31; size of, 87n., 115, 139, 241–42, 260; women and, 178–210, 243–44, 249–51. *See also* fraternalism; Freemasonry

fraternalism: artisans and, 13–14, 16–17, 145–77; corporatism and, 4, 38–42, 150–52, 169–71, 175–76, 211–12; domesticity and, 162–64, 173–77, 179, 185–93; early modern, 21–52; as fictive kinship, 15, 36–38, 175, 221–22; funerals and, 34–35, 42–43, 117; labor organizations and, 30–32, 40–42, 139–44; masculinity and, 14, 17, 45–52, 130, 173–77, 178–210, 258–59; mutuality and, 32, 92–94, 120–21, 170–71, 221–27; ritual, 3, 17–18, 43–45, 238–41; as social form, 4, 38, 135–38, 243–44; symbolism of, 255–56. *See also* fraternal orders; Freemasonry

fraternity, contrasted to fraternalism, 6

free-labor ideology, 169–70

Freeman, Jo, 7–8, 206n

Freemasonry, 15–16, 52; anti-Masonry, 115–18, 186–87, 188; architecture and, 56–57; artisans and, 74–75, 78, 81–82; British, 3, 53–83; Grand Lodge of England, 53–54, 75, 80–81, 113–14, 132, 134; Grand Lodge of the Ancients, 75; Jewish members, 77; latitudinarianism and, 65–73; membership, 7, 73–76, 95–96, 115, 117; nonsectarianism, 76–77; Prince Hall Masons, 132–33, 134; ritual and, 74–75, 81, 127–29, 228–29; symbolism of, 55, 73, 76–83, 243, 255–56; Templaric

or Scottish, 79–80, 114–15, 233, 236; United States, 87, 112–18; women and, 182–91. *See also* fraternal orders; fraternalism
Friedlander, Peter, 251
funerals, 34–35, 42–43, 117

Galilean Fisherman, Grand United Order of, 132
Geertz, Clifford, 228
Gennep, Arnold van, 196n
Gerson, Judith M., 10, 245, 247
Gilkeson, John, 95
Gillis, John R., 27n.12
Goodwyn, Lawrence, 5
Goody, Esther, 24
Gordon, David M., 148, 165
Gramsci, Antonio, 12
Grand Army of the Republic, 124, 230
Grange. *See* Patrons of Husbandry
Green, Burt Wilder, 208
Griffith, D. W., 218
guilds. *See* trade associations
Gusfield, Joseph, 162
Gutman, Herbert G., 251

Hay, James M., 101
Hersey, Daniel, 120
Hill, Christopher, 58
Hobsbawm, E. J., 211

individualism, 14, 77, 169–70
insurance. *See* fraternal orders, life insurance and
Interrante, Joe, 246

Jacob, Margaret C., 66
Jayne-Weaver, Ida, 204
Johnson, Paul, 155, 157, 158, 159
Jones, G. P., 56
journeymen's associations: compagnonnages, 3, 30–32, 40–42, 47,

51, 175; corporatism and, 40–41; United States, 111, 121, 151–53
Junior Order of United American Mechanics, 131
Junis, John J., 138

Katznelson, Ira, 9–10, 247
Keller, Evelyn Fox, 182
Kelley, Oliver U., 136
King, George, 103
kinship: as model for social relations, 22–25, 175; fictive, fraternalism as, 15, 36–38, 40, 221–22
Kiwanis Clubs, 261–63
Knights of Columbus, 130
Knights of Father Matthew, 131
Knights of Honor, 100, 124
Knights of Khorassan, Dramatic Order of, 232–33
Knights of Labor: as fraternal order, 4, 6, 138; goals of, 142–44, 169
Knights of Pythias, 96, 180, 263; in Belleville, Ill., 3, 98–101; in Buffalo, N.Y., 103–6; membership, 103–5, 107–8, 241–42; Uniform Rank, 234–38; women and, 200, 205
Knights of Pythias of North and South America, Europe, Asia and Africa, 132
Knights of St. Crispin, 137
Knights of the Globe, 126–27
Knights of the Golden Eagle, 129
Knoop, Douglas, 56
Koerner, Gustave, 101
Ku Klux Klan, 4, 130, 218–19

labor organizations: labor reform associations, 137–38, 139–43; trade unions, 3–4, 102–3, 136–37, 237; United States, 111. *See also* journeymen's associations
latitudinarianism, 66–73
Laurie, Bruce, 154

Lee, John, 244
League of Friendship, Supreme Mechanical Order of the Sun, 138, 141
Legion of Honor, 221
Lions Clubs, 261–63
Lipson, Dorothy Ann, 113, 117
Locomotive Engineers, Brotherhood of, 137
Locomotive Firemen, Brotherhood of, 139
Lodge of Adoption, 183–85, 192
Lynd, Robert S., and Helen M., 260

Maccabees, Knights of the, 124
Maccoy, Robert, 202
Machinists and Mechanical Engineers, Order of United, 137
McWilliams, Wilson Carey, 6
"Magic Flute, The," 183–84
Maloney, William R., 214
Marx, Karl, 90, 149–50
masculinity: class identity and, 45–52, 153–55, 170–72; drinking and, 161–64; Enlightenment concepts of, 182–85; fraternalism and, 4, 45–52, 170–77, 178–79, 196–97, 256–59; twentieth century, 262–63. *See also* fraternalism; Freemasonry; women
Masons. *See* Freemasonry
Mathiot, Augustus, 120
Middletown, 260, 260n.22, 261
Modern Woodmen of America, 176, 180, 219; exclusionary policies, 134, 226; founding, 124; fraternal agents, 217, 217n; life insurance and, 221, 225–27; military branch, 235, 243; ritual, 129, 176, 180
Montague, John, Duke of, 69
Montgomery, David, 7, 89, 137, 165, 167, 171
Moose, Loyal Order of, 4, 219, 263

Morgan, William, 115–17
Morris, Robert, 188–91, 202
Mozart, Wolfgang Amadeus, 183
mutual benefit societies, European, 34, 92–94. *See also* fraternal orders, life insurance and
mutuality: drinking and, 156–57, 257–58; fraternalism and, 14, 41–42; as ideal, 169–71, 221–22, 225, 242. *See also* corporatism

Napier, John, 58
National Council of Women, 204
National Labor Congress, 138
Nelson, Halvor, 127
Newton, Sir Isaac, 58, 70; ideas of, 54, 56, 65–73. *See also* latitudinarianism
Norris, George P., 120, 121

Oberschall, Anthony, 7, 211
Odd Fellows, Grand United Order of, 132–33
Odd Fellows, Independent Order of, 96, 100, 118–81, 230, 263; drinking and, 119–21, 160–61; history of, 118–23; membership, 7, 242; ritual, 122–23, 234–35; women and, 187–89, 191–93
Order of Twelve, 132
Owen, William E., 100

patriarchalism, early modern, 25–33, 45–52
Patrons of Husbandry (Grange), 4, 136, 208–9
Peiss, Kathy, 10, 245, 247, 250, 258
Phillips, Anne, 258
Powderly, Terence, 138
Prince Hall Masons, 132–33, 134
processions and parades, fraternal, 43, 44–45, 75, 151, 238. *See also* charivari

unions. *See* labor organizations: trade unions
Upchurch, John J., 126, 140–44

veterans organizations, 124
Vitruvius, 56–57

Washington, George, 113–14
Washingtonian movement, 161, 163
White, Harrison, 91
Wildey, Thomas, 118
Wilentz, Sean, 82, 107, 147, 150, 151, 152, 159, 168
Wilson, Darius, 214
women: domesticity and, 173–77, 185–93; Enlightenment concepts of, 182–85; fraternal auxiliaries, 195–99, 204–5, 206–10, 244, 250n; fraternal orders and, 130, 178–210, 243, 249–51; honorary degrees for, 188–92; twentieth-

century conceptions of, 209–10, 262–63; voluntary associations and, 194, 250. *See also* masculinity
Women's Christian Temperance Union, 162, 179, 194
Woodmen of the World, 218, 219
Workmen, Ancient Order of United, 96, 177, 180, 230; fraternal agents and, 216–17; life insurance and, 143, 221, 222; labor movement and, 139–44; membership, 139; ritual, 127–28
Wuthnow, Robert, 12

Yates, Frances, 60
youth: early modern fraternalism and, 27–33, 47–49, 243; military branches and, 235

Zelizer, Viviana A., 221

QMW LIBRARY
(MILE END)